DELUSIONS
of
GRANDEUR

DELUSIONS
of
GRANDEUR

The United Nations and Global Intervention

edited by Ted Galen Carpenter

CATO
INSTITUTE
Washington, D.C.

Library of Congress Cataloging-in-Publication Data

Delusions of grandeur : the United Nations and global intervention /
edited by Ted Galen Carpenter.
    p.   cm.
Includes bibliographical references and index.
ISBN 1-882577-49-3. — ISBN 1-882577-50-7
1. United Nations. 2. Carpenter Ted Galen.
JX1977.D43 1997
341.5′84—dc21   97-16247
                                                CIP

Printed in the United States of America.

CATO INSTITUTE
1000 Massachusetts Ave., N.W.
Washington, D.C. 20001

To David F. Healy, who taught us that in international affairs there are no easy answers; there is only a daunting array of important questions that deserve to be asked.

Contents

Acknowledgments

This book is the outgrowth of an October 1996 Cato Institute conference on the United Nations. Many people deserve appreciation for helping to make that event a success. I wish to thank Edward H. Crane, president of the Cato Institute, for his consistent and enthusiastic support of the conference, the subsequent book, and, indeed, the entire UN evaluation project. Scott Wallace, Julie Briggs, Elizabeth Kleinknecht, David Lampo, Mark Fondersmith, Peggy Ellis, and other members of the institute's administrative staff did an excellent job of handling the conference's many logistical requirements. Jonathan Clarke, John Hillen, Fred Smith, and Edward Hudgins generously donated their time to moderate the various panels. Rep. Joe Scarborough (R-Fla.) took time from an extraordinarily busy schedule to deliver a thoughtful and provocative luncheon address.

I owe special thanks to my colleagues Barbara Conry and Ian Vásquez, who helped organize the panels and supervised the planning and implementation of the conference at every stage. Without their untold hours of dedicated labor, the conference would never have been possible.

An additional debt of gratitude is owed to those who have worked on the book project. My copyeditor, Elizabeth W. Kaplan, did her usual splendid job of preparing the manuscript for publication. Jeanne Hill labored diligently and with unfailing good humor to incorporate the revisions made by the authors. She also demonstrated a remarkable ability to decipher my sometimes cryptic instructions. Andrew Stone tracked down a number of elusive references.

Most of all, I want to thank the authors for their cooperation and enthusiasm. It has been a pleasure to work with all of them, and I believe that together we have made a major contribution to informed discussion and debate on the future of the United Nations.

Introduction

The United Nations is an increasingly controversial institution, especially in the United States. Many champions of that world organization viewed the end of the Cold War as the dawn of a new era in international affairs in which the UN would play a leading role. A standing army at the call of the Security Council would impose peace on warring nations and engage in "nation building" in so-called failed states. A host of UN-brokered international agreements on issues ranging from the environment to health to urban planning, funded by the World Bank and the regional development banks, would serve as the basis for a global "Great Society."

The more ambitious the initiatives, however, the more glaringly apparent the organization's problems. Critics point to a more than a half century of inefficiency, corruption, and disastrously mismanaged peacekeeping ventures, culminating with those in Somalia and Bosnia. Some critics have even begun to question whether the UN should continue to exist at all. During the 104th Congress, Rep. Joe Scarborough (R-Fla.) and several cosponsors introduced legislation to rescind the United Nations Participation Act and terminate America's membership in the organization. A few months later, Sen. Jesse Helms (R-N.C.), chairman of the Senate Foreign Relations Committee, published a scorching article in *Foreign Affairs,* demanding that the UN adopt major reforms or go out of business.[1]

Defenders of the UN insist that the problems have been exaggerated and that, on the whole, the institution has performed well. They add that most of the UN's difficulties have been the result of ill-advised actions on the part of key member nations, most notably the United States. In their view, the U.S. Congress's strategy of withholding funds to compel the United Nations to implement reforms has been especially counterproductive and led to financial and organizational chaos. Missteps in the peacekeeping arena, UN defenders argue, resulted from overly ambitious mandates given to the organization by the five permanent members of the Security Council—led by the United States.

Unfortunately, the debate about the future of the United Nations has frequently been characterized by smear tactics and overblown rhetoric. Multilateralists sometimes act as though the United Nations should be above criticism. The scornful attitude of National Security Council aide Richard Clarke is all too typical. According to Clarke, there is overwhelming support for the United Nations among the American people "despite the fact that there is a small vocal minority who believes in black helicopters coming to take their lawn furniture."[2] That kind of dismissive response—one that seeks to equate any negative appraisals of the United Nations with the rantings of a few conspiracy buffs—justifiably infuriates reasonable critics. It is not isolationism, much less know-nothingism, to insist that the role of the United Nations—and America's relationship to the world body—be carefully examined and that the UN's performance be subject to a rigorous cost-benefit analysis.

Both critics and defenders of the United Nations might improve the quality of the debate by lowering the temperature of their rhetoric. Ironically, extreme members of both factions tend to attribute more importance to the organization than it probably deserves—a point made by Robert Oakley, Michael Stopford, and other contributors to this volume. Some ardent globalists insist, as their intellectual predecessors did in 1945, that the UN is humanity's "last best hope for peace." They formulate elaborate (and sometimes wildly unrealistic) plans to give the organization independent taxing authority, an independent military force, a permanent war crimes tribunal with extensive powers, and control over all nuclear weapons. It is such inflated conceptions of the United Nations that the title of this book, *Delusions of Grandeur*, seeks to puncture.

Some opponents of the UN, however, have their own inflated notions of the organization's power and influence. Those who see the United Nations as an insidious world government that is constantly concocting plots to destroy American sovereignty and liberty chase after phantom threats. Their critique is simply another manifestation (essentially a mirror image of the pro-UN globalist stance) of delusions of grandeur. The United Nations has an ample number of faults, but a credible scheme for global hegemony is not among them.

The analyses in this book adopt more sober and reasoned approaches. Whatever the differences in their perspectives, the authors realize that the United Nations is neither savior nor satan.

Even the strongest critics of the UN acknowledge that the organization has had some worthwhile accomplishments—such as helping to end civil wars and fostering democracy in Namibia and El Salvador. And even the strongest defenders of the UN admit that the organization has had its share of problems with corruption, mismanagement, and sometimes overly ambitious policy agendas—problems that cannot be solved merely by greater injections of cash or the acquisition of additional powers.

The book is divided into five sections. In part I, "The United Nations in Perspective," three authors present overviews of the UN's problems and prospects. I begin the discussion in chapter 1 by examining the assumptions underlying the doctrine of global collective security, which is the conceptual foundation of the United Nations. I question whether collective security is either desirable or feasible on a global basis and suggest that regional arrangements might prove more durable and beneficial. I propose that the United States act as the "balancer of last resort" in a complex and inevitably somewhat turbulent international system.

In chapter 2 Michael Stopford examines the various problems faced by the United Nations and the reasons why reform efforts have repeatedly proven futile. He argues that it is a common mistake of UN critics to see the organization as a truly independent entity, when in reality it has very little autonomy. Until the principal member states summon the will and unity to adopt a meaningful reform agenda, Stopford contends, there will continue to be far more rhetoric than substantive change.

John R. Bolton traces the history of the United Nations in chapter 3 and contends that the UN has been successful only when the United States has exercised decisive leadership. He bluntly argues that the value of the United Nations ought to be measured by its ability to advance American interests. During much of the Cold War era, especially during the 1970s, it failed that test. Conversely, when the Reagan and Bush administrations pressured the organization to respect American values and policy goals, it responded well, as evidenced by its endorsement of Washington's objectives in the Persian Gulf crisis. According to Bolton, the gulf war, not the vague multilateralism embraced by the Clinton administration, should be the model for a constructive relationship between the United Nations and the United States.

In part II, "The United Nations as Peacemaker and Peacekeeper," four authors examine the central function of the UN: prevention and resolution of armed conflicts. Doug Bandow argues in chapter 4 that UN-led military interventions are a dangerous snare for the United States. Interfering in subregional or intrastate conflicts will, in his view, usually prove futile, as the aborted UN missions in Somalia and Bosnia demonstrated. Such conflicts may be tragic for the people involved, Bandow contends, but they will rarely impinge on vital American interests and, therefore, do not warrant the commitment of U.S. armed forces to UN peacekeeping missions. Such blood sacrifices should be made only in defense of essential American security interests.

Robert B. Oakley agrees with Bandow that the Somalia and Bosnia missions turned out badly and that the United States must be cautious about UN military missions. Nevertheless, he insists in chapter 5 that some UN ventures have been quite successful and that the various types of peace operations can often advance important U.S. goals. The United Nations Emergency Force for the Sinai, established in 1973, and the United Nations Disengagement and Observer Force for the Golan, established in 1974, were essential complements to U.S. diplomacy in ending the 1973 war and stabilizing the Middle East. The UN has failed when the United States and other key members have asked the organization to pursue ambitious missions without giving it the financial and military resources to succeed. Oakley contends that the blame for overreaching, most notably in Somalia and Bosnia, lies primarily with the permanent members of the Security Council, especially the United States, not the UN itself.

In chapter 6 Alan Tonelson charges that American proponents of a global interventionist foreign policy see the United Nations as a mechanism for involving the United States in a plethora of military missions without congressional authorization—or public support. He notes that President Harry S Truman sent troops to Korea in response to a UN Security Council resolution and that President George Bush argued that a similar resolution was sufficient for the deployment of more than 500,000 U.S. troops to the Persian Gulf region—although he did seek congressional approval at the 11th hour. Tonelson contends that such presidential war making under UN auspices is unconstitutional and undermines the entire principle of democratic accountability. He warns that the Clinton administration's enthusiasm for U.S. participation in UN peacekeeping missions portends a strengthening of the imperial presidency.

In chapter 7 John Hillen urges the UN to return to basics when it comes to military operations. He argues that the UN has done relatively well in implementing peacekeeping missions where the objectives have been limited, only a small number of peacekeepers have been needed, and there has already been a stable cease-fire among the belligerents. It did noticeably less well in the Congo during the 1960s and more recently in Somalia and Bosnia where such conditions were absent. In particular, the United Nations is not equipped organizationally to handle missions involving large numbers of peacekeepers attempting to disarm belligerents and orchestrate complex political settlements. Hillen warns that unless the UN returns to the modest goals of traditional peacekeeping, it risks destroying its credibility and effectiveness.

The authors in part III, "Funding, Bureaucracy, and Corruption," examine some of the organizational problems that have increasingly bedeviled the UN. In chapter 8 Stefan Halper presents numerous examples of excessive bureaucracy and outright corruption throughout the entire UN system. He argues that the root of such problems has been the disconnect between voting power in the General Assembly and the sources of funding for the organization. Nations that pay virtually nothing toward UN operations control a majority of the votes while most of the funds are provided by 14 Western nations. He contends that any meaningful reform must give the principal donor countries a larger voice in budgeting and spending decisions. Beyond that change, Halper proposes a comprehensive, independent audit of all UN operations, not only to identify the narrow problems of waste, fraud, and abuse, but to determine which UN missions have failed to fulfill their promise and should be scaled back or eliminated.

Daniel Gouré examines the question of whether the UN should be given the authority to levy taxes in chapter 9. He concludes that proposals for such powers are impractical at best and dangerous at worst. The principal danger, in his view, is not that the UN would become an all-powerful world government if it were granted taxing authority, but that all UN operations would become controversial

5

issues in the domestic politics of member states. That greater prominence, and the bitter debates that would follow, Gouré fears, could
end up destroying the United Nations.

Edward Luck assesses the prospects for reform in chapter 10. He
contends that many proponents of reform, especially conservatives
in the United States, harbor hidden agendas. He wonders how many
of them would really like to see a more efficient, and hence more
capable and powerful, United Nations. Given their broader criticisms of UN missions and objectives, he suspects that at least some
critics of the United Nations are using the call for reform as a pretext
for constraining and weakening the organization. Luck concedes
that a variety of management reforms is needed, but he argues that
they must be implemented in a way that does not undermine the
UN. Moreover, the U.S. Congress's policy of unilaterally withholding funds is especially unhelpful.

The authors in part IV examine the UN's social and environmental
agenda. In chapter 11 Sheldon Richman sharply criticizes the
assumptions and programs of the United Nations Population Fund.
He contends that the fund embraces discredited Malthusian assumptions about population growth and resources. Even worse, the organization has supported and funded coercive population control measures in China and other countries. Citing examples from around
the world, Richman argues that there is no correlation between high
population densities and high rates of poverty. To the contrary,
many prosperous nations (e.g., Taiwan, Japan, and the Netherlands)
have extremely high population densities, while some of the most
poverty-stricken countries (e.g., Somalia and Chad) are sparsely
populated.

Ronald Bailey takes issue with the UN's environmental programs
in chapter 12. The resolutions adopted at the conference held in Rio
de Janeiro, as well as other measures, betray a pervasive UN bias
toward intrusive governmental activism, according to Bailey.
Indeed, environmental issues frequently seem to serve as a pretext
for advancing an agenda of global economic regulation—in some
cases virtually the same agenda that was pushed in the 1970s under
the guise of promoting greater economic equity between industrialized and developing countries. Bailey argues that the UN programs
are obsessed with such nonexistent or greatly exaggerated environmental problems as global warming and that the UN's proposed

"solutions" would retard global economic progress and do little to address legitimate environmental concerns, such as safe drinking water and improved air quality in the Third World.

Gareth Porter presents the opposite thesis in chapter 13, arguing that the Rio conference and other UN initiatives have made a major contribution to a cleaner and healthier environment. Porter also contends that the UN is an essential institution for coordinating international environmental efforts. Relying on the marketplace, national governments, or ad hoc multilateral initiatives, he insists, would not prove sufficient.

In chapter 14 Richard E. Wagner examines the record of the World Health Organization and concludes that, on balance, American taxpayers have not received good value for their money. Wagner concedes that the WHO has done some worthwhile work, such as the successful campaign to eradicate smallpox, and he notes that the organization's public relations strategy focuses on such enterprises to generate public support. An analysis of the WHO's budget, however, suggests that a disproportionate percentage of financial resources and personnel is involved in work on "trendy" health issues (such as anti-smoking campaigns) that are popular with the health ministries of developed states. A surprisingly small percentage of resources and personnel is devoted to addressing the health problems of poor societies.

The authors in part V discuss the UN's role in economic development. In chapter 15 Roy D. Morey insists that the UN and its affiliated agencies have contributed to economic advancement in many parts of the developing world. They have especially assisted those societies making the difficult transition from command economies to market-oriented economies. Moreover, Morey emphasizes that the UN's agenda is not economic growth for the sake of economic growth; the more important part of that agenda is equitable development. The wide diffusion of economic benefits, he argues, will ensure development that is sustainable over the long term, providing populations with a stake in their societies' economic progress and contributing to overall social and political stability.

Nicholas Eberstadt reaches a very different conclusion in chapter 16. He contends that there has been no positive correlation between UN development activities and the economic progress of recipient countries. Indeed, the bulk of the evidence suggests that there may be a negative correlation. Some UN projects, he argues, have clearly proven harmful, as UN agencies have encouraged governments throughout the developing world to adopt highly intrusive regulatory and fiscal policies. Many of the economic success stories in East Asia and elsewhere, Eberstadt concludes, have occurred in spite of UN developmental programs, not because of them.

Michael Maren presents an even harsher thesis in chapter 17. He notes that even the most critical accounts of the United Nations tend to spare the organization's humanitarian relief programs and especially exempt the nongovernmental organizations (NGOs) that work closely with the relevant UN agencies. Maren contends that such favorable interpretations are erroneous. Drawing from nearly two decades of experience in Africa, he paints a disturbing picture of self-serving institutional collusion bordering on incest among UN agencies that fund humanitarian programs, think tank and university scholars who both propose and evaluate such programs, and NGOs that receive UN funds and implement the programs. Most UN-sponsored efforts, Maren argues, have proven ineffective or destructive. Using recent developments in Somalia as an example, he contends that populations frequently fare better without the "help" of the UN and its NGO allies.

In the final chapter Ian Vásquez examines the record of the World Bank and the International Monetary Fund. He notes that the IMF and the two components of the World Bank (the International Bank for Reconstruction and Development and the International Development Association) are considered UN "specialized agencies" and that their activities must be considered in any assessment of the UN's overall contributions to economic development. Vásquez contends that the World Bank has funded and encouraged disastrous economic policies throughout the developing world. Bank loans have paid for "white elephant" industrial projects that now litter Asia, Africa, and Latin America. Worse, the bank's largesse has often shielded regimes from the consequences of their own economic folly, thus delaying badly needed reform efforts. The performance of the IMF has not been materially better, in Vásquez's judgment. Indeed, the IMF's typical blueprint for austerity and higher taxes has caused needless suffering among Third World populations.

This book contains a diversity of views on both the current condition of the United Nations and the prospects for meaningful change.

Despite the differing assessments and policy prescriptions, however, there is widespread agreement that the UN is now under greater stress than at any previous time in its history. The UN has entered a critical phase, and its new secretary-general must confront a daunting array of financial problems and growing doubts in the most important member state about whether the organization can ever play the role that its founders intended.

It is quite likely that the fate of the United Nations will be decided in the next decade, and the outcome of the debate in the United States may well have a decisive impact. The chapters in this book are presented in the hope that they will make a contribution to that important debate.

Notes

1. Jesse Helms, "Saving the UN: A Challenge to the Next Secretary-General," *Foreign Affairs* 75, no. 5 (September–October 1996): 2–8.
2. Quoted in Warren P. Strobel, "Clinton Says Most Americans Support U.N.," *Washington Times*, September 25, 1996, p. A1.

PART I

THE UNITED NATIONS IN PERSPECTIVE

1. The Mirage of Global Collective Security

Ted Galen Carpenter

The United Nations was created a half century ago with the expectation that it would be an effective organization for preserving world peace. Indeed, proponents of collective security hailed their new creation as mankind's "last best hope" for peace. It is difficult to escape the conclusion that the United Nations has failed to live up to such lofty ambitions.

During the Cold War the organization was largely irrelevant in the security realm, as the rivalry between the United States and the Soviet Union paralyzed the Security Council. Ardent internationalists believed that with the end of the Cold War, the United Nations would finally be able to function as its founders had intended. The UN's highly visible role during the 1990–91 Persian Gulf crisis reinforced those expectations.

UN secretary-general Boutros Boutros-Ghali epitomized the burgeoning optimism in his June 1992 report to the Security Council, *An Agenda for Peace*.[1] Responding to the council's request for a specific proposal to strengthen the UN's ability to resolve conflicts around the world, Boutros-Ghali presented a plan to establish a stand-by military force. Each member state was to make available up to 1,000 troops for peace-enforcement, peacekeeping, and deterrent operations at the call of the Security Council.

An Agenda for Peace was hardly unique. The immediate post–Cold War period witnessed a blizzard of books, articles, and studies by UN enthusiasts, both inside and outside the organization, presenting blueprints for the UN's expanded post–Cold War role.[2] Not only did most of the authors advocate a more robust UN military capability, many of them called for increased powers in other areas, such as revitalizing the Trusteeship Council and giving it the authority to assume control of so-called failed states.

Such ambitious plans foundered on the rocks of international political realities. Despite the widespread belief that the Cold War's end would finally enable the United Nations to function effectively, its record in the post–Cold War period has been generally unimpressive—especially in the realm of conflict resolution. The UN nation-building project in Somalia (which was to be the model for rehabilitating failed states) produced a bloody fiasco. The UN mission in Bosnia, essentially an attempt to manage a civil war, fared little better, merely prolonging the agony by preventing a decisive battlefield verdict.[3] Even the UN's much-touted success in ending the long civil war and fostering the emergence of democracy in Cambodia appears increasingly tarnished as the incumbent Cambodian regime displays blatant authoritarian characteristics.

To be sure, the UN has not been without successes. The organization played a constructive role in helping to end the armed conflicts in El Salvador, Mozambique, and Angola (although the latter settlement remains extremely fragile) and supervising elections that brought independence and democracy to Namibia. Nevertheless, the failures were decidedly more spectacular than the successes and emphasize the UN's inherent limitations.

Even on nonmilitary matters, the UN's performance has been uninspiring. Now in its sixth decade, the organization is plagued by problems of mismanagement and corruption.[4] Much of the UN's energy and funds has been devoted to pushing such pernicious measures as the Law of the Sea Treaty and holding pretentious summits on the environment, world population, and other issues.[5] Delegates to those gatherings habitually embrace the discredited notion that more government intervention and regulation are the solution to any problem. Given the manifest problems and abuses at the United Nations, it is hardly surprising that hostility to the world body is rising among portions of the American public. Perhaps more relevant to the organization's future, anger is rising rapidly in the U.S. Congress.

Critics have suggested a number of important changes in Washington's policy toward the United Nations. Sen. Jesse Helms (R-N.C.) and other congressional hard-liners believe that the United States should reduce its financial support for the organization and insist, not ask, that it trim its bloated, corrupt bureaucracy. Other reform proposals call for a comprehensive audit that would go beyond an examination of the UN's finances and management to scrutinize the UN's missions and eliminate those that are unrealistic or of dubious value.[6] Critics also argue that the United States should use its veto on the Security Council to block efforts to have the United Nations undertake overly ambitious missions, such as those in Somalia and Bosnia. According to that thesis, the UN should confine itself to traditional peacekeeping operations—those involving a small number of personnel policing a cease-fire that is reliably supported by the erstwhile belligerents.

Such suggested changes are commendable, but they skirt the central issue. Ultimately, the United States needs to reexamine its enthusiasm for the entire concept of collective security. Although it has been the conventional wisdom among liberal internationalists since the days of Woodrow Wilson that collective security is a noble ideal and an attainable objective, there is reason to question both assumptions. We should no longer accept on faith that it is either feasible or wise to attempt to "globalize" civil wars and minor cross-border conflicts. Yet that will be the inevitable outcome if the United Nations is strengthened and attempts to play the role that its founders envisaged.

The United Nations and the Chimera of "Stability"

Policy prescriptions that advocate that Washington support measures to strengthen the security function of the United Nations are based on an implicit premise: that it is both possible and in the best interests of the United States to help prevent "aggression" and "disorder" throughout the international system. That premise should be carefully examined.

The United Nations itself has embraced the objective of "stability" since the inception of the organization. That fondness for the status quo should not be surprising. The UN was, after all, primarily a postwar continuation of the alliance of the victors in World War II. Even the UN Charter designated Germany and Japan as "enemy nations"—a curious provision for an organization that purported to represent the entire international community. Throughout its history, the UN has exhibited a noticeable preference for supporting incumbent regimes (although ideological considerations have sometimes overridden that preference) and especially for preserving the territorial integrity of member states—even against internal opponents. The bias against secessionist movements has been glaringly evident at times. A prime example was the massive "peacekeeping" effort to prevent the breakup of the Congo (Zaire) in the 1960s. A more recent example has been the refusal of the UN and its leading member states to recognize the independence of Somaliland, even though that political entity broke away from Somalia and has maintained a de facto independence for more than five years.[7] (Somaliland has also largely managed to avoid the massive bloodshed and chaos that has afflicted the rest of Somalia.)

Making the UN's stability agenda the lodestar of U.S. policy is dangerously misguided. The immediate future is likely to be one of the most turbulent periods in world affairs. There are several factors that are contributing to the turbulence.

Many regions are still dealing with the legacy of the imperial age in which colonies or client states were established without reference to long-standing linguistic, cultural, and economic patterns. It is not surprising that those imposed artificial political settlements are now being challenged. Iraq's attempted annexation of Kuwait; the turmoil in the former Yugoslavia; the unraveling of Zaire; the Kurdish rebellion (in both Iraq and Turkey); the massive bloodshed in Somalia, Burundi, Rwanda, and Afghanistan; and the disintegration of the last multinational empire, the Soviet Union (which led to subsequent conflicts in Tajikistan, Georgia, and Nagorno-Karabakh) are all examples of post–Cold War era turbulence.[8]

Even in regions where the detritus of colonialism is not the dominant consideration, there are other factors that are threatening the geopolitical status quo. Many of the UN's member states are highly fragile entities that are increasingly under siege from two sides. One threat comes from the globalization of economic ties. By their very nature, such links tend to be transnational, involving individuals and companies from different nations and regions. Frequently, the participants in those economic transactions bypass (either deliberately or inadvertently) the authority of national governments. Regional bodies (e.g., the European Union) or subnational ones (e.g., provinces and municipalities) may gain power and influence simply because they are more immediately relevant to the economic participants involved in a specific transaction. In some cases, *all* governmental entities are bypassed as creative economic actors pursue their objectives entirely in the private sector—even when such transactions may technically violate certain laws.

Whatever the specific manifestation, the globalization of the economy and the diffusion of economic transactions have already undercut the prestige and authority of the nation-state and are likely to do so to an even greater degree in the future.[9] Stable political states with relatively homogenous populations, unifying ideologies or ideals, and a strong sense of nationhood may be able to weather that erosion of power. States that are held together by little more than the commanding presence of a single political personality or a governing party are far less likely to survive.

Adding to the woes of such countries are pressures coming from the opposite side. Whereas the global economy bypasses and undermines the nation-state and promises a more cosmopolitan world, the growth of movements based on ethnic, linguistic, or religious separatism presents a frontal challenge. (Indeed, it appears that such separatism is at least partly a reaction to the cosmopolitan implications of the global economy. Groups that feel threatened by that development redouble their efforts to establish or protect what they see as their distinct—and now beleaguered—cultural identities.)[10]

There is little doubt that such separatism is on the rise. The breakup of the Soviet Union and Yugoslavia are among the most obvious examples. But there are others, and some of them are occurring in surprising places—portions of the world that were thought to have stable, entrenched nation-states. The "velvet divorce" between the two regions of Czechoslovakia, the mounting drive to partition Italy and establish a northern Italian state, the quiet but surprisingly strong surge of Scottish nationalism, and the ongoing secessionist campaign in Quebec provide ample evidence that separatism is not confined to Africa and Asia.

The strength of the countervailing trends of economic globalism and cultural parochialism reinforces the likelihood of political turmoil and often wrenching changes in international affairs throughout the coming decades. Shaky, artificial states are especially vulnerable to being ground between the millstones of such powerful disintegrative forces. The evidence of the resulting turmoil is all around us. According to the Stockholm International Peace Research Institute, there were 30 major (producing at least 1,000 casualties in the previous 12 months) internecine and cross-border conflicts in 1995.[11]

Boutros-Ghali and other leaders warned that if the international community failed to stem the disintegration of such states as Somalia and Bosnia, within a generation or so there might be several hundred "ministates," many of which would be dominated by narrow, intolerant ethnic or religious agendas. Such warnings may well be proven right, but it is the essence of hubris to assume that the United Nations or any other international body will be able to prevent that result. If the forces chipping away at the foundations of existing nation-states are indeed so pervasive and powerful, it is highly improbable that the United Nations will be able to stem, or even manage, the political turbulence that has already begun to sweep the post–Cold War world.

Globalism or Regionalism?

Any collective security system would be hard-pressed to succeed, given the extent of disintegrative trends. But a *global* collective security system is especially impractical. It assumes that militarily capable nations will choose to expend financial resources and put their troops at risk to deter or suppress conflicts that have little or no relevance to their national security interests. Such manifestations of altruism are exceedingly rare in the long history of international affairs.

Moreover, it is not clear that it would be wise to encourage great powers to meddle in local conflicts outside their own regions even if they were so inclined. Among other problems, the globalist strategy increases the danger of friction among those powers unless their agendas are fully compatible. Even if friction does not arise at the start of a UN-sponsored mission, it can occur with a change of policy or regime in one of the major powers. Pat Buchanan rightly warns of the danger of making minor conflicts the concern of outside great powers. Referring to the intervention in Bosnia, he states that such a policy has already "made the Balkan war what anyone with a sense of history hoped it would not again become: a playground for great power rivalry."[12]

It is both safer and more realistic to deal with disorders on a regional, and sometimes even a subregional, basis. That approach maximizes the likelihood that there will be one or more significant powers with a stake in dampening the conflict. Those countries have an incentive to contribute military personnel to a peacekeeping operation and to help pay its costs. They also have an incentive to get other, smaller countries in the region to join the enterprise. True, the fact that major regional powers have a stake in the conflict may skew the results, producing unjust outcomes, but as discussed below, globalism rarely ensures equitable results either.

The alternative to regional initiatives is to hope that distant, disinterested parties will be willing to make the necessary investments and sacrifices. But that is a forlorn hope in most cases. One cannot expect Japan or China to have a burning concern about events that transpire in West Africa, or the United States to be as concerned as the European Union about developments in the Balkans, or Russia to fret about disorders in Central America and the Caribbean. It is both more practical and more equitable to expect nations on the scene, rather than outside powers, to take responsibility for dealing with conflicts in their regions.

The regionalist approach can be implemented either through formal regional security organizations or, where such organizations are nonexistent or underdeveloped, on an ad hoc basis. Europe and the Western Hemisphere appear to be ahead of other regions in developing capable regional security organizations. The Organization of American States has been in existence almost as long as the United Nations and has been involved in a number of peacekeeping missions. Europe has one comprehensive security association, the Organization for Security and Cooperation in Europe, and several subregional bodies that have considerable potential—most notably the Western European Union. (NATO is also attempting to transform itself from a traditional military alliance into an organization with a focus on peacekeeping. But NATO's Cold War baggage and the probability that an enlarged NATO will provoke Russia make it an unsuitable institution for dealing with the security problems of post–Cold War Europe.)[13]

The prospects in other regions are not as favorable. The Organization of African Unity has some promise, but it has thus far been timid and ineffectual in confronting crises in such countries as Somalia, Sudan, Burundi, and Rwanda. The Economic Community of West African States showed greater initiative in trying to end the civil war in Liberia, albeit with mixed results. Regional and subregional security institutions are either absent or terribly underdeveloped in the Middle East, Central and South Asia, and the Far East—although the greater interest in security issues shown recently by the Association of Southeast Asian Nations offers some hope for the emergence of an effective body in that region.

Washington should encourage the strengthening of regional security organizations whenever possible. The proposal by former secretary of state Warren Christopher to help African states develop a rapid-reaction force to respond to armed conflicts and humanitarian emergencies was constructive.[14] (Even in that case, the security system must be organized and managed by the countries in the region; such programs cannot be designed, funded, or run by the United States.)

Although regional and subregional collective security systems are more feasible than the globalist version, there may be many cases in which even such smaller scale enterprises prove impractical. To the extent that stability can be fostered at all, it may have to be done through informal balance-of-power arrangements or regional hegemony exercised by a dominant power. There may also be occasions when the best policy may be to let a conflict run its course and not attempt to suppress it or orchestrate elaborate political settlements. Even those foreign policy practitioners who are obsessed with the alleged virtues of stability ought to recognize that sometimes when a conflict ends with a definitive victory for one faction, it produces greater stability in the long run than would be the case were a battlefield verdict thwarted by outside parties.

Collective Security as a Facade for Injustice

In addition to emphasizing the objective of stability, proponents of global collective security insist that it increases the likelihood of equitable results. But there is, at the very least, an inherent tension between stability and justice. Moreover, throughout the history of the UN, the preference has clearly been for stability even when the results have been manifestly unjust. Interventions have been highly selective and marked by more than a dollop of hypocrisy.

Part of the reason is the structure of the UN system itself. The veto power exercised by the five permanent members of the Security Council ensures not only that they will never be subject to UN-sanctioned coercive measures but also that none of their allies, clients, or friends will be either. Such measures will be disproportionately directed against the handful of pariah states—and of course against insurgent movements that threaten influential regimes that have a stake in the status quo.

That underscores the point that there is nothing sacred—or even fair—about stability, and American policymakers make a serious error when they sign on to a global collective security agenda designed to protect the status quo. There are many instances in which radical change might produce a result measurably better than the current situation. Why, for example, should the Kurds have to remain a stateless people, brutalized and discriminated against by the governments of Iraq, Iran, and Turkey? Why should Serbs and Croats be forced to remain citizens of a Bosnian state when they have emphatically demonstrated that they desire other arrangements? Why should the black Christians of southern Sudan have to live under an Islamic regime that treats them as third-class citizens and has committed atrocities against them for decades? Such examples could be multiplied almost endlessly.

For the United States, helping to implement a global collective security strategy is an especially bad deal. By globalizing otherwise minor, localized conflicts, the United States, as the UN's most powerful member country and a permanent member of the Security Council, becomes entangled in obscure disputes. That is both expensive and risky. Revisionist governments or movements tend to view "stability" as a euphemism for a conspiracy of satisfied powers, led by the United States, to preserve an unjust global status quo. Washington risks becoming the principal target of their wrath, thereby creating adversaries that would otherwise have no incentive to challenge the United States.

Must the United States Embrace Collective Security?

Despite the doubtful feasibility and dubious morality of global collective security, proponents insist that the United States must embrace that mission to protect its own security. That contention is based on the belief that international disorder per se threatens American interests. (Indeed, the original U.S. decision to ratify the UN Charter and participate in a collective security framework was a product of such reasoning.) But is it a valid assumption? The best case for that proposition was made during the Cold War, when it was plausible to argue that minor regional or internecine conflicts actually had larger implications, since they typically involved surrogates of the other superpower or at least could be exploited by that rival. In a strategically bipolar world, the reasoning went, there were no geopolitical peripheries; a victory by a pro-Moscow regime or movement was a corresponding defeat for the U.S.-led "free world."

That thesis greatly oversimplified a complex international system even during the worst stages of the Cold War, and it led to such foolish commitments as the Vietnam intervention. But even if the reasoning had been valid in the Cold War setting, it would be inapplicable in the post–Cold War environment. The United States no longer faces a would-be hegemonic rival, nor is any credible challenger on the horizon. That is a watershed event, and it should fundamentally change the way we view regional or internecine conflicts. In most cases such disorders will not impinge on vital U.S. security interests. Washington can, therefore, afford to view them with detachment, intervening only as a balancer of last resort when a conflict cannot be contained by other powers in the affected region and is expanding to the point where America's security is threatened.

Critics invariably cite the Persian Gulf crisis as evidence that ostensibly minor conflicts in distant regions will frequently threaten U.S. interests and that collective security is, therefore, a crucial element of American foreign policy. That argument is erroneous. In reality, the gulf episode was a classic example of U.S. policymakers' confusing a limited threat that could have been contained by other Middle Eastern states with a dire menace of global proportions. Even Saddam Hussein's alleged ability to control world oil supplies and gain a "stranglehold" on Western economies does not hold up under scrutiny.[15] Moreover, the principal result of the "UN victory" in the gulf war has been to make the entire Persian Gulf region a U.S. military protectorate. Not only is that set of obligations entangling the United States in the myriad and complex political struggles of the region, but there is no prospective end to the mission.[16]

Collective Entanglements

A global interventionist policy within a collective security arrangement is the worst of all possible policy alternatives for the United States. Unilateral interventionism at least leaves U.S. officials extensive latitude to determine when, where, and under what conditions to use the nation's armed forces. Working through the UN

Security Council to reach such decisions reduces that flexibility and creates another layer of risk and obligation. That is certainly true if Washington is serious about collaborating in genuine collective security operations and does not merely seek to employ the United Nations as a multilateral facade for U.S. policy objectives.

Of course, U.S. officials have used the United Nations to give U.S. initiatives a multilateral patina.[17] That was true as far back as the Korean War. The commander of "UN forces" in that conflict was always an American, and the United States provided nearly 90 percent of the troops and weaponry. Crucial decisions, such as whether to cross the 38th parallel and liberate North Korea, were made in the Pentagon and White House, not UN headquarters.

The Persian Gulf intervention was only marginally more of a bona fide collective security partnership. President George Bush was content to work through the United Nations as long as the other Security Council members—and other members of the international coalition—were willing to endorse Washington's policy agenda. The administration was even willing to engage in some bargaining, if the input from other parties did not affect core U.S. objectives. The military decisionmaking authority and the command structure, however, were overwhelmingly American, just as they had been in Korea. Washington was unquestionably more subtle in creating a multilateral facade for the Persian Gulf intervention than for the Korean "police action," but it was still a facade.

Some advocates of multilateralism apparently believe that the Persian Gulf model can be used for future peace-enforcement operations. That is highly improbable. Aside from the obvious point that no collective action can be taken if a permanent member of the Security Council is the "aggressor" or regards the accused aggressor as an important ally or client, there are other reasons why it would be difficult to replicate the gulf operation. Other key international actors acquiesced to a dominant U.S. role because of the convergence of several factors peculiar to the gulf crisis. Even those powers that harbored doubts about the course charted by Washington realized that the cost of opposing U.S. policy would be high (China, for example, knew that opposition would probably mean the end of its most-favored-nation trade status) and did not deem the stakes important enough to justify the risk.[18]

That will not always be the case. (Indeed, the disarray of the Persian Gulf coalition when Washington launched air strikes against

23

Iraq following Saddam's September 1996 military offensive against Kurdish-held areas in northern Iraq illustrated how atypical the unity achieved at the time of the gulf war may have been.)[19] Other powers are likely to insist on far more policy input—a genuinely collaborative decisionmaking process—as the price of their cooperation in future collective security enterprises. Such a development automatically means a loss of decisionmaking autonomy for the United States.

U.S. leaders must also face the reality that they will not be able to use the United Nations only when it is convenient for Washington. The other permanent members of the Security Council (and such crucial actors—and probable future permanent Security Council members—as Japan, India, and Germany) will have their own security priorities for which they will want UN support, and they will insist on a quid pro quo from Washington. Such diplomatic "logrolling" has disturbing implications. The inexorable logic of the tradeoffs required by coalition diplomacy could entangle the United States in an assortment of irrelevant conflicts.

That danger exists even at the embryonic stage of an enhanced UN security role in which responses to crises must still be formulated on a largely ad hoc basis. It would be greatly magnified if a permanent peacekeeping force that included U.S. units were created.[20]

Instead of traveling down the perilous and ultimately unrewarding road of global collective security, we should seek to maximize U.S. decisionmaking independence. But the proper alternative is not a Pax Americana, under which an arrogant United States plays the role of the swaggering "sole remaining superpower." There is a more benign option: a policy of cautious unilateralism, or strategic independence.[21] With such an approach, American lives and resources would be reserved for the defense of vital American security interests.

It is crucial that Washington adopt such a policy. Global collective security should be objectionable to Americans on both strategic and constitutional grounds. In terms of strategic considerations, the United States needs to focus its attention and energy on dealing with *large-scale* adverse changes in the international system. Those developments have the potential to pose a threat to America's own security and well-being. The United States cannot afford to become bogged down in an assortment of petty conflicts under the banner of UN peacekeeping. Put bluntly, the behavior of a great power like China in a strategically important region like East Asia matters to the United States. Serbia's behavior in the Balkans, the status of Nagorno-Karabakh, or the fate of Somalia does not.

The pursuit of global collective security is also destructive to America's constitutional system. The federal government was designed to be a limited government with carefully defined powers. Providing for the common defense is a legitimate (indeed, essential) constitutional role; participating in UN nation-building enterprises or other global collective security schemes is not.

Realism about the United Nations

A policy of strategic independence would include a restrained and somewhat skeptical relationship with the United Nations. The belief that the UN was mankind's last best hope for peace was erroneous when the organization was established in 1945, and it is erroneous today. The United Nations is not an independent actor in the international system, the guardian of global peace, or the institutional conscience of humanity. If the United Nations is to play a constructive role in international affairs, we need to dispense with such overblown notions.

A dose of realism about the United Nations is overdue. The United Nations has limited but important utility as an international forum for the airing of different points of view and a mediation service to resolve quarrels. It also can play (and indeed has played) a useful role in coordinating humanitarian relief efforts. But the notion of the United Nations as a powerful global security body is unrealizable and undesirable. The organization's most ardent enthusiasts may inadvertently be its worst enemies. Proponents of "assertive multi-lateralism"—including, initially at least, some Clinton administration officials—want the United Nations to perform functions far beyond its capabilities. By pushing the organization to pursue such missions, with the almost inevitable subsequent failures, they risk discrediting the UN entirely.

The United Nations is merely an association of the world's *governments*—not, it should be emphasized, the world's peoples. As such, it is and should be only a marginal player on the global geopolitical stage. Once that limitation is fully accepted, the UN can perform some modestly useful functions—provided that it is properly focused on its core missions and is able to overcome its serious management problems.

Indeed, the American people should not want it any other way. The United Nations as an embryonic world government with an independent taxing authority and the other powers of a political state would pose a threat to individual liberty wherever it existed. Most UN members are ruled by authoritarian regimes that rarely even make the pretense of being democratic, and the culture of governance at the United Nations itself is hardly sympathetic to the values of individual rights and tethered government.

Even the more limited version of an activist United Nations, with a standing military force and a mandate to rebuild "failed states" around the planet, would constitute a dangerous entanglement for the United States. Not only is it dubious wisdom to make parochial conflicts a matter of global concern and intervention, but the lives of American military personnel should be put at risk only to defend America's vital security interests. Their lives should never be sacrificed for the abstract and unattainable principle of global collective security.

Notes

1. Boutros Boutros-Ghali, *An Agenda for Peace* (New York: United Nations, 1992).

2. Examples include Richard N. Gardner, "The Comeback of Liberal Internationalism," *Washington Quarterly* 13, no. 3 (Summer 1990): 23–39; Brian Urquhart, "Who Can Stop the Civil Wars?" *New York Times*, December 29, 1991; David Boren, "The World Needs an Army on Call," *New York Times*, August 26, 1992; Bruce Russett and James S. Sutterlin, "The UN in a New World Order," *Foreign Affairs* 70, no. 2 (Spring 1991): 69–83; Joseph S. Nye Jr., "What New World Order?" *Foreign Affairs* 71, no. 2 (Spring 1992): 83–96; *Collective Security and the United Nations: An Old Promise in a New Era*, 26th United Nations of the Next Decade Conference, 1991 (Muscatine, Iowa: Stanley Foundation, 1991); Alan K. Henrikson, "How Can the Vision of a 'New World Order' Be Realized?" *Fletcher Forum* 16 (Winter 1992): 63–79; Indar Jit Rikhye, *Strengthening UN Peacekeeping: New Challenges and Proposals* (Washington: U.S. Institute for Peace, 1992); Robert C. Johansen, "Lessons for Collective Security," *World Policy Journal* 8, no. 3 (Fall 1991): 561–74; Edward C. Luck and Toby Trister Gati, "Whose Collective Security?" *Washington Quarterly* 15, no. 2 (Spring 1992): 43–56; David J. Scheffer, "Toward a Modern Doctrine of Humanitarian Intervention," *University of Toledo Law Review* 23 (Winter 1992): 253–93; and Timothy W. Stanley, John M. Lee, and Robert von Pagenhardt, *To Unite Our Strength: Enhancing the United Nations Peace and Security System* (Lanham, Md.: University Press of America, 1992).

Such proposals have not entirely gone out of fashion. See Lukas Haynes and Timothy W. Stanley, "To Create a United Nations Fire Brigade," *Comparative Strategy* 14 (January–March 1995): 7–21; Carl Conetta and Charles Knight, *Vital Force: A Proposal for the Overhaul of the UN Peace Operations System and the Creation of a UN Legion*

The Mirage of Global Collective Security

(Cambridge, Mass.: Commonwealth Institute, October 1995); Frederick Bonnart, "It's Time for a Standing UN Rapid Reaction Force," *International Herald Tribune,* January 22, 1997, p. 9; and Carl Kaysen and George W. Rathjens, "Send in the Troops: A UN Foreign Legion," *Washington Quarterly* 20, no. 1 (Winter 1997): 207–28.

3. John F. Hillen III, "Killing with Kindness: The UN Peacekeeping Mission in Bosnia," Cato Institute Foreign Policy Briefing no. 34, June 30, 1995.

4. See Stefan Halper, "A Miasma of Corruption: The United Nations at Fifty," Cato Institute Policy Analysis no. 253, April 30, 1996; Jesse Helms, "Saving the U.N.: A Challenge to the Next Secretary-General," *Foreign Affairs* 75, no. 5 (September–October 1996): 2–7; and "The United Nations," *Cato Handbook for Congress: 104th Congress* (Washington: Cato Institute, 1995), pp. 285–89.

5. For discussions of the Law of the Sea Treaty and its many flaws, see Doug Bandow, "Do Not Endorse the Law of the Sea Treaty," Cato Institute Foreign Policy Briefing no. 29, January 27, 1994; and Doug Bandow, "Faulty Repairs: The Law of the Sea Treaty Is Still Unacceptable," Cato Institute Foreign Policy Briefing no. 32, September 13, 1994.

6. Halper, pp. 16–19.

7. In fact, the UN peacekeeping mission in Somalia in the early 1990s had as an explicit goal the reunification of all Somalia—apparently regardless of the wishes of the inhabitants of Somaliland. Ted Galen Carpenter, "Foreign Policy Peril: Somalia Set a Dangerous Precedent," *USA Today Magazine,* May 1993.

8. For an early discussion of such developments, see Ted Galen Carpenter, "The New World Disorder," *Foreign Policy* 84 (Fall 1991): 32–34.

9. Discussions of such trends include Joel Garreau, *The Nine Nations of North America* (Boston: Houghton-Mifflin, 1981); Kenichi Ohmae, *The End of the Nation State: The Rise of Regional Economies* (New York: Free Press, 1995); John Newhouse, "Europe's Rising Regionalism," *Foreign Affairs* 76, no. 1 (January–February 1997): 67–84; and Jessica T. Mathews, "Power Shift," *Foreign Affairs* 76, no. 1 (January–February 1997): 50–66.

10. That is a point stressed in Benjamin R. Barber, *Jihad vs. McWorld: How Globalism and Tribalism Are Reshaping the World* (New York: Random House, 1995).

11. Stockholm International Peace Research Institute, *SIPRI Yearbook, 1995: Armaments, Disarmament and International Security* (New York: Oxford University Press, 1995), pp. 1, 16–20.

12. Patrick Buchanan, "Power Rivalries Revisited," *Washington Times,* February 23, 1994, p. A16.

13. For an extended discussion, see Ted Galen Carpenter, *Beyond NATO: Staying Out of Europe's Wars* (Washington: Cato Institute, 1994).

14. Thomas W. Lippman, "U.S. Calls for All-Africa Crisis Force," *Washington Post,* September 28, 1996, p. A1.

15. Space considerations preclude a detailed discussion of these points. See Ted Galen Carpenter, "Bush Jumped the Gun in the Gulf," *New York Times,* August 18, 1991; Christopher Layne and Ted Galen Carpenter, "Arabian Nightmares: America's Persian Gulf Entanglement," Cato Institute Policy Analysis no. 142, November 9, 1990; David R. Henderson, "Do We Need to Go to War for Oil?" Cato Institute Foreign Policy Briefing no. 4, October 24, 1990; Doug Bandow, "The Myth of Saddam's Oil Stranglehold," *New York Times,* September 17, 1990; and Christopher Layne, "Why the Gulf War Was Not in the National Interest," *Atlantic Monthly,* July 1991.

16. See F. Gregory Gause III, "The Illogic of Dual Containment," *Foreign Affairs* 73, no. 2 (March–April 1994): 56–66; and Barbara Conry, "Time Bomb: The Escalation of U.S. Security Commitments in the Persian Gulf Region," Cato Institute Policy Analysis no. 258, August 29, 1996.

17. For a discussion of that ploy, see Ted Galen Carpenter, "Direct Military Intervention," in *Intervention into the 1990s: U.S. Foreign Policy in the Third World*, ed. Peter J. Schraeder (Boulder, Colo.: Lynne Rienner, 1992), pp. 159–61, 168–69.

18. For a discussion of China's shifting and frequently ambivalent policy regarding UN military missions, see M. Taylor Fravel, "China's Attitude toward UN Peacekeeping Operations since 1989," *Asian Survey* 36, no. 11 (November 1996): 1103–21.

19. Ted Galen Carpenter, "Misguided Missiles," *New York Times*, September 12, 1996.

20. On the problems associated with the idea of a permanent UN military force, see Doug Bandow, "Avoiding War," *Foreign Policy* 89 (Winter 1992–93): 156–74; and Jeffrey R. Gerlach, "A UN Army for the New World Order?" *Orbis* 27, no. 2 (Spring 1993): 223–36.

21. For more detailed discussions of strategic independence, see Ted Galen Carpenter, *A Search for Enemies: America's Alliances after the Cold War* (Washington: Cato Institute, 1992), pp. 167–204; and Ted Galen Carpenter, "Toward Strategic Independence: Protecting Vital American Interests," *Brown Journal of World Affairs* 2, no. 2 (Summer 1995): 7–13.

2. The United Nations and the Politics of Reform

Michael Stopford

It is impossible to discuss the current status of the United Nations without considering the vexed issue of reform. Indeed, the chief political debate revolves around reform: Is it feasible? Can it be reconciled with competing political priorities? Can U.S. demands ever be satisfied? Is the new secretary-general willing and able to carry out reform? The UN's role in the post–Cold War era is inextricably bound to prospects for reform.

The cause of UN reform has a history almost as venerable as the organization itself. To offer an anecdotal example, I recall the first book I read on the UN in 1979 when, as a junior member of Her Majesty's Diplomatic Service, I was considering joining the UN Secretariat; it was Labour Parliamentary Under-Secretary Evan Luard's account of the UN based on his years as a delegate in the late 1960s. The work finished with a chapter titled "Can the System Be Reformed?" Among Luard's points were that conflicts were increasingly civil and internal; human rights were of ever greater importance; the Secretariat should concentrate more on "early warning" issues; the Security Council should be expanded to include West Germany, Japan, India, and Brazil; peacekeeping should be rethought, UN financial problems resolved, and the economic development agencies better coordinated through an "up-graded ECOSOC" (Economic and Social Council) so as to at the very least "eliminate overlap and duplication"; and that "any serious attempt to improve the UN must include improvement of the Secretariat."[1]

That list has a familiar ring to it. In fact, Luard's proposals from nearly two decades ago could have been presented to the secretary-general as a timely contribution to the UN's 50th anniversary commemoration in 1995. A considerable proportion, unfortunately, of the UN reform agenda shares that distressing sense of déjà vu. If the refrain is constant and the precepts repetitious, some fundamental questions need to be answered: Why has reform proven so difficult to achieve? In whose interests is a strong and streamlined UN? Can any degree of consensus be found on reform priorities—or indeed on program priorities in general? The reports and reviews commissioned for the 50th anniversary, while offering several proposals for change, reform, and renewal, provided few insights into those basic dilemmas.

It is certainly misleading to view the entire UN system through the same prism, since that obscures the underlying political issues. The scope and the feasibility of reform vary among programs—and between principal UN organs and Secretariat bodies. It is clearly more overtly political to recommend enlargement of the Security Council than abolition of a Secretariat department. Nevertheless, even apparently management decisions such as the latter are always imbued with political considerations at the UN.

At this point, it is perhaps useful to conduct a brief review of the reform issues before various UN components, from the intergovernmental bodies to the internal Secretariat entities.

The Security Council

Little has changed in discussions of reform of this most important of UN bodies since Luard's day. In his 1993 annual report to the General Assembly, Secretary-General Boutros Boutros-Ghali declared rather too optimistically, "The question of the Security Council's membership structure is of crucial importance, and I look forward to the issue being resolved by the time of the 50th Anniversary of the Organization."[2] With that anniversary long past, the issue is no closer to resolution.

One of the major reports produced for the 50th anniversary, *The UN in Its Second Half-Century*, by the Independent Working Group on the Future of the UN, sought to curtail the use of the veto to "Chapter VII or other decisions entailing the use of military personnel" while pressing for the council's expansion to 23 members.[3] Progress toward expansion has been stymied by the obvious questions: who would be added from the "South" to "balance" the addition of Germany and Japan, and what would be the eventual veto arrangements for new permanent or semipermanent members?

The significance of the issue—like so much else at the UN— grows in proportion to the real relevance of the body involved. Hence, when the Security Council was at the height of its power and prestige, in the period during and shortly after the Persian Gulf War, its alleged lack of legitimacy appeared to be a serious problem. According to Professor José Alvarez of the University of Michigan, "To avoid the fate of its illustrious but failed predecessor, the League of Nations, the UN needs to shore up its floundering legitimacy." Alvarez wrote of the council's "democratic deficit" and of its power without accountability, lamenting that the United States had merely gone along with council membership for Germany and Japan "essentially on the grounds that [their] participation would lessen the pressures on the United States for peacekeeping funds." He commented that "oddly enough, the possible restructuring of what is potentially the most powerful supranational organ in the world has not generated much heat in Washington."[4] Council reform is no doubt low on Washington's list of foreign policy priorities.

The General Assembly

Intended to be the UN's supreme decisionmaking body, the assembly probably reached its nadir in the mid-1970s—at least from a U.S. perspective—when its resolutions appeared increasingly declamatory and devoid of any meaningful impact. The assembly's less dramatic, but ultimately more significant, role as the incubator of international opinion has more recently been usurped by the series of global conferences it has called. Persuaded that only such mega-gatherings—on the environment in Rio, population in Cairo, women in Beijing, and others—can constitute sufficient catalysts to address pressing global issues, the assembly perhaps inadvertently hastened its own irrelevance. Those conferences have varied in effectiveness—from the serious progress reached at Rio and Cairo to the vague premises of the "Social Summit" in Copenhagen.

The assembly's annual sessions, particularly when given over to anniversary celebrations as was the case in 1995, have not ceased to attract high-level participation; the lure of delivering an address from the General Assembly rostrum proves irresistible, although the true intended audience is frequently domestic. The formal results of those VIP segments are negligible: witness the instantly forgettable declarations produced. Opportunities for diplomatic contacts are generally considered the more valuable benefits.

31

The Clinton administration has served notice that it intends to push for the assembly to refocus on major global themes in the future and put a moratorium on mega-conferences.[5] That would undoubtedly channel assembly energies along more productive lines, although it may prove hard to resist the centrifugal tendencies of the "general debate." The assembly retains final say over budgetary matters, which may become more politicized as financial constraints increase.

Economic and Social Council

The unanimity that proves so elusive on UN reform questions at least appears in the almost universal agreement on ECOSOC's ineffectiveness. The need for a complete reform of ECOSOC's competence, procedures, and structure has been acknowledged for decades. As former assistant secretary of state Charles William Maynes put it on August 31, 1995, in an address to the National Assembly on the U.S. in the UN, "The decisions of ECOSOC have little relationship to reality." Criticizing the lack of coordination, he urged radical restructuring.[6]

Two of the major reports for the UN's 50th anniversary contained similar recommendations. *The UN in Its Second Half-Century* called for the establishment of a 23-member economic council to integrate all the economic agencies, and the Commission on Global Governance called for ECOSOC's replacement by an economic security council with broad oversight powers.[7] As Under-Secretary of State Tim Wirth acknowledged, "Clearly ECOSOC has not worked very well. That is why we have conferences in Rio, Cairo, Copenhagen, Istanbul. If the UN was working the way it ought to, we would not need these conferences."[8] Others are less enthusiastic about the prospects of expanding the UN's economic reach. New Zealand's prime minister Jim Bolger argues, "The concept of international bureaucrats sitting in New York trying to direct world economic policy is a non-starter."[9]

The UN System

The UN system of specialized agencies was conceived on the premise that it was possible to insulate the functional agencies of the international system from the central UN's political preoccupations. In many cases, it might be argued that that produced the worst of both worlds: the agencies have not been immune to political pressures, in particular over Middle East issues, while the system has suffered from lack of any central coordination. The agencies have also been beset by the same lack of accountability with respect to their management that has affected the UN proper.

The United States has taken the decisive step of withdrawing from UN agencies on several occasions. Such action has generally been the final result of growing financial pressures from Congress. For example, the U.S. withdrawal from the International Labor Organization in 1977 was preceded by congressional reduction in funding for the agency. Congressional action similarly preceded the withdrawal in 1984 from the UN Educational, Scientific, and Cultural Organization (UNESCO).[10] The latest agency to be identified for U.S. withdrawal is the UN Industrial Development Organization (UNIDO), based in Vienna. The proposal to shut down UNIDO, as well as the UN Conference on Trade and Development (UNCTAD), was first made in the report of the Commission on Global Governance, which lent international credibility to the U.S. action.[11]

The reasons given for withdrawal are not uniform: it is hard to disagree with the authors of *Our Global Neighborhood* that "the UN system must from time to time shut down institutions that can no longer be justified in objective terms."[12] The rationale for leaving UNESCO, however, was related, not to that organization's underlying purpose, but to its excessive politicization and severe mismanagement. Once out, however, it is hard to go back in. The domestic constituency for doing so is evidently less than overwhelming. Hence, despite what Maynes and others acknowledge as the "important reforms completed" by the clearly competent director-general of UNESCO, the administration decided in December 1994 not to reenter that organization.[13]

Peacekeeping

The vexed question of peacekeeping—and the underlying issue of the limits of international intervention—merits a far longer and more in-depth treatment than is possible here. On the budget front, the unpredictable nature of peacekeeping expenses has long been a source of political and financial woes. The simple expedient of reserve funding has proved difficult to implement. The past two years have seen problems in meeting commitments for new UN mandates in Haiti, Guatemala, El Salvador, and Rwanda. The proposed 1998–99 budget, however, contains an additional $70 million for "special missions extensions or to anticipate new ones."

The Secretariat

Criticism of the Secretariat's efficiency and quality is nearly as universal as that of ECOSOC. According to Maynes, "The personnel policies of the UN . . . remain an institutional scandal."[14] Much of the blame for the alleged poor quality of Secretariat performances has been laid to the charter's careful balance; its article 101 says that in employing staff the "paramount consideration . . . shall be the necessity of securing the highest standards of efficiency" and that "due regard shall be paid to the importance of recruiting the staff on as wide a geographical basis as possible." In their 1995 session, the American Assembly participants declared unequivocally, "The principle of geographical representation should be clearly subordinated to the merit principle in hiring, with the aim of significantly raising the quality of staff."[15]

It is simplistic, however, to blame geographic distribution for all of the Secretariat's ills. The principle has certainly been abused by managers, and the tendency to enforce a quota system at every level is obviously a mistake. The Secretariat would benefit from a far more fundamental reordering—perhaps taking a cue, as Elliott Richardson once suggested, from the corporate world's "reduction in middle management and increased productivity" brought about by such measures as vastly increased use of information technology.[16]

A succession of American under secretary-generals—from Richard Thornburgh to the present incumbent, Joseph Connor—has been accorded the invidious task of administrative reform and some downsizing at the Secretariat. Despite their best efforts, the results so far reflect the American Assembly document's advocacy of limited measures, "to approach the pruning process rationally."[17] A more extensive redesign of the landscape might yield a hardier plant in the long term.

Much has been made of the Secretariat's pervasive "lack of accountability" and of the various recent initiatives to enhance both accountability and oversight—most notably the establishment of the Office of Internal Oversight Services. The conventional wisdom appears to be that the jury is still out on the new office. In his first report to the General Assembly, Under Secretary-General for Internal Oversight Services Karl Paschke acknowledges candidly that "overlapping and duplication of responsibility have not been adequately addressed, let alone eliminated." Paschke continues in the same refreshingly frank tone to note that "while the need of internal structural reform is widely acknowledged, the energy to bring it about is in short supply." Nevertheless, despite such admissions and the suggestion that "managerial and administrative skills are not well distributed in the Organization," prescriptions for action refer again to "pruning" and "weeding out."[18]

The actual investigations conducted appear to cover a wide range of activities. Paschke notes that his aim is to ensure steady oversight rather than to offer up "spectacular and short-lived actions." His specific management observations cover such crucial areas as human rights, a vital and truly significant sphere of UN activity, which recently suffered from the decision to superimpose a high commissioner on an existing Secretariat structure without implementing essential administrative reforms. Paschke correctly called for reappraisal, restructuring, and reorganization. On balance, it would seem that the new office is making a positive contribution, although it remains to be seen whether it will be given sufficient resources and cooperation to carry out its mandate.

The Secretary-General

In light of the acrimonious conflict over the secretary-general's election, Maynes's remarks in August 1995 were prescient:

> Relations between the Secretary-General . . . and the administration are at an all-time low. U.S. officials state off the record their sharp criticism of the current Secretary-General, suggesting his chances of re-election resemble those of a "snowball in hell." . . . We should begin the search for the successor to Boutros-Ghali now. Whatever his attributes or however unfair some of the criticism has been, it is clear that it will require new leadership at the UN to turn around the American attitude.[19]

The Clinton administration subsequently announced its intention to block a second term for Boutros-Ghali. The issue was affected by domestic considerations surrounding the presidential elections. It is nevertheless hard to disagree with Maynes's basic premise about the secretary-general and the state of U.S.-UN relations. The broader issue, however, is also enunciated by Maynes in the same address: "The U.S. should begin to promote the idea that no one should be elected to the position of Secretary-General who has not presented to the Security Council and General Assembly his program for UN reform."[20] Or as the recent report of the Council on Foreign Relations (chaired by financier George Soros) recommended, "The U.S. should work for the election of a UN Secretary-General who will act decisively to improve the performance of the Organization."[21]

The call for a comprehensive search for candidates for the position of secretary-general was elaborated most extensively by Brian Urquhart and Erskine Childers, senior officials of the UN and the UN Development Programme, respectively, in their 1990 study, "A World in Need of Leadership." The authors criticize the current practice of leaving the secretary-general's election to a thoroughly reactive, political process and call for a proactive, serious search and discussion. They dismiss the venerable principles of geographical rotation and of not considering a candidate from the "permanent five." They suggest a single, seven-year term. They also propose other high-level management changes, such as the introduction of a system of three deputies, and posit the key link with UN reform: "The revitalization of the UN system and the quality of its leadership are closely related."[22]

The hope for reform tied to renewed political leadership at the UN has been echoed in the international media, together with the same expressions of exasperation at the manner in which the secretary-general is habitually chosen. The *Times* of London declared on June 6, 1996—before the U.S. announcement of opposition to a second term for Boutros-Ghali—that "the process of choosing the UN 'chief administrative officer' is haphazard to the point of irresponsibility. There is no search committee, no deadline of application, no requirement of candidates to set out their plans for the organization." The paper concluded that "the time for reform is now, but that if the current incumbent should win a second term by default, governments will have proved that they do not, in reality, care whether the UN wrestles its way into the modern world or continues its present slide into financial insolvency and political irrelevance."[23]

The last point is ominously difficult to rebut. The same arguments were made broadly by *Washington Post* columnist Jessica Mathews, by Morris Abram in the *Wall Street Journal*, and—after the U.S. decision—by *The Economist* in its lead editorial.[24]

Almost all of the recommendations made by Urquhart and Childers seem more valid and urgent today than they did when they were written—at the time of the last election of a secretary-general in 1990–91. Their proposals were ignored then; it seems they will also be ignored today. Perhaps it is naive to expect to secure the independent and objective treatment the authors suggest for such a political selection. A still more cynical but pervasive view would hold that an independent, strong-minded secretary-general is precisely what the leading UN members would not countenance. It is, after all, asserted that Dag Hammarskjold's independence came as a surprise. The question remains: in whose interest would be an effective and strengthened UN?

Money and Reform

In an organization in which obligatory membership dues are assessed proportionate to a member's economic product, while programs are decided on by a majority of unweighted votes, the major contributor has historically found itself in a difficult position. Organizational reforms called for by the United States have seemed, according to Gregg, "almost impossible to achieve in the prevailing political climate at the UN."[25] It was in the Reagan era that the perhaps inevitable consequences of the dichotomy began to appear. It was then that the United States "undertook to compel the UN to change its ways by withholding a sizable portion of its sizable financial assessment." Although earlier years had seen selective withholdings of contributions, chiefly for political programs such as those advancing the interests of the Palestine Liberation Organization, with which the United States then disagreed, the Reagan years were the first to see financial leverage exerted wholesale to secure comprehensive reform—or at least to try "to force the UN to perform as the United States wanted it."[26]

Congressional action paralleled the administration's attitude in some of the most significant measures adopted, most notably the Kassebaum amendment of 1985. That amendment mandated a reduction of U.S. contributions to 20 percent if weighted voting on budgetary matters was not introduced. One of the more effective intergovernmental administrative reform groups at the UN (the so-called Group of 18 chaired by then permanent representative to the UN and now Norway's ambassador to Washington, Tom Vraalsen) resolved the issue by helping to introduce the basics of consensus voting on budgetary questions. But it must be admitted that the congressional amendment had the desired effect: financial leverage secured a major change.

Senator Kassebaum argued that "the history of the UN has shown conclusively that it requires Congress, rather than executive branch action, to bring the UN and it agencies under control."[27] The power of the purse has been potent. Congressional appetite for unilateral action with respect to the UN has not diminished over the years. When peacekeeping expenses were at their height, two years ago, with the political burden compounded by setbacks in Somalia, carnage in Rwanda, and confusion in the former Yugoslavia, Congress decided to reduce its assessed share from over 31 percent to the same level as the regular budget—25 percent.[28] Downward pressure on the regular budget figure has now resumed, with agreement tentatively edging toward 20 percent.

Nevertheless, to decry such unilateral action does not mean it will not work: the latest staff cuts at the UN and the round of efficiencies introduced must be attributed to determined U.S. pressure—whether from Congress, the administration, or both. As the *Washington Post* noted, "U.S. pressure has had some successes . . . that will help the UN meet its approved 'no growth' budget of 2.6-billion dollars."[29] Ambassador Madeleine Albright declared, in fact, that the UN's proposed budget outline for 1998–99 is a "responsive step towards the fiscal reform mandated by the General Assembly" and that its adoption would be "a priority for the U.S."[30] The budget proposes a $179 million decrease from current spending levels to be achieved through staff reductions and efficiency gains.

Politics and Priorities

Where does this compendium of pruning, reorganization, and downsizing leave the overall state of reform at the UN? Can we envisage a sufficiently comprehensive renewal to ensure a future for the UN? According to Sen. Jesse Helms (R-N.C.), writing in the pages of *Foreign Affairs*, if the next secretary-general demonstrates insufficient reformist zeal, the next incumbent "could—and should—be the last."[31]

For the former chairman of Volvo, Pehr Gyllenhammar, the answer is also simple: "Close it down and start again!"[32] With that sweeping, no-nonsense corporate attitude, he asserts that "the UN should declare bankruptcy and conduct a fundamental reorganization and downsizing—all at the same time." The clean-slate approach has its appeal. Gyllenhammar is also convinced that "an organization to deal with today's conditions and tomorrow's world" is essential. That is more, of course, than Stefan Halper's policy study for the Cato Institute would concede, suggesting as it does that "it may well be that the international body is no more relevant to the world's problems than the Holy Roman Empire was in its waning decades. If that is the case, we should rid ourselves of the UN as Napoleon did Europe of the empire in 1808."[33] (Ironically, it was Napoleon's ambition and subsequent defeat that perhaps led to the first seeds of collective security ideas after the Congress of Vienna.)

Halper and Gyllenhammar even use the same language in calling for a radical overhaul. Yet their message has so far eluded the illustrious series of UN reformers. Professor Leon Gordenker of Princeton University notes that "the organizational translations of the tasks assigned to the UN have resulted in a web of structures whose formlessness even the sloppiest spider would reject." He endeavors, like many others, to see whether possibilities exist for "reorganizing, eliminating or adapting some of the web." And he notes, in the same vein as Gyllenhammar's call for an organization that "would deal with today's conditions and tomorrow's world," that with respect to the UN system "old organizational construction burdens the present."[34]

All bureaucracies—national and international—have grown skillful at resisting change. Here Halper is doubtless right that "bureaucratic bric-a-brac once established are almost never eliminated even though their usefulness has long since come to an end."[35] Moreover, it is certainly discouraging to see some of the same reform ideas produced at regular intervals, with little to show for implementation in the intervening years. One example I recall most vividly occurred during Secretariat-wide brainstorming on the relentless lack of coordination among humanitarian relief organizations in 1990. My older colleagues remarked that precisely the same issues had been raised and similar recommendations made by Sir Robert Jackson, an experienced "disaster" hand, in the 1960s.[36] Meanwhile, the latest organizational structure created in 1992 to meet coordination needs (the Department of Humanitarian Affairs) has been deprived of the resources and the authority to play any fundamentally meaningful role.

Gordenker is forced to conclude that "no thorough-going organizational reform of the UN system has either been undertaken or succeeded—despite occasional pressure from some governments."[37] Even the pruning and trimming of parts of the system that have progressed have done so against great resistance and with considerable difficulty. And once again, they have not touched the foundations, only the periphery. (The same could be said of the U.S. decisions to withdraw from UNIDO or UNCTAD.) There is thus a disheartening Catch-22 quality to those minor reform goals. Gordenker notes "some rather rococo structures . . . if some of them disappeared tomorrow, their loss would hardly be felt outside the UN enclaves." He asks, "What holds back such an effort?" and suggests that "declining organizations" should be allowed to "become moribund," and then reformers should "administer the coup de grace."[38]

Ultimately, however, the disappointing achievements of UN reform cannot fully be laid at the door of bureaucratic inertia. Nor can a complete transformation be expected from a new secretary-general, even though a candidate chosen with the care prescribed by Urquhart and others would no doubt make a difference. The challenge of reform is in the last analysis a challenge of politics. What is to be reformed is part of the larger question of what the UN is to do today. Reform priorities are policy priorities. And there the intergovernmental "world organization" can hardly achieve a consensus. The result is all too frequently, as Gordenker describes it, the lowest common denominator: the outcome of a long bargaining process, a compromise after much horse-trading. International diplomacy is not geared to the adoption of clear solutions corresponding to majority wishes, as the simpler, more partisan agenda of national politics tends to be. Special interests multiply at the international level.

Reform at the most direct management level cannot answer the basic questions. Halper argues that the "real audit" he calls for "cannot be limited to fraud, waste, and outright theft, narrowly defined. . . . The audit needs to determine, not only whether the various bodies are effectively performing their missions, but also whether a particular mission is worth pursuing in the first place."[39] That is impossible. The member governments cannot unload the responsibility for their own inability to make tough political decisions onto a management-consultancy audit operation. They have tried to do so, but the consultants' and auditors' reports have been rapidly shelved for the same political reasons that made their work necessary from the start.

To attribute the greater part of the blame to sovereign member governments is not to make light of the difficulties involved. The often illogical and incoherent structure of international organizations reflects, as Gordenker puts it, "changing perceptions among governments and the ideas of those who influenced them regarding the needs for transnational cooperation."[40] What is the proper subject for such cooperation, and how extensive or intrusive should it be? One has to go no further than the constant dissent over the level of international activity to be permitted on human rights issues to see how little consensus has yet been reached about the scope of international cooperation.

Recently, that question has again come to the fore with the U.S. response to Saddam Hussein's renewed aggression. Whether there is an international responsibility to prevent Saddam from abusing and oppressing part of the Kurdish population in northern Iraq—which is still officially Iraqi territory—is a key element in the military action taken. It recalls the crucial debate in the Security Council in 1991 over the brief but pivotal Resolution 688 concerning international protection of the Kurds. In condoning a degree of international enforcement of human rights protection through the Security Council, that resolution went as far as the Security Council has ever ventured.

The post–Cold War and gulf war era of international interventionism, of "assertive multilateralism," of extensive UN peacekeeping and peace enforcement, of a highly activist secretary-general, was short-lived. The subsequent retrenchment has perhaps left still less basis for agreement about the proper role of UN multilateralism—and hence still less consensus as a basis for reform.

Yet in the last analysis I do not believe it is beyond our capacity to agree on a limited number of core functions for the UN—and to build the nucleus of a reformed structure around them. The charter remains both valid and visionary: we are fortunate we do not have to draft it today, when the Declaration for the 50th anniversary is forgotten no sooner than the ink is dry. As Gyllenhammar says, "The UN has a wonderful charter."[41] Meanwhile, the current U.S. reform plan wisely calls for "focusing the UN on its core missions," as David Birenbaum, former ambassador at the U.S. mission to the UN, puts it. The plan calls for "peace and security, humanitarian relief, sustainable development and establishing human rights norms and international technical standards."[42] My own "core list" would comprise human rights, international protection of the environment, sustainable development, health, nuclear nonproliferation, and population. Issues of peace and security are last on the short list, reflecting the reality that the UN has provided an invaluable mechanism for dealing with those issues but does not always have a comparative advantage. Sometimes, as the Council on Foreign Relations' report affirmed, ad hoc coalitions will be preferable.[43]

The notoriously difficult task of producing criteria for evaluation and reform requires a modicum of prior agreement on overall objectives. The central issue, as a commentator on the report of the Commission on Global Governance put it, is, indeed, "In whose interest is it to reform the UN and why should anyone do it?"[44] If we keep the focus tight, I believe we can demonstrate that it is in the universal interest. And if reform follows that focus, the overhaul will be radical and comprehensive. Business as usual, of course, would be the ultimate proof of indifference.

Notes

1. Evan Luard, *The UN: How It Works and What It Does* (London: Macmillan, 1979), pp. 164, 167, 165.

2. Boutros Boutros-Ghali, *Report on the Work of the Organization* (New York: United Nations, 1993), p. 12.

3. Independent Working Group on the Future of the UN, *The UN in Its Second Half-Century: The Report of the Independent Working Group on the Future of the UN* (New Haven, Conn.: Yale University Press, 1995).

4. Jośe E. Alvarez, "The Once and Future Security Council," *Washington Quarterly* 18, no. 2 (Spring 1995): 5, 12.

5. U.S. Department of State, "Preparing the UN for Its Second Fifty Years," April 1996.

6. Charles William Maynes, Address to National Assembly on the U.S. in the UN, August 31, 1995, Washington.

7. Independent Working Group on the Future of the UN; and Commission on Global Governance, *Our Global Neighborhood* (Oxford: Oxford University Press, 1995).

8. Timothy Wirth, "The Commission on Global Governance," *Update*, October 1995, p. 8.

9. Jim Bolger, "The Commission on Global Governance," Speech delivered at World Economic Forum, Davos, Switzerland, January 31, 1995, p. 4.

10. Robert Gregg, *About Face? The US and the UN* (Boulder, Colo: Lynne Rienner, 1991), p. 65.

11. Commission on Global Governance, pp. 279–82.

12. Ibid., chap. 7, "A Call to Action," p. 346.

13. Maynes, p. 4.

14. Ibid., p. 14.

15. The 87th American Assembly, "U.S. Foreign Policy and the UN System," Final report, April 1995, p. 14.

16. Elliott Richardson, Letter to the UN secretary-general, July 26, 1993. Copy in the possession of the author.

17. The 87th American Assembly, p. 5.

18. Karl Paschke, *Report of the Secretary-General on the Activities of OIOS* (New York: United Nations, October 1995), Preface, pp. 7–9.

19. Maynes, pp. 3–4, 20.

20. Ibid., p. 20.

21. Council on Foreign Relations, *American National Interest and the United Nations* (New York: Council on Foreign Relations, 1996), Recommendations, p. 9.

22. Brian Urquhart and Erskine Childers, "A World in Need of Leadership," Dag Hammarskjold Foundation, Uppsala, Sweden, 1990, p. 40.

23. "Change the UN Guard," *Times* (London), June 6, 1996.

24. Jessica Mathews, "Filling the Top Spot at the UN," *Washington Post*, June 10, 1996; Morris Abram, "Time for a Woman to Run the UN," *Wall Street Journal*, May 16, 1996; and "A Funny Way to Fill the World's Top Job," *The Economist*, July 20, 1996.

25. Gregg, p. 60.

26. Ibid.

27. *Congressional Record*, June 7, 1985, quoted in Gregg, p. 84.

28. *Foreign Relations Authorization Act, Fiscal Years 1994–95*, P.L. 103–236, 103d Cong., 2d sess.

29. John Goshko, "Conflicts Bedevil Push to Reform UN," *Washington Post*, June 23, 1996.

30. Madeleine Albright, Statement of August 16, 1996, cited by *UNA/USA Washington Weekly Report* 22, no. 25 (August 30, 1996): 1–2.

31. Jesse Helms, "Saving the UN: A Challenge to the Next Secretary-General," *Foreign Affairs* 75, no. 5 (September–October 1996): 3.

32. Pehr Gyllenhammar, "Close It Down and Start Again," *International Herald Tribune*, August 14, 1996.

33. Stefan Halper, "A Miasma of Corruption: The UN at 50," Cato Institute Policy Analysis no. 253, April 30, 1995, pp. 19–20.

34. Leon Gordenker, "The UN Tangle: Policy Formation, Reform, Reorganization," World Peace Foundation, Cambridge, Mass., report no. 12, 1996, p. 2.

35. Halper, p. 16.

36. Robert Jackson, *The Capacity of the UN Development System* (New York: United Nations, 1969).

37. Gordenker, p. 30.
38. Ibid., pp. 48, 52.
39. Halper, p. 17.
40. Gordenker, p. 13n 29.
41. Gyllenhammar, p. 8.
42. David Birenbaum, "Our Reform Plan for the UN," Letter to the editor, *Washington Post*, July 16, 1996.
43. Council on Foreign Relations, p. 9.
44. M. Desai, "The Commission on Global Governance," *Times* (London), Higher Education Supplement, March 24, 1995, p. 5.

3. The Creation, Fall, Rise, and Fall of the United Nations

John R. Bolton

American foreign policy must be based on identifying our vital national interests and then advancing and defending those interests around the world. We can do so in a variety of ways—through formal alliances such as NATO, through informal coalitions as we did in Desert Storm, or on our own if necessary, as we did in Grenada and Panama. Those were the successful ways in which Presidents Reagan and Bush protected American lives and interests for 12 years.

By contrast, the Clinton administration, from its outset, chose to rely heavily on the United Nations. The administration scorned traditional definitions of the national interest, welcomed the watering down of American influence that UN-centric diplomacy entailed, and ignored the loss of American independence and flexibility caused by becoming wrapped around the UN axle. Although the administration has been more circumspect about its policies recently—to the extent, that is, that we can guess what the policy is on any given day—the basic Clinton attitudes have never really disappeared. I believe that President Clinton—unconstrained because he will never have to face the voters again—will return to his UN-centered approach to foreign policy. His selection of Madeleine Albright, U.S. ambassador to the UN, to be secretary of state in his second term strongly suggests such an approach. America has been seriously harmed by Clinton's policy mistakes in the last four years and could be gravely weakened in his second term.

The 1996 election provides a useful vantage point, one year after the hype of the UN's 50th anniversary celebrations, from which to reflect on the organization's history and prospects. That history falls into two broad periods: (1) the first 40 years after the UN's founding in 1945 and (2) the last 11 years, corresponding to the second half of the Reagan-Bush period and the Clinton administration to date.

Original Intent: Creation and First Fall

After World War II there was broad, bipartisan support for creating an international organization to prevent another global conflict. The Preamble to the UN Charter speaks eloquently of the need "to save succeeding generations from the scourge of war, which twice in our lifetime has brought untold sorrow to mankind."[1] Realistic American drafters, however, also carefully circumscribed the reach of the UN, by limiting its role to cases that presented a threat to "international peace and security," in the hope of avoiding giving the UN a global license for international social work. American officials also insisted on veto power in the Security Council as a sine qua non for U.S. membership, to ensure that no majority of UN members could ever threaten our national interests.

The Soviet Union's designs for global hegemony, and the Cold War they caused, largely consigned the idealistic original intent of the charter to gridlock and obscurity. Within just a few years after its founding, the UN was so obviously ineffective that the United States, and those in the world who shared our values, turned to more realistic approaches to protecting our basic national interests. Nuclear deterrence and strong political-military alliances such as NATO quickly became the preferred instruments for both protecting our liberty and preventing "the scourge of war."

During the 1960s and 1970s anti-Western and anti-American UN General Assembly majorities regularly and enthusiastically trashed our values. Led by the Communist bloc, those dictatorial or authoritarian governments mocked democracy through resolutions in the General Assembly and other UN bodies in an attempt to advance a thoroughly anti-democratic agenda. They assaulted America's world leadership and integrity in resolutions condemning U.S. foreign policies, year after year after year. They attacked our friends and allies, for example, in the 1975 General Assembly resolution that equated "Zionism" with "racism," a blood libel of the legitimacy of the state of Israel. They undermined economic liberty and global prosperity by endorsing Soviet-backed policies such as the New International Economic Order, a socialist dream of forcing redistribution of wealth to the Third World. And, all the while, the UN bureaucracy grew and grew, just like a coral reef—no planning, no system, no goal, yet blessed with apparently eternal life.

Incredible as it may sound today, the Carter administration was hardly troubled by any of those developments. President Carter's foreign policy team, much of which now serves President Clinton, thought that the hateful venom from the UN General Assembly was just a way for the Third World "to let off a little steam." After all, they said, each nation has one vote in the General Assembly, and they acted as though each nation's opinion was equally valid and entitled to the same deference. In the Carter years, America was just one more vote in the "parliament of man."

Sensible Americans, however, realized that the idealism of 1945 had long since been replaced by an organization we no longer recognized. They rejected the UN for any mission of real importance to American foreign policy.[2] Sen. Daniel Patrick Moynihan (D-N.Y.), former U.S. ambassador to the UN, correctly called it "a dangerous place" for American interests.[3] Since the UN had turned away from its principal founder, it is no wonder that the United States turned away from the UN.

The Rise and Second Fall

When Ronald Reagan became president, things began to change. Congressional majorities were thoroughly disenchanted with the United Nations, and they announced a dramatic transformation in American policy: play time at the UN was over. The United States would no longer reflexively and automatically pay for the privilege of being savaged.

In the mid-1980s President Reagan actually withdrew the United States from the UN Educational, Scientific, and Cultural Organization (UNESCO) because it had become bloated and wasteful, served virtually no legitimate American interests, and routinely attacked liberties central to the health of free societies. (The withdrawal was a noteworthy achievement, which the Clinton administration sought to reverse by having the United States rejoin UNESCO. As of now, however, there is no serious prospect that the United States will *ever* rejoin UNESCO.)

In addition, Congress, during several annual appropriations cycles in the mid-1980s, refused to pay the full U.S. assessments to other parts of the UN system to protest the waste, fraud, and abuse that were so rampant throughout the UN and to protest the charade that the UN somehow amounted to a "parliament of man." That may have been the most important development of all, because when the U.S. financial gravy train slowed down, even the somnolent bureaucrats at the UN were shocked into attention.

The United States also took on the fundamental hypocrisy of many UN members by challenging the human rights record of Cuba and other leaders of the Third World. President Reagan appointed Armando Valladares as the U.S. representative to the UN Human Rights Commission, so he could tell the world directly about the Castro regime's brutality. The Communist bloc and Third World countries were shocked, and they acted as though the UN rules did not allow the United States to defend itself.

Suddenly, it was the United States that was "letting off steam," and a lot had been accumulating over the years. By so doing, the Reagan administration advanced American interests, instead of simply defending them against the constant attacks of the Soviets and their Third World sycophants. We rejected the Carterite counsel, those cynics posing as idealists, who said that the UN could never really be changed and that trying to do so was not worth the effort. In effect, we said, "Change, or else!" President Reagan always understood that standing up for U.S. interests in the UN never required an apology.

Americans welcomed that new assertiveness in our foreign policy. In fact, President Reagan's policy laid the groundwork for rare opportunities to use the Security Council constructively, especially as "new thinking" in Soviet policy emerged during his second term:

- In the late 1980s the UN helped negotiate and monitor the truce in the war between Iran and Iraq to help protect the world's oil supply from disruptions in the Persian Gulf.
- Under American leadership, the Security Council supervised a process that brought free and fair elections to Namibia, the last colony in Africa, thus leading it out of apartheid and into independence.
- The UN provided monitors at the end of major Cold War conflicts, as Soviet troops withdrew from Afghanistan and Cuban troops withdrew from Angola.

Thus, traditional UN peacekeeping techniques advanced American interests through the Security Council. Even in those instances, however, we must understand the limited role actually played by the UN. Traditional UN peacekeeping requires that any UN involvement have the consent of all of the parties to a dispute, that UN troops and civilian personnel act in a consistently neutral fashion, and that UN troops use force only when necessary for self-defense. And, in all of those cases, the UN was an instrument of American policy, not a policymaker itself.

Even more dramatic and important, in the Persian Gulf crisis, America led the Security Council to perform for the first and only time in its entire history as the charter's framers had intended. (The Soviet boycott of the council during the early stages of the 1950 Korean crisis was the principal reason the council was able to function on that occasion; unfortunately, when the Soviets resumed full participation, gridlock again ensued.) The UN authorized the U.S.-assembled international coalition to use force to defeat and reverse the unprovoked Iraqi aggression against Kuwait.

After Saddam Hussein's armies of aggression had been humiliated, America used the Security Council and the coalition's military forces in the unprecedented humanitarian rescue of the Iraqi Kurds. To provide at least some compensation for the victims of Iraq's invasion, we had the Security Council establish a system to force the Iraqis to pay compensation. Even more important, we created a program, endorsed by the Security Council, to find and eliminate Iraq's weapons of mass destruction and their delivery systems. By so doing, we hoped to make it impossible for Iraq ever again to threaten its neighbors or our vital interests in the Persian Gulf. In each of those instances, American leadership made the difference. And, in each of those cases, the UN was an instrument of that leadership—a useful instrument to be sure, but only an instrument.

In addition, the Reagan and Bush administrations prevailed upon the UN General Assembly to repeal the odious and hateful "Zionism is racism" resolution. We gained UN approval for economic sanctions against Libya's terrorist regime in retaliation for the mass murder of the passengers and crew of Pan Am Flight 103. We fostered democratic elections in Central America, clearing away another legacy of the Cold War, even as we continued to hammer away at the Castro regime in Cuba. We created the concept of the "unitary UN" as a systematic basis for sweeping reform of the galaxy of UN agencies, to reduce waste and mismanagement. We rolled back politicization in the specialized agencies, to try to reconcentrate them on their technical missions rather than have them resolve such issues as whether the Palestine Liberation Organization was entitled to UN membership. Unfortunately, however, none of those accomplishments was easy, and the very difficulties we faced underscore the fundamental problems still remaining throughout the UN system.

Even so, the lesson was plain. When there was a vital U.S. interest at stake, the UN could serve a useful role as an instrument of U.S. policy. When the United States led, the UN could work.

Unfortunately, many misread or ignored that lesson, particularly then-governor Bill Clinton. He missed the point that the UN's "successes" after 1985 had been brought about by tough-minded American leadership. He did not see or understand that the UN was only an instrument of American policy, not the policy itself. He ignored the enormous effort that had been required to achieve even the first steps toward true reform in the UN system.

Even worse, Clinton took office believing that U.S. foreign policy could largely be run through the UN system. Indeed, in many respects, he and his advisers longed to make the conduct of American foreign policy subordinate to the UN, so uncomfortable were they with the unashamed, unembarrassed American leadership exercised by Presidents Reagan and Bush.

The Carter foreign policy team reemerged from hibernation, after 12 years of failing to learn from their own mistakes. Having given away the Panama Canal, been paralyzed by the Soviet invasion of Afghanistan, been driven to their knees by the Communist-led Sandinista revolution in Nicaragua, been humiliated by the Iranian kidnapping of our diplomats in Teheran, and sabotaged our national defense readiness by inattention and ineptness, the Carter team came back for another turn at the plate.

This time led by the naive and inexperienced Bill Clinton, they proclaimed a policy of "assertive multilateralism."[4] That policy, the meaning of which varied from day to day, was at best confused and at worst dangerous to U.S. interests. It clearly signaled, however, subordination of our international leadership, a turning away from a global role in the American Century, and a search for respite from hard choices. Even at the outset of his first term, we saw President Clinton tacking and triangulating, desperately trying to avoid the responsibility of U.S. leadership. After all, if foreign policy is always multilateral, there are plenty of others to bear the blame for failure.

Throughout its foreign policy, and especially under the banner of assertive multilateralism, the administration displayed an instinct for the capillaries, pursuing illusory concepts unrelated to tangible U.S. national interests. In endless multilateral meetings, from Copenhagen to Cairo and from Beijing to Istanbul, Clintonites have talked and talked, while real international threats to America and its friends—from the proliferation of weapons of mass destruction to state-sponsored terrorism—have grown and grown.

President Clinton basically lost interest in American leadership, around the world generally and in the UN specifically. He forgot that the UN was an instrument to be used to advance *America's* foreign policy interests, not to engage in international social work and ivory-tower chattering. His policy was to commit the United States through the UN to major involvements in peripheral conflicts, with little or no thought to the risks and costs involved. The results of the Clinton policy were calamitous.

First came tragedy, death, and disgrace in Somalia. There, we saw Clintonite foreign policy in its most pristine form, before spin control and reelection politics were able to camouflage the substance. By turning a generous, humanitarian relief operation launched by President Bush, and unmistakably led by the United States, into a test case of assertive multilateralism, President Clinton eviscerated America's ability to lead its own operation and left American troops in considerable peril.

President Clinton decided that Somalia would be a fitting place to engage in something called "nation building." Former secretary of defense Les Aspin said explicitly on August 27, 1993, "We went there to save a people, and we succeeded. We are staying there now to help those same people rebuild their nation."[5] It turned out that nation building was a vague and expansive policy President Clinton could neither understand nor implement.

By following misguided, dangerous policies in Somalia, the Clinton administration achieved what might have seemed impossible: it took a desert country and turned it into a quagmire for the United States. Eighteen Americans died in Mogadishu on October 3, 1993, because of assertive multilateralism. Still, President Clinton did not understand. Instead, he sent Secretary Aspin and Secretary of State Warren Christopher to brief Congress. The *Wall Street Journal* reported that Secretary Aspin was "the picture of confusion" and

51

"contradictory in his statements," and that Secretary Christopher "sat virtually silent."[6] So much for American leadership. Unfortunately, the whole world saw the entire episode as an example of U.S. policy disarray.

Next came neglect, indecision, and hypocrisy in the former Yugoslavia. To avoid hard choices, President Clinton sought to pawn off responsibility for Bosnia on the seemingly anonymous UN and the UN Protection Force (UNPROFOR). Thoroughly misunderstanding the nature of UN peacekeeping, the administration urged conflicting and inconsistent mandates on UNPROFOR and then failed to supply basic political leadership to correct the mess it had made.[7]

Virtually the president's first action after his inauguration was to torpedo the Vance-Owen peace plan. While there was much to object to in that plan, the administration had no substitute of its own, other than platitudes, and no idea what to do once it had vitiated the very strategy it had called for while campaigning. Even when it managed to generate policy ideas, the administration failed to lead the Western alliance. For many Americans—and our allies—the low point came early in 1993 when Secretary Christopher was sent to "consult" with other NATO members about an alliance strategy for the former Yugoslavia. To their amazement, the NATO governments found that Christopher had no real plan to offer.[8]

Then, even after the debacle in Somalia, the Clinton administration watched passively as UNPROFOR, in both its military and its civilian capacities, became ever more entwined with NATO efforts. Fundamental political-military issues such as command relationships, lines of operational control, and ultimate political responsibility were hopelessly muddled. Assertive multilateralism came more and more to look like mass confusion. All the while, the Bosnian Muslim victims of Serbian aggression were denied the means of defending themselves because of the administration's interpretation of an out-of-date Security Council weapons embargo.

That abdication of American leadership only made the ongoing tragedy of the former Yugoslavia worse. Ultimately, U.S. hesitancy required a much larger and riskier American presence on the ground than would have been needed had President Clinton not sought cover under the UN. Stronger American leadership earlier would have obviated the need to place so many in harm's way and to keep them in Bosnia for the lengthy period to which the administration has agreed.[9]

And while American lives were put at risk in UN missions by President Clinton, inattention to the UN's underlying management problems resulted in waste and paralysis in the UN system. We should not be surprised that the administration has been as unsuccessful in restraining waste, fraud, and abuse throughout the UN system as it has been in restraining domestic federal spending. In fact, as was the case in the 1980s, the only thing keeping UN expenditures in line is the withholding of payments by Congress, once again outraged at the UN's lack of responsiveness to true management reform.

But more is at stake here than just wasting American tax dollars, although that is bad enough. By the Clinton administration's own admission, it has deceived the American public about UN reform for the last four years. During testimony before congressional committees, in public speeches, and in private conversations, the Clinton team argued repeatedly that Secretary-General Boutros Boutros-Ghali was committed to major administrative and management reform. They made those claims even after the American under secretary-general for management and administration, selected by the Clinton administration, was fired for being unsuited for the job. They made those claims even after the first Office of UN Inspector General was exposed as a toothless watchdog. And they even made those claims while the secretary-general was recalling and shredding the comprehensive report on UN reform by former under secretary-general Richard Thornburgh.[10]

While uttering the demonstrable falsehood that Boutros-Ghali was serious about reform, the Clinton administration acted as though continued concern in Congress about UN waste, fraud, and abuse was the equivalent of bean counting. "All is well," said the Clinton team, "just pay the U.S. assessment, and our problems will be solved. Boutros-Ghali is on top of UN reform, and Congress needs to get behind him and his cost-cutting efforts." Boutros-Ghali strongly supported the Clinton policy of assertive multilateralism, and the president seemed to stand by his man. Indeed, Ambassador Albright scorned U.S. critics of the UN by saying, "Maybe their problem with the UN is that there are just too many foreigners there, but that can't be helped."[11]

Imagine the surprise, then, when the Clinton administration announced that Boutros-Ghali was being thrown off the train, obviously as an unnecessary obstacle to the president's reelection efforts.

Suddenly, the hero of UN reform had become an albatross. But what does that casual, Clintonite stab in the back tell us about three and a half years of assurances to Congress and the American public that all was well with UN reform? It should make clear that UN reform was nothing more than another pose, another foreign policy charade, by a president who changes policies like some people change clothes.

The administration professes to be deeply involved in the Middle East peace process, yet the public cat fight with Boutros-Ghali has humiliated the government of Egypt, a key actor in that process, and embarrassed the United States. Ironically, many supporters of Boutros-Ghali still hoped that President Clinton would win reelection, believing that, having successfully fooled the American people, the president would turn around and acquiesce in Boutros-Ghali's reelection. The final administration decision to veto Boutros-Ghali was, in fact, almost certainly motivated by fear of the domestic U.S. political consequences of not carrying out the threat. The result of Clinton's failed UN policies is that American interests are in retreat across the board, and the organization itself is virtually paralyzed.

Climbing Out of the Ditch

So, what do we do now? Some Americans simply want to withdraw from the United Nations, believing that it can never really be fixed. I understand the frustrations and the disappointments that lead to that view, even though I disagree with it. We should tell the world community instead, "Let's make one last effort to put things right in the UN. And make no mistake, our patience is not unlimited." We should stress the following specifics.

The New Secretary-General Must Deliver on Reform

President Clinton ambushed incumbent Secretary-General Boutros-Ghali. Now, after the fact, the administration has, through press leaks, taken credit for covertly supporting the ultimately successful candidate, Kofi Annan of Ghana. However, the administration's mishandling of the entire Boutros-Ghali affair, ironically, made it even more difficult than before to elect a secretary-general who sees the world—and the UN—the way we do.

So eager was the administration to appease those who argued that Africa was *entitled* to its candidate for a second term in the secretary-general's position, that it acquiesced in a Security Council procedure virtually guaranteed to produce an African winner.

Indeed, the administration seemed so desperate that it led many to believe that it might accept Salim A. Salim, the head of the Organization of African Unity. He is the man who, as Tanzania's ambassador to the UN in 1971, danced joyously in the General Assembly's aisles when Taiwan was denied representation in the UN over American objections.

The winner, Kofi Annan, was certainly preferable to Salim. Virtually all of Annan's career has been within the UN system, frequently in management and personnel positions. Few know "the system" better than Annan. He is, therefore, in the best possible position to deliver on reform, for bureaucratic trials, jargon, and obfuscation are not likely to distract him if he is truly engaged. From January 1, 1997, forward, the world can judge his performance—and his will.

But one should not invest excessive hope in any secretary-general. The UN Charter describes the secretary-general as the UN's "chief administrative officer." He is not the president of the world. He is not a diplomat for all seasons. He is not Mr. Friend of the Earth. And, most definitely of all, he is not the commander in chief of the World Federalist Army. He is the *chief administrative officer.* Nothing less than that, to be sure, but, with even greater certainty, nothing more.

Stick with Traditional UN Peacekeeping

Traditional UN peacekeeping, together with the often-important role the agencies of the UN system play in the international delivery of humanitarian assistance, can work and should be continued. Although peacekeeping has had only limited use throughout much of the UN's history, it is an option that we should preserve for appropriate use, such as the UN Disengagement Observer Force along the Golan Heights between Israel and Syria.

What should be relegated to history's junk pile at the first opportunity, however, are the chimerical Clinton notions of UN "peace enforcement," "nation building," and "enlargement." Those unworldly concepts have resulted in American personnel and resources being committed to UN operations far removed from vital American interests. Those concepts are based on misreadings of what happened in the world and in the UN in the late 1980s and early 1990s. In fact, they represent the triumph of those who have always felt uncomfortable with American world leadership, those who prefer a subdued, tamed America to one that unashamedly proclaims its vision and its interests.

Most important of all, American troops should almost never be placed under UN command. Americans face unique risks of being targeted, captured, and killed by fanatics and lunatics, as the tragic case of Colonel Higgins in Lebanon proved so dramatically just a few years ago. Even in traditional peacekeeping, with only the rarest exceptions where the highest American interests are at stake, Americans should not wear blue helmets—that is, participate in peacekeeping forces. In fact, we should revive the convention, which served us well for many years, that no troops from the five permanent members of the Security Council be involved in UN peacekeeping.

We should also reverse the Clinton administration's policy of indiscriminately sharing sensitive intelligence information with the UN Secretariat. That fuzzy-minded policy risks exposing sensitive intelligence sources and methods, as well as degrading our ability to act rapidly and independent of the UN when we choose to do so. When it serves palpable and immediate U.S. interests, such as helping to eliminate Iraq's weapons of mass destruction, we should consider limited exceptions, but only on a case-by-case basis and under the strictest possible safeguards. For similar reasons, there is no need to create any intelligence-gathering capability in the UN itself.

Finally, even in traditional peacekeeping operations, forces under UN command should operate under the control of the Security Council, not under that of the secretary-general. That is the arrangement the framers of the UN Charter intended, and we should require it. The chief administrative officer of the UN should stick to administration and stay out of military matters.

Do Not "Reform" the Security Council

Yet another example of the Clinton administration's pie-in-the-sky approach to the world was evidenced right at the start by the desire of officials to remake the Security Council through a kind of international quota system. Following theories that only liberal academics take seriously, the administration wanted to enlarge the council; add new permanent members, balanced geographically, perhaps on a rotating basis; and throw in additional nonpermanent members as well.[12] The next step, of course, would be the elimination of the veto power, the single greatest protection the United States has in the UN.

The bottom line is, leave the veto alone, and leave the Security Council's membership alone. Presidents Reagan and Bush worked hard to fix the council. The desire to remold the Security Council now to conform to theoretical models of contemporary global politics should not obscure our present ability to make the council function effectively, at least in certain circumstances.

Management and Financial Reform Remains Essential

We know what needs to be done to eliminate wasteful overstaffing; overlapping agency jurisdictions; endless and duplicative international conferences, meetings, and publications; and corruption and favoritism in contracting and procurement. If we revitalized the unitary UN approach to management and budget issues, we would have a comprehensive framework by which to judge our strategy and our progress, instead of the episodic, anecdotal, and uncoordinated efforts of the Clinton administration. Congress, on a bipartisan basis, should simply no longer tolerate waste, fraud, and abuse in the UN system.

Even more important, and of far more long-range significance, we need a dramatic change in the way UN agencies are financed. President Clinton's favorite professors already have their own idea—they want to give the United Nations the authority to tax various international transactions.[13] That authority would give the UN a revenue base independent of its member governments, a prospect that warms the hearts of those who do not much like the influence of the United States to begin with. Such proposals are completely unacceptable.

Congress has already pointed us in the right direction by ordering that the U.S. share of the cost of peacekeeping operations be no higher than its present assessment level in most UN specialized agencies—25 percent of the overall budget. We should go further and eliminate assessments altogether, moving toward a UN system that is funded entirely by purely voluntary contributions from the member governments. Such a system of voluntary contributions would allow each government to judge for itself whether it was getting its money's worth from the UN and each of its component agencies.

That would go a long way toward making the UN system responsive to the major contributors—especially to the United States, the largest contributor of all. If we were displeased with an agency's actions, we would simply lower our voluntary contribution until our views were taken seriously. For those agencies that were doing particularly good work, we might even consider a contribution level higher than our present assessment. And, if things were really bad, we should follow Ronald Reagan's example and withdraw from one or two agencies. That would really get their attention.

We need to explain to our allies just how serious we are about reform, make sure they understand the strength of our opinions, and persuade them to "get with the program" on unitary UN reform. That task is a major challenge for American leadership generally in the international system, including in the international financial institutions such as the World Bank and the regional development banks. It is a challenge that the Clinton administration has failed utterly to meet.

Face Reality

Above all, let us be realistic about the United Nations. It can be a useful tool in the American foreign policy kit. The UN should be used when and where we choose to use it to advance American national interests, not to validate academic theories and abstract models. But the UN is only a tool, not a theology. It is one of several options we have, and it is certainly not invariably the most important one.

Conclusion

The UN has arisen, fallen, risen, and fallen again in our esteem, all in just 51 years, and especially in the last 11. The UN was an admirable concept when conceived; it has served our purposes from time to time; and it is worth keeping alive for future service. But it is not worth the sacrifice of American troops, American freedom of action, or American national interests. The real question for the future is whether we will know how to keep our priorities straight.

Notes

1. *Charter of the United Nations* (San Francisco: United Nations, June 26, 1945), Preamble, p. 1.

58

2. See, for example, *Report on the U.S. and the U.N.: A Balance Sheet*, ed. Burton Yale Pines (Washington: Heritage Foundation, 1984); and Harris O. Schoenberg, *A Mandate for Terror: The United Nations and the PLO* (New York: Shapolsky, 1989).

3. Daniel P. Moynihan, *A Dangerous Place* (Boston: Little, Brown, 1978).

4. Thomas W. Lippman, "African Crises Test Limited U.S. Commitment," *Washington Post*, June 13, 1993, p. A33.

5. Quoted in John Lancaster, "Aspin Lists U.S. Goals in Somalia," *Washington Post*, August 28, 1993, p. A1.

6. Jeffrey H. Birnbaum and David Rogers, "Clinton to Set Pullout Date for Somalia but Plans to Boost Troop Strength First," *Wall Street Journal*, October 7, 1993, p. A3.

7. John Hillen, "Killing with Kindness: The UN Peacekeeping Mission in Bosnia," Cato Foreign Policy Briefing no. 34, June 30, 1995.

8. Daniel Williams and John M. Goshko, "Reduced U.S. World Role Outlined but Soon Altered," *Washington Post*, May 26, 1993, p. A1.

9. William Drozdiak, "NATO Endorses New Bosnia Mission," *Washington Post*, November 19, 1996, p. A16.

10. Dana Priest, "House Votes to Reduce Payments to UN," *Washington Post*, February 17, 1995, p. A1.

11. Quoted in Thomas L. Friedman, "Dissing the World," *New York Times*, February 19, 1995, p. E13.

12. Commission on Global Governance, *Our Global Neighborhood* (New York: Oxford University Press, 1995), pp. 233–41.

13. Ibid., pp. 296–302.

PART II

THE UNITED NATIONS AS PEACEMAKER AND PEACEKEEPER

4. UN Military Missions as a Snare for America

Doug Bandow

The collapse of the Soviet Union and end of the Cold War have forced a long-overdue reevaluation of American security policy. Traditional containment is dead, since there is no longer an opposing, hegemonic power to contain. What new strategy, then, should replace containment?

Various unilateral approaches have been suggested, ranging from strategic independence to benevolent hegemony.[1] Absent from both the unilateral noninterventionist and the unilateral interventionist perspectives is reliance on other countries, especially through multilateral organizations. An important alternative strategy, however, is collective security. That approach is inherently interventionist, but it posits that American military activity would be carried out within a multilateral framework. Some advocates would prefer to pursue collective security through regional military and political alliances, such as an expanded NATO, but the more commonly suggested mechanism is the United Nations.

In fact, a diluted form of collective security has long been an aspect of American foreign policy. For instance, the United States gained the UN's imprimatur for combat in South Korea and more recently in the Persian Gulf and has backed various forms of UN peacekeeping around the globe. But there is significant support today for "strengthening" collective security, particularly by granting the UN both the authority and the means to mount military operations to punish aggressors and preempt, and perhaps even settle, civil disorders and wars. Despite the good intentions of those who desire a UN able to make and enforce peace around the globe, such a strategy risks ensnaring the United States in costly and bloody conflicts that are rarely solvable by outside parties or worth the price necessary to enforce even a tenuous peace.

Wilsonian Roots

The roots of collective security go back to President Woodrow Wilson's crusade for democracy and his successful campaign to pull the nation into World War I. In fact, at the peace talks in Versailles Wilson stated that "armed force is in the background" of his proposal and that "if the moral force of the world will not suffice, the physical force of the world shall."[2] However, it was the allied success in World War II that led to a more serious attempt to achieve an international order policed by the world's countries collectively. Even such a one-time isolationist as Republican Sen. Arthur Vandenberg of Michigan hoped that the United Nations would provide an effective system of collective security.

The UN Charter explicitly vests the Security Council with "primary responsibility for the maintenance of international peace and security." The charter goes on to establish procedures for dispute resolution, enforcement activity, and use of armed forces provided by member states. Most of those provisions have never been used, largely because the Cold War disrupted what was expected to be continued cooperation among the members of World War II's "Grand Alliance" as the Soviet Union used its veto to deadlock the Security Council.

In theory the UN has enormous authority. Article 42 empowers the Security Council to "take such action by air, sea, or land forces as may be necessary to maintain or restore international peace and security." Article 45 orders member states to "hold immediately available national air-force contingents for combined international enforcement action" so that the UN can "take urgent military measures." Plans for military action are to be drafted by the Military Staff Committee. Of particular interest is article 43, which specifies how the UN can raise a military by reaching agreements for armed forces to be made available to the Security Council.

With the end of the Cold War and with Moscow's cooperation in the Persian Gulf War, proposals to resurrect that original UN function began to appear. Indeed, in 1990 President George Bush declared before the UN, "Not since 1945 have we seen the real possibility of using the United Nations as it was designed, as a center for international collective security."[3]

Before leaving office, Bush advocated expansion of UN peacekeeping and promised that Washington would "emphasize training of combat, engineering and logistical units for the full range of peace-keeping and humanitarian activities."[4] For a time his successor seemed prepared to go much further. Candidate Clinton called for a UN rapid-deployment force for use in tasks other than peacekeeping, "such as standing guard at the borders of countries threatened by aggression" and "preventing mass violence against civilian populations."[5]

In his report, *An Agenda for Peace,* Secretary-General Boutros Boutros-Ghali advocated implementation of article 43 and much more. He asked that member states provide troops on short notice and fund a $50 million revolving fund and a $1 billion endowment for peacekeeping.[6] Nineteen governments have since placed their names on a standby roster for UN use. (Not that they seem willing to actually commit their forces. None of them offered any units for service in Rwanda, despite the secretary-general's request.) In January 1995 Boutros-Ghali revisited the issue, calling for creation of "a strategic reserve for the Security Council's deployment," specially trained units deployed in their home nations but on permanent call by the UN. He demanded that the UN have sole command of such forces and that member governments drop their tendency "to micro-manage."[7]

Assorted Punditry

A host of former UN officials, academics, pundits, and other interested parties has come up with its own suggestions. Ideas have ranged from revitalizing the Military Staff Committee, to gaining binding commitments for standby forces from member states, to creating an independent UN military (*New York Times* columnist Flora Lewis suggested recruiting Nepal's Gurkhas). A commission sponsored by the United Nations Association of the United States proposed a tripartite UN force: a "standing ready force" deployable within hours, a rapid-deployment force of tens of thousands drawn from member states, and an even larger promised contingent that could "overwhelm a midsized opponent."[8] Finally, there have even been proposals to go outside the UN, if necessary. Suggests liberal writer Ronnie Dugger,

> The world's 1,500 nongovernmental organizations . . . could collectively create a world body comprised of citizen-members who would convene neighborhood, local, regional and

eventually world assemblies. By democratic vote, they could elect a world parliament that would enact a new body of binding international criminal and civil law, and create a voluntary military force to back it up.[9]

Two different models have been offered for expanding the UN's collective security responsibilities. The first is the organization's traditional peacekeeping activities. The second is the UN's more ambitious "peace-enforcement" ventures in Korea (1950–53) and Iraq (1990–91).

Peacekeeping

The UN is currently undertaking about a dozen different peacekeeping operations encompassing some 26,000 soldiers, all volunteered by their respective nations. (At their height in 1993, 18 such operations, including that in the Balkans, involved 78,744 personnel.) Recent enterprises have varied dramatically in scope, ranging from 40 observers in Kashmir to thousands of soldiers in Angola, Bosnia, and Cambodia. In 1995 John Hillen of the Heritage Foundation counted 38 UN peacekeeping missions, of which he classified 21 as observation missions, 6 as traditional peacekeeping, 9 as new forms of peacekeeping, and 2 as larger enforcement actions.[10] Many proposals have been made to establish UN peacekeeping forces elsewhere for different purposes, no matter how implausible. In 1987, for instance, one columnist suggested creating a multinational naval force under UN auspices to ensure freedom of transit in the Persian Gulf during the Iran-Iraq war.

Peace Enforcement

Quite different from the UN peacekeeping operations were the two large-scale conflicts undertaken under the authority of the Security Council. In 1950, with the Soviet delegate boycotting the Security Council to protest the failure to seat China's new revolutionary government, the Security Council authorized, under chapter 7 of the UN Charter, the creation of a multinational force to repel North Korean aggression against the Republic of Korea. The UN forces were predominantly American (who joined Seoul's numerically strong but qualitatively weak forces). U.S. General Douglas MacArthur was designated the commander of the UN forces, but he never reported to the Security Council, and Washington unilaterally made all of the war's major decisions—to cross the 38th parallel into North Korea, for instance.

In the Persian Gulf War the Security Council exercised marginally greater influence, but it still did not create a UN joint command. Although the United States formally observed the conditions of the council's resolutions, Washington had considerable latitude in deciding how to implement them. America provided the bulk of the UN forces, as it had in the Korean War. Washington's ongoing involvement in the region reflects similar U.S. dominance. U.S. military raids on Iraq, though officially said to be based on the UN's proclamation of a protected zone for the Kurds, were conducted despite the opposition of Middle East nations and most members of the UN Security Council.

Is Collective Security Desirable?

Collective security assumes that it is in America's interest to work to eliminate international disorder and instability, including by preventing aggression and squelching civil conflicts. Indeed, the cornerstone of a policy of collective security is stability. Whatever the formal rhetoric of policymakers about human rights and democracy, the primary goal of collective security is, at base, to prevent unauthorized border crossings and ensure popular submission to the relevant national government. Observes Anthony Arend of Georgetown University, "States must also be willing to act no matter how 'just' the cause of aggression may seem to be. In this system, the international community has determined that the highest goal of the system is the preservation of peace; even 'just causes' do not justify aggression."[11]

But instability in the post–Cold War world is an increasingly inescapable reality. For decades the two superpowers were largely successful in suppressing often severe cultural, ethnic, linguistic, nationalistic, and religious differences among and within allied states. That international "lid" has now disappeared.

Of course, it would be best if previous political settlements, however artificial, were not challenged violently. But the fundamental issue for Washington is how best to advance America's security interests. The question, then, should be, does maintaining the international status quo make America more secure? (The well-being of people in other nations is obviously an important moral concern, but the foremost duty of the U.S. government is to protect the American people's lives, property, freedom, and constitutional system.)[12]

Global disorder per se does not threaten the United States. If Washington was wrong to view every local conflict as instigated by the Soviet Union during the Cold War, at least that perspective was understandable.[13] But the end of the Cold War has terminated the potentially zero-sum nature of international relations. The disintegration of Somalia, a onetime U.S. ally, is tragic but has few security implications. Liberia's three-sided civil war threatened no important American interests. Even the Yugoslavian civil war, occurring in the ever-unstable Balkans, could have been viewed with detachment from Washington. Indeed, perhaps more than any other conflict, it demonstrated how little instability matters if surrounding parties are determined to avoid participating in a spreading war: the series of Yugoslavian civil wars lasted longer than World War I without ensnaring a single outside state.

Even where stability is deemed to be important, interested regional players are often capable of responding. For instance, Iraq's neighbors would seem to be capable of containing a still-weakened Saddam Hussein. Of course, such cooperation between distrustful states may not be easy to arrange. However, in situations without great consequence for Washington, regional arrangements, however tenuous and imperfect, would seem to be a better solution to the problem of instability than direct U.S. intervention.

Is Collective Security Feasible?

The objection to collective security is not purely theoretical. There are also a number of practical pitfalls. "For a collective security system to work," argues Arend, "there must be an absolute commitment of all states. They must be willing to combat aggression, wherever and whenever it may occur." As impartial judges, countries "must also be willing to act no matter who the perpetrator may be. Special relationships or alliances are not allowed to interfere with the duty of states to confront aggression."[14]

Unfortunately, however, the UN has never demonstrated a capacity for impartially settling international disputes.[15] The original organizers of the UN thought that the countries united by war would remain united in peace "in supervising, and if necessary, enforcing world peace," in the words of former UN under secretary-general

Brian Urquhart.[16] That assumption proved unrealistic, and Moscow's new willingness to cooperate should not obscure the fact that for 45 years the UN was merely another international battleground.

Even today, UN policy is at the mercy of Beijing, which possesses a veto in the Security Council and may have expansionist ambitions of its own. The comic-opera squabbling between America and France over the linguistic background of the new secretary-general shows the difficulty of cooperation even between Western states. And while more states are moving toward democracy, a majority of the UN's members are still dictatorships. Thus, even if the growing number of free states survives, collective security in the near future is likely to be ineffective so long as the aggressor is a permanent member of the Security Council, a client state of a permanent member, or a country able to amass eight votes from the Security Council's 15 members, many of whom will still be ruled by venal autocrats. Indeed, it is conceivable that even Western democracies might act to shield friendly states from UN censure and enforcement action. Consider Washington's likely attitude should Israel or South Korea launch a preemptive attack against Syria or North Korea, respectively. France might take a similarly protective attitude toward its client states in Africa.

A more practical problem involves the UN's inherent weakness in managing what are largely volunteer operations, since they depend on military contributions from member states. Hillen goes so far as to contend that the organization is unable "to be a functional military manager for complex and ambitious second generation peacekeeping operations."[17] The Somali mission, in particular, was marked by serious dissension. The Italian commander disagreed with the UN strategy of targeting warlord Mohamed Farah Aideed and refused to attack his forces; some other UN commanders blamed the Italians for the deaths of UN troops; and the Nigerian commander accused the Italians of making payoffs to Aideed's soldiers.[18] And while an independent military force might avoid some of those problems, the UN has never been noted for its management abilities in other areas of responsibility.

The Inadequate Peacekeeping Models

Neither of the supposed models for UN enforcement of collective security offers much hope. True, traditional UN peacekeeping may

69

help prevent small incidents that could spread and thereby threaten a fragile peace accord and may give responsible officials an excuse to resist domestic political pressure to provoke a conflict. In the end, however, UN peacekeeping can only prevent fighting where both parties desire peace for other reasons. For instance, it is Israel's military superiority, not the presence of UN troops, that prevents Syria from attempting to reclaim the Golan Heights; similarly, it was Egypt's and Israel's unwillingness to go to war, not a UN force in the Sinai, that led to a durable peace. The desire of the various combatants in Cambodia to stop fighting had little to do with UN peacekeeping efforts. UN forces have been in Cyprus since 1964 without bringing that dispute any closer to resolution. The organization has maintained 328 peacekeepers in the Western Sahara since 1991, theoretically to hold a referendum on its future—again, with no apparent practical effect.

Where a desire for peace does not exist, the UN, whether or not backed by Washington, can do little. International peacekeepers proved to be little more than impotent targets in Bosnia; even the succeeding effort backed by NATO military power is not likely to ultimately yield a united Bosnia of the sort desired by international diplomats. Observers disagree sharply over the likely permanence of democratic and economic reforms in Cambodia. Even worse was the experience in Somalia, where UN contingents became active combatants when their mission changed from peacekeeping to nation building. The *Washington Post* reported that even UN officials admitted that they "had no idea who the Mogadishu police—outfitted and trained with UN money—really work for."[19] An observer group of 49 members has patrolled the Indo-Pakistan border since 1948, yet that did not prevent a full-scale war from breaking out in 1971 and would not forestall renewed fighting in Kashmir if the two nations were otherwise willing to risk conflict. Forces in the Sinai did not prevent the 1967 war between Israel and its neighbors; UN troops in southern Lebanon do not constrain Israeli, Palestinian, or Shi'ite military activity in that area. In short, the UN cannot stop war by determined participants.

The problem is not just failure. UN peacekeeping is not cheap. Only because of congressional action has the U.S. share of peacekeeping costs fallen to 25 percent, from the 31.7 percent set back in 1973. In 1995 peacekeeping assessments on Washington hit $760 million.

John Whitehead, chairman of the United Nations Association of the
United States of America, calls that cost "a small offset against the
$34 billion annual savings in reduced defense spending that the end
of the Cold War has given us."[20] However, the official figure seriously
understates U.S. costs—the incremental U.S. expenses (including
air- and sealift, for instance), aside from the salaries of American
soldiers and the implicit cost of equipment use, ran another $2
billion in 1995. Although even that price might appear to be minor
compared to a $265 billion military budget, choices always have to
be made among competing priorities. Rep. Curt Weldon (R-Pa.)
charged that while Washington was paying the housing costs *and
salaries* of Bangladeshi, Guatemalan, and Nepalese troops participating in the UN force in Haiti, troops from the Second Armored
Division stationed at Fort Hood, Texas, had to pretend to be tanks
in their training exercises, because the Army lacked sufficient funds
for fuel and maintenance.[21]

Unnecessary Conflicts

Even more serious, UN operations also draw nations, particularly
the United States, into irrelevant conflicts around the globe. American military personnel are particularly enticing targets since U.S.
casualties will receive pervasive media coverage in the world's most
influential state. The 1993 spectacle of the body of an American
soldier being dragged through the streets of Mogadishu was enough
to cause even the Clinton administration to draw back from its
expansive plans for "assertive multilateralism." In 1994 it issued
narrowed conditions for U.S. involvement in UN operations and
disclaimed any support for a UN military.

The costs go beyond individual casualties. The entire nation is
drawn into bitter foreign struggles and becomes a potential adversary of one or more opposing forces. Washington may also find
itself at serious odds with other major states—say, Russia, which
has long-standing ties to the Serbs. U.S. citizens also become potential targets of terrorism, since that is the only way for some groups
and nations to strike back at the planet's strongest military power.

Those concerns are not purely academic. The UN has, at times,
put Washington back into areas from which it had only recently
disengaged after years of meddling. In Somalia, for instance, the
United States was finally rid of its Cold War client Mohamed Siad

Barre when he was overthrown in January 1991—despite having been aided and armed by Washington. But America almost immediately ended up back in the country as a de facto combatant.

Even worse is the situation in the Balkans. The UN Protection Force (UNPROFOR) was largely ineffective in halting barbarities against civilians and prisoners, let alone stopping the fighting. Nor did it offer even a pretense of a long-term political solution. Instead, the UN intervened on behalf of the Muslim-dominated central authorities in Bosnia, an artificial state that had only recently seceded from the larger nation of Yugoslavia and was perceived, rightly, by Bosnian Serbs as an adversary. When member states raised the possibility of withdrawing the UN forces in mid-1995, President Clinton promised not to leave those forces "in the lurch," even though American troops were not present.[22] He pledged to intervene with ground forces, if necessary, to aid UNPROFOR. Then came NATO military strikes, the Dayton accord, and U.S.-led NATO intervention. Thus, a UN action in which the United States was not participating, and which Congress had not approved, ultimately led to significant U.S. military intervention in a region devoid of serious American security interests.

The Undesirable Peace-Enforcement Model

The two major wars fought under the UN flag offer no better model for a stronger UN role. Korea and Iraq were UN conflicts in name only. An American commitment to intervene, even without allied support, was the critical factor in both wars. While UN authority provided a convenient and politically popular patina, it was not necessary to prosecute the war. Nevertheless, the United States had to pay a price for the UN's imprimatur. Washington's desire for Soviet support against Iraq forced the administration to ignore the USSR's crackdown in the Baltic states. China's abstention from the critical Security Council vote authorizing the use of force probably was aided by the issuance of new World Bank loans, which were approved shortly thereafter, and reduced pressure on human rights issues. Many of the 10 nonpermanent members, who had a voice in shaping Persian Gulf policy, were interested in gaining additional Western financial assistance, if nothing else. While such logrolling might be expected, it hardly augurs well for the creation of an effective system of collective security.

In the future other nations might expect not only bribes but also real influence. The late French president François Mitterrand, for instance, apparently advanced his proposal to rejuvenate the Military Staff Committee because he thought it would break America's military monopoly on UN actions. His foreign minister later argued that Europe and the UN should help counteract U.S. power: "American might reigns without balancing weight," he complained.[23] Moreover, increasingly wealthy and influential Germany and Japan may demand not only permanent seats on the Security Council but also a say in any future military operations. Similarly, India, which possesses a potent military, may not be so quiescent about a future peace-enforcement action. Other states, like Brazil, have also indicated an interest in permanent Security Council membership.

There is nothing intrinsically wrong with turning what has been a Potemkin collaborative security enterprise into a real one. But it is doubtful that such a system, subject to the usual vagaries of any international organization, especially the UN, is going to either achieve its purpose or advance American interests. Not only might the UN be unduly restrictive where Washington felt intervention was necessary, but more important, a genuine collective security system could drag the United States into conflicts that have no connection to American interests and should be solved without Washington's assistance. What if, for instance, Armenia, Russia, and Turkey proposed UN intervention in Azerbaijan? Should America, which would otherwise wisely remain aloof, become a major combatant, perhaps consigning thousands of citizens to their deaths in a potentially bloody, interminable conflict with no impact on U.S. security?

Proposals to give the UN an independent combat force to be used at the secretary-general's discretion are even less attractive. Whatever the international body's value as a debating chamber within which to let off steam, it has never demonstrated principled leadership unhampered by multitudinous and arcane political pressures. Today, of course, the UN's potential for abuse is tempered by the role of the Security Council, but if the UN gained the sort of influence that would come with an independent armed force, a coalition of smaller states might attempt to move security power back to the General Assembly. In fact, smaller nations have periodically pressed to "democratize" the organization. Ironically, the United

States itself sought ways to circumvent Soviet obstructionism during the UN's intervention in the Congo during the early 1960s. The consequences of a more "democratic" UN with its own military would be unpredictable, but not likely positive, and Washington would almost certainly be drawn into a number of local conflicts as a result. So long as the UN is governed by a majority of nation-states, many of which are ruled by some of the worst thugs on earth, the UN should not be trusted with even one soldier.

An Alternative: U.S. Nonintervention

Despite the good intentions of those who advocate collective security, the UN has proved unable to impose peace on unwilling parties or remake failed societies. Whether it really understands its limitations, even after the "peacekeeping" fiascos in Somalia and Bosnia, is unclear. After all, humility has never been a virtue of the organization. Back in 1989, after the UN's phones were shut down as part of New York City's telephone strike, a spokesman commented that he hoped "nuclear war does not break out today, because if it does, there is nothing we can do."[24] What the UN could have done in such an instance even if the phones worked was left unexplained.

This is not to say that the UN can't be helpful where parties want peace and need an outside mediator. Mozambique and Namibia appear to have been such cases. But in both instances, a formal UN troop presence was at best a minor contribution, and U.S. participation was not needed. The UN's primary virtue remains its role as a forum for the airing of international grievances, with at least the possibility of offering specific diplomatic assistance in defusing disputes.

True, some advocates of collective security argue that there is no alternative. For example, Rep. Jim Leach (R-Iowa) says that without U.S.-supported UN peacekeeping, "we'll have to look for much more expensive alternatives" for solving international problems.[25]

But that assumes that Washington has to solve all such problems. There is a score of wars, civil conflicts, domestic disorders, and national implosions that are as deserving of international attention as are, say, the Balkans. Even former assistant secretary of defense Joseph Nye acknowledges that "a foreign policy of armed multilateral intervention to right all such wrongs would be another source of enormous disorder."[26] Thus, Washington should learn to say no.

Secretary of State Madeleine Albright worries that cutting U.S. support for UN missions will kill international peacekeeping, forcing America "to act alone or not at all."[27] Just what is wrong with not acting when America has no critical interest at stake?

The dramatic international changes of recent years have truly yielded a "new world order," one providing America with a unique opportunity to reassess its global role. For nearly five decades the United States has acted more like an empire than a republic, creating an international network of client states, establishing hundreds of military installations around the world, at times conscripting young men to staff those advanced outposts and fight in distant wars, and spending hundreds of billions of dollars annually on the military. Indeed, that globalist foreign policy badly distorted the domestic political system, encouraging the growth of a large, expensive, repressive, secretive, and often uncontrolled state.

Disappearing Justifications

The justification for such an interventionist military strategy, so alien to the original American design, was the threat of totalitarian communism. With that threat gone, the United States should return to its roots, rather than look for another convenient enemy or enemies. And that requires a much more limited foreign policy with much more limited ends.

Of course, while the threat of war involving vital U.S. interests seems to be the smallest in six decades, that does not mean that the entire globe is destined to enjoy a golden era of peace. The end of the Cold War has released long-standing ethnic and nationalist tensions in Eastern Europe; the collapse of the USSR has loosed similar bloody disputes throughout Eurasia; the Third World remains riven with warfare between tribes, religions, and nations. To combat those threats many policymakers and analysts are now advocating reliance on collective security, particularly through the UN, though without compromising regional alliances, such as NATO. Explains Albright, "It's important for the President to have a variety of tools to do the job. The UN is clearly a useful tool for some of the jobs and not so useful for others. Sometimes you need a hammer, sometimes you need a screwdriver and sometimes you need a chisel, but you don't throw away one tool just because you don't use it all the time."[28]

But most fundamental is the question of American interests. Put bluntly, what policy will best protect the lives, property, and constitutional system of the people of this nation? Entangling Washington in a potentially unending series of international conflicts and civil wars through the UN? Or remaining aloof from struggles that do not affect the United States? If one's chief concern is preserving American lives and treasure, the latter position is clearly preferable. The Republican-controlled House of Representatives has taken some useful steps, voting to bar the president from putting U.S. forces under foreign command and having American personnel wear the UN insignia without congressional approval. But the president, or Congress if the president refuses to act, should further lower the share of UN expenses covered by the United States and bar American military participation in UN missions.

Today there is no Soviet Union to contain and local and regional quarrels are no longer of vital concern as a result of their being part of the overall Cold War. Moreover, those states that were once possible victims of aggression—underdeveloped Korea, defeated Germany and Japan, war-torn France and Britain, and even smaller nations like Australia and New Zealand—have developed potent militaries and are capable of meeting any likely threats to themselves, their neighbors, or their regions. Collective security was not desirable or practical even during Woodrow Wilson's era. It has even less appeal as a strategy today.

Notes

1. For examples of the former, see Ted Galen Carpenter, *A Search for Enemies: America's Alliances after the Cold War* (Washington: Cato Institute, 1992); and Eric Nordlinger, *Isolationism Reconfigured: American Foreign Policy for a New Century* (Princeton, N.J.: Princeton University Press, 1995). Examples of the latter include Joshua Muravchik, *The Imperative of American Leadership: A Challenge to Neo-Isolationism* (Washington: American Enterprise Institute, 1996); and William Kristol and Robert Kagan, "Toward a Neo-Reaganite Foreign Policy," *Foreign Affairs* 75, no. 4 (July–August 1996): 18–32.

2. This was an oft-repeated theme of Wilson's. See, for example, M. V. Naidu, *Collective Security and the United Nations* (New York: St. Martin's, 1974), pp. 4–5.

3. "Transcript of President's Address to U.N. General Assembly," *New York Times*, October 2, 1990, p. A12.

4. Quoted in Thomas Friedman, "Bush, in Address to U.N., Urges More Vigor in Keeping the Peace," *New York Times*, September 22, 1992, p. A14.

5. Quoted in Alison Mitchell, "Clinton's About-Face," *New York Times*, September 24, 1996, p. A8.

6. Boutros Boutros-Ghali, *An Agenda for Peace* (New York: United Nations, 1992), p. 42.

7. Quoted in Julia Preston, "U.N. Aide Proposes Rapid-Reaction Unit," *Washington Post*, January 6, 1995, p. A23.

8. Robert Greenberger, "Outspoken U.N. Chief Takes Strong Role, Irking Some Nations," *Wall Street Journal*, December 17, 1992, p. A14.

9. Ronnie Dugger, "Create a World Army," *New York Times*, June 27, 1995, p. A17.

10. John Hillen, "Peace(keeping) in Our Time: The United Nations as a Professional Military Manager," Paper presented at the Biennial Conference of the Inter-University Seminar on Armed Forces and Society, Oxford University, October 20–22, 1995, p. 8.

11. Anthony Arend, *Pursuing a Just and Durable Peace: John Foster Dulles and International Organizations* (New York: Greenwood, 1988), pp. 39–40.

12. See Doug Bandow, *The Politics of Envy: Statism as Theology* (New Brunswick, N.J.: Transaction Publishers, 1994), pp. 91–106.

13. Unfortunately, Washington's devotion to stability led it to make many a bargain with the Devil, or at least with his surrogates. American aid for Iran's shah, Nicaragua's Somoza, Zaire's Mobutu, the Philippines' Marcos, and Sudan's Nimiery all placed the United States on the side of unsavory regimes, created some degree of local anti-Americanism, and ultimately generated various forms of regional instability.

14. Arend, p. 39.

15. Among the more egregious examples of the politicization of the UN was the multiyear campaign for a "new international economic order." See Doug Bandow, "Totalitarian Global Management: The U.N.'s War on the Liberal International Economic Order," Cato Institute Policy Analysis no. 61, October 24, 1985. More broadly, international organizations, particularly those within the UN system, have often contributed to a number of global problems. Some people, writes Wesleyan University professor Giulio Gallarotti, "have traditionally been overly optimistic about the ability of multilateral management to stabilize international relations and have generally ignored the fact that [international organizations] can be a source of, rather than a remedy for, disorder in and across issue-areas." Giulio Gallarotti, "The Limits of International Organizations: Systematic Failure in the Management of International Relations," *International Organizations* 45, no. 2 (Spring 1991): 218–19.

16. Brian Urquhart, *A Life in Peace and War* (London: Weidenfeld and Nicolson, 1987), p. 93.

17. Hillen, p. 13.

18. Julia Preston, "U.N. Faces Fiscal Crisis and Uncertain Role," *Washington Post*, September 27, 1993, p. A16.

19. Rick Atkinson, "Marines Close Curtain on U.N. in Somalia," *Washington Post*, March 3, 1995, p. A30.

20. John Whitehead, "Best Bargain in the World: The U.N.," Letter to the editor, *Wall Street Journal*, August 29, 1996, p. A11.

21. John McCaslin, "Clank, Said the Tank," *Washington Times*, February 22, 1995, p. A6.

22. Quoted in John Harris, "Clinton Vows Help for U.N. Troops in Bosnia," *Washington Post*, June 1, 1995, p. A1.

23. "France to U.S.: Don't Rule," *New York Times*, September 3, 1991, p. A8.

24. "Phone Strike Hangs Up U.N.," *Washington Post*, October 25, 1989, p. A9.

25. Quoted in Carla Anne Robbins, "GOP Bid to Downgrade U.N. Peacekeeping Role Is Likely to Gain Steam in House Vote Today," *Wall Street Journal*, February 16, 1995, p. A16.

26. Joseph Nye Jr., "The Self-Determination Trap . . .," *Washington Post*, December 15, 1992, p. A23.
27. Quoted in Robbins.
28. Quoted in Mitchell.

5. Using the United Nations to Advance U.S. Interests

Robert B. Oakley

A discussion of the United Nations as peacemaker and peace-keeper should be conducted in the context of whether, how, and to what degree the UN can advance U.S. interests. One of the reasons for the controversy over the value of the UN as a whole has been excessive attention to peacekeeping, the importance of which has been seriously exaggerated by critics and supporters. This chapter does not address the issues of whether or not successive U.S. administrations have been correct in deciding to intervene and use the UN peacekeeping mechanism in various crises or whether U.S. interests might have been better served by passivity. Given space limitations, the discussion assumes that the past crises brought to the UN for action, by or with the support of the United States, touched U.S. interests and that similar occasions will occur in the future. There have been and will be occasions, however, when that is a questionable assumption.

The Importance of Definitions

There are several different definitions of both peacemaking and peacekeeping. The United Kingdom, for example, uses the former as the United States uses the term "peace enforcement"—the application of considerable military force to bring about peace, by imposing it if need be. For purposes of this chapter, peacemaking is defined as diplomacy, mediation, conflict prevention, or conflict resolution. There can, on occasion, be a small number of military personnel, such as observers, used in peacemaking, as a supplement to diplomacy.

Peacekeeping was traditionally defined as the deployment of a lightly armed UN (or other) military force with the consent of two states to assist them in maintaining an agreement between them to end hostilities. However, over the past five years, that concept has changed. As used in this chapter, "peacekeeping"covers intervention within a single state, usually pursuant to a Security Council mandate, sometimes without the explicit permission of indigenous authorities. For purposes of discussion, it also extends to what some call expanded or complex peacekeeping and peace enforcement. A typology of these definitions, plus the concept of humanitarian support, is given in Table 5.1.

Background

Attitudes in the United States, and other countries, about the utility of the UN for peacekeeping have fluctuated widely over the past 50 years. The UN Charter provides an elaborate system for peacekeeping under article 43, including provisions for a standing UN military force and a UN military directorate made up of military representatives of the five permanent members of the Security Council. The United States, following the vision of President Franklin D. Roosevelt, took the lead on that during the drafting of the UN Charter. However, the vision rapidly faded as idealism gave way to the reality of the Cold War. No standing force or even an on-call force was created, nor was the Military Committee ever activated.

Nevertheless, 13 UN peace operations or peacekeeping missions of various kinds took place between 1945 and 1988, most of them in the Middle East, aimed at discouraging the renewal of conflict after a cease-fire between hostile states had been concluded. Those missions used unarmed or lightly armed observers acting in concert with UN diplomats. Outside the Middle East, the United States and the USSR were usually at loggerheads over the idea of UN intervention, with the latter vetoing most proposals. In the Middle East, both countries were more supportive of UN missions, seeking to prevent hostilities in a very sensitive region from pulling the two military superpowers into direct confrontation.

Peacekeeping

The first two operations began in 1947: the United Nations Military Observer Group for India and Pakistan, observers of the cease-fire between those countries; and the United Nations Truce Supervisory Organization, observers of the cease-fire and truce between Israel and its Arab neighbors. Interestingly, those operations continue

Table 5.1

TYPOLOGY OF HUMANITARIAN SUPPORT AND PEACE OPERATIONS

	Mandate Roles	Peace Accord	Degree of Opposition	Size & Complexity
Peacemaking	Self-defense only (6)	No; incipient	None; peace force seen as impartial	Small (under 500). Observers and mission support
Peacekeeping	Self-defense, observation, verification	Yes	None; peace force seen as impartial	Medium (500–6,000). Observers; some peace building
Expanded peacekeeping	Force in support of diplomacy	Not normally	Episodic clashes; peace force seen as ambivalent	Large (20,000+). Some combat capability; peace building
Peace enforcement	Use of all necessary means (7)	No	Peace force seen as antagonist	Large. Offensive combat capability
Humanitarian support	Variable (6 or 7)	Variable	Variable	Variable

NOTE: Numbers in parentheses are those of chapter of the UN Charter invoked for the operation.

81

today, a sign of at least marginal utility. Before 1989 UN peacekeeping missions were, with two exceptions, limited to observing and patrolling demilitarized zones and force-limitation zones and monitoring cease-fire agreements. Such operations had mixed results. The 1956 mission in the Sinai helped prevent war for a decade but was compelled to withdraw at Egypt's insistence in 1967, powerless to prevent another Arab-Israeli war. A subsequent UN Sinai mission in 1973 facilitated the successful transition to the U.S.-negotiated Camp David peace treaty in 1979. The UN Golan Heights peacekeeping mission negotiated by Secretary of State Henry Kissinger in 1974 has helped Israel and Syria avoid even a single incident. On the other hand, the operation in South Lebanon, begun in 1972, has proved impotent to prevent conflict. Its continued presence follows the Security Council's judgment (and that of the United States and Israel) that the situation would be even more volatile if it were withdrawn. That is also true of the Cyprus operation, which began in 1964 at the instigation of the United States and the United Kingdom, was disrupted by a major war in 1974, but still has shown some utility in helping the parties avoid another major war.

A much larger mission began in 1960, when the Security Council established the UN Operation in the Congo (UNOC), which built up to a force of some 20,000 and undertook such functions as humanitarian support, temporary public administration, and the demobilization and retraining of militaries. It was used alongside some very astute, difficult diplomacy (peacemaking) by Secretary-General Dag Hammerskjold. The United States used its assets (including the Central Intelligence Agency) in the Congo (later Zaire) and pursued bilateral measures with other African states, Belgium, and France, in addition to working closely with the UN. That effort eventually resulted in the pro-Soviet premier Patrice Lumumba and other rebellious factions losing out and the installation of successive pro-U.S. governments, culminating with that of Joseph Mobutu (Mobutu Sese Séko), who assumed power in 1965. The UNOC provoked a major attack by the USSR and its allies on the institution of the secretary-general, who was seen as too pro-U.S., and on the idea of peacekeeping; the USSR refused to pay its assessed peacekeeping dues in protest.[1]

In 1962, over Soviet objections in the Security Council, a UN General Assembly action—taken at U.S. instigation—created the

UN Temporary Executive Authority (UNTEA) for West New Guinea to avoid an impending war between Indonesia and our NATO ally the Netherlands. The UNTEA successfully provided security and an interim administration for the territory, turned it over to Indonesia after seven months, and organized "an expression of popular opinion"'on the future. That episode prefigured the more complex and challenging sort of peacekeeping operation that has arisen in the post–Cold War period.

Since the late 1980s many UN operations have combined traditional military and diplomatic peacekeeping activities with humanitarian support for civilian populations conducted by military units, usually to save lives and alleviate suffering on a large scale, and with other tasks such as helping revive civil administration, assisting elections, and disarmament. Moreover, most of those operations have taken place within violently troubled states, rather than in the context of conflicts between states. The missions have varied in size, and they have taken place under various mandates, in both permissive and hostile environments. The United States has been the most active supporter of all such operations. On occasion (e.g., Somalia and Bosnia), the initial protection of humanitarian activities by peacekeeping forces has evolved into expanded (or complex) peacekeeping on a large scale and has even evolved into peace enforcement. Postconflict nation-building assistance or peace-building activities—disarming factions, conducting elections, rebuilding local administrations, economic assistance, and other measures to strengthen a weakened or collapsed state—have also frequently been incorporated.

Between 1988 and 1995 there were some 26 new peace operations authorized and commanded by the UN. Starting in 1987–88 a positive attitude emerged in Moscow toward both UN peacekeeping and cooperation with Washington in resolving regional conflicts. The ensuing cooperation produced a much more assertive approach by the United States, the other permanent members of the Security Council, and other key UN members to peace operations. Military forces of the permanent members also began to participate in peacekeeping for the first time. In addition, the United States organized, outside the formal UN framework, two major coalition peace operations (Restore Hope in Somalia and Uphold Democracy in Haiti) as well as a more limited multinational mission (Provide Comfort in

Iraq)—all three formed with UN approval. In Somalia and Haiti, UN-led peace operations replaced those led by the United States. France and Russia also organized and led peace operations outside the UN framework but with its concurrence: France in Rwanda in 1994 and Russia in Georgia and Tajikistan in 1994–95 (through the Commonwealth of Independent States). The latter episode underscored the increased involvement of regional and subregional organizations in peacekeeping during that period (e.g., the Organization of American States in Haiti, NATO in Bosnia, the Organization of African Unity in Burundi, and the Economic Community of West African States in Liberia).

Over the past five years, the U.S. military has become heavily involved in peace operations around the globe, through both direct and indirect participation and as a source of transportation, logistical support, and equipment. The participation of U.S. military units in post–Cold War peace operations qualitatively boosted their effectiveness. Superior U.S. communications, command, control, and intelligence (C³I) capabilities and experience in managing coalitions have proven to be major assets in planning and coordinating multilateral operations, and valuable skill specialties—such as civil affairs, psychological operations, special forces, engineering, and advanced logistics (including tactical and strategic airlift)—have been contributed by the United States. Few other military establishments can provide such assets to the UN. When there has been danger of conflict, U.S. combat units participating in UN peace operations have remained under the operational command and control of U.S. senior officers, as in Somalia and Haiti. On occasion, for temporary duty, U.S. military personnel have served under operational or tactical control of other military commanders, including those of NATO, but always under U.S. command. The U.S. National Command Authority has ultimate responsibility for U.S. forces on peacekeeping duty and can countermand orders from UN or other commanders.

In keeping with the growth of operations, the number of UN peacekeeping personnel increased from 10,664 in 1988 to a high of nearly 79,000 in 1994, and assessments for UN peace operations rose from approximately $254 million in 1988 to $2.8 billion in 1995.[2] (Those figures did not include the costly U.S.-led operations in Iraq, Somalia, and Haiti.) Starting in 1994, however, the UN secretary-general, the United States, and the Security Council all adopted a more cautious attitude. There was a clear recognition that the UN did not have and would not have the capability to conduct large-scale peacekeeping or peace-enforcement operations and should not be asked to do so. Those in Haiti, Angola, and Tajikistan were the only new UN peacekeeping missions undertaken in 1994–96. The UN Protection Force (UNPROFOR) in the former Yugoslavia was reinforced, and the NATO-led Implementation Force (IFOR), which succeeded UNPROFOR completely by 1996, was created for Bosnia. The number of UN peacekeeping personnel was down to 26,000 in September 1996.

Simultaneously, in 1994, there arose in Congress a strong movement for a drastic reduction in U.S. contributions to and support of future UN peace operations, as well as tight limits on the use of U.S. forces. The backlash resulting from the failed mission in Somalia, the agonizing dilemmas of the operation in Bosnia, and the need for deep cuts in the overall U.S. budget generated serious concerns about the utility of UN peacekeeping and made it an inviting political target. The Clinton administration favored tighter restrictions on the UN and issued a presidential decision directive (PDD-25) spelling out those restrictions and overall policy. But the administration opposed drastic cuts and overly restrictive constraints and argued for the continued utility of selective, more effective, and usually less costly peace operations. At the same time, it assisted in substantial improvements in the peacekeeping capabilities of the UN Secretariat, particularly in the areas of logistics, planning, and C³I.

Peacemaking

Alongside or as part of peacekeeping, there has been UN peacemaking, diplomatic activity, or assistance in negotiations between hostile states or hostile factions within states. Before 1992 such initiatives normally required a Security Council or General Assembly resolution empowering the secretary-general to undertake an initiative, and there were not many diplomatic actions. Since then, the secretary-general has been given general authorization by the Security Council to engage in peacemaking on his own initiative, and the pace of diplomacy has increased greatly. Notable examples of successful peacemaking activities include negotiating an end to the Iran-Iraq war; helping conclude peace agreements for Namibia, Angola, and Mozambique; facilitating an agreement by the USSR to pull out of Afghanistan; consolidating and formally implementing agreements to end the civil wars in El Salvador and Nicaragua; and working with the permanent members of the Security Council to implement the agreement by the three major Cambodian factions to end the conflict in that country. In none of those situations was the UN solely responsible for the success achieved, but in all of them its role was vital to a positive outcome. Notably less successful peacemaking efforts have included those in the Arab-Israel confrontation (1967–73), Haiti, Somalia, the former Yugoslavia, Rwanda, and Burundi. However, the UN was not the sole actor involved and cannot fairly be given total blame for failure.

Legitimization

There is another, less direct but sometimes more important, UN role in peacekeeping, namely the legitimization of an operation undertaken outside the formal UN framework. In 1950 the Security Council passed a resolution calling for member states to assist the Republic of Korea in repelling the North Korean invasion. The Soviets, fortunately, chose to absent themselves rather than veto, making it easier for the United States to obtain international support for its effort to force the North Koreans out of the South. Without the UN's imprimatur, fewer nations would have volunteered and the burden on the United States would have been greater.

Similarly, in 1990 the Security Council called on member states to use all available means to assist Kuwait and repel Iraqi aggression. That resulted in a broad multinational military coalition of Western, Asian, and Muslim countries, led by the United States. Without legitimization by the UN, a number of those states would not have participated, given the domestic political controversy associated with joining the United States in fighting against Iraq. It is questionable whether the Muslim states, in particular, would have participated. Their absence would have made Desert Storm much more difficult, an apparent case of Christians versus Muslims. It is also unclear whether the United States would have had such free access to ports, airfields, and other installations in the gulf and elsewhere for its aircraft and ships. Nor would it have had the benefit of such large payments to reimburse its expenses, many of which were made pursuant to the Security Council resolution via a UN trust fund. The Security Council also legitimized U.S.-led ad hoc multinational coalitions in Somalia, Haiti, and Bosnia. Other countries attach much more importance to both the international legal niceties and the political cover they afford than we do, and they would probably not have participated in those operations without UN approval.

Examining the Canards

There are those who really believe that the UN is engaged in undermining U.S. sovereignty. Some believe that it is actively doing so by employing black helicopters in the West, raising the UN flag over Ft. Polk, and pursuing other subversive actions. Others see evil omens in U.S. soldiers' wearing blue berets or UN shoulder patches.[3] And there are those who, for political or ideological reasons, make such allegations but do not really believe them. That is not new. We saw the same reaction to President Woodrow Wilson's proposal that the United States join the League of Nations and in response to the campaigns of the World Federalists and the Trilateral Commission. Naturally, none of those "plots" has been in any way substantiated. There was, and is, nothing there.

On the other hand, there are those who believe the UN (or before it, the League of Nations) can and should be the organization to solve almost all the world's problems, assuming primacy if not actual sovereignty over unilateral or extra-UN actions by the United States and other nations. That is as unrealistic as fears of UN black helicopters. The most violent U.S. public and political reactions to the UN (or the League of Nations) have tended to come in response to extremely strong commitments to global organizations—such as Wilson's advocacy of the league and President Clinton's initial enthusiasm for UN peacekeeping and "assertive multilateralism," including a standing UN military force.

Then there are those who assert that the UN has gotten itself into trouble and demonstrated its generic institutional incompetence and impotence in such peacekeeping operations as those in Somalia and Bosnia. One of the flaws in that allegation also applies to claims that U.S. sovereignty has been compromised: the United States has veto power on the Security Council and can just say no anytime it does not approve of a proposed operation, thus avoiding any possibility that U.S. forces would be involved, or that the UN would do something the United States does not like. The United States can also use its veto power to modify a council resolution or block its adoption until and unless Washington is satisfied with the objectives and wording of the resolution and what it requires of a peace force or until and unless Washington is satisfied that the peace force has the means needed to achieve its objective.

The United States voted for 85 Security Council resolutions or presidential statements spelling out what UNPROFOR should do. Yet many were unrealistic, or the means were clearly not available to implement them, or both. For example, designating safe areas such as Srebrenicza for protection when the UN forces on the ground were obviously inadequate was a major error by the Security Council. Yet it was actively supported by the United States, despite warnings by the secretary-general's military advisers and the UN commanders (who happened to be our NATO allies France and the UK) that UNPROFOR would not be able to do the job if challenged because its forces were too weak and too hamstrung by limits that the Security Council had placed upon their ability to act decisively. However, in this country, almost all the blame is placed on the UN, which has been sharply criticized by the administration, Congress, and public opinion for alleged weakness.[4]

Again, in Somalia, the United States took the lead in drafting and obtaining approval for the Security Council resolutions spelling out what the second UN Operation in Somalia (UNOSOM II) should do, including activities that have come to be denigrated and called "nation building" and the pursuit of clan leader Mohammad Farah Aideed. It is simply incorrect to place the blame entirely on the UN for a mission that the United States instigated, supported, and voted for. Nor is it correct to blame the UN for not having the military resources to make good on its mission, since in Somalia, as in Bosnia and all other operations, the members must provide the resources. (The United States sharply reduced its military forces in Somalia in the first half of 1993 and saw others follow suit, even while pressing the UN to take on a much expanded, more dangerous mission).[5] The UN has no military resources of its own—nor in my judgment should it have them except for the small military staff of the Peacekeeping Directorate of the UN Secretariat.

Finally, there has been a campaign to charge the UN with having been in command and operational control of U.S. forces in Somalia, ordering them into danger and thereby having the responsibility for their being killed or wounded. Some who make the allegation are genuinely ignorant of the facts, but there has been a deliberate effort by some Republican politicians to spread that untruth even when they know better. The Senate Armed Services Committee and its House counterpart conducted in-depth inquiries during 1993–94 into what happened to U.S. forces in Somalia. They found that all U.S. forces who took part in combat operations were at all times under the command and operational control of U.S. commanders. Even after UNOSOM was established, their orders came down the U.S. chain of command, from the commander in chief, not from or through the UN.[6]

Both U.S. generals who had served in Somalia testified in open hearings before the Senate Armed Services Committee that they, not the UN, were in command and control of U.S. forces. All other U.S. military and civilian officials made the same point to members of the Senate and House committees who questioned them.[7] Unfortunately, the Clinton administration has not forcefully refuted the false allegations of UN command and control—thereby adding to their unwarranted credibility. Also, with respect to Somalia as well as Bosnia, the Clinton administration has on occasion joined the chorus of critics who place responsibility for trouble on the UN, as if it were a totally independent entity and the members of the Security Council had no responsibility at all. That has added to the public and political misunderstanding and criticism of the UN.

Net Assessment

When one looks at the record of the past 50 years, it is clear that the actual role of the UN in peacekeeping has been badly distorted and its importance exaggerated—by both critics and advocates. Among those who expected too much, thereby arousing false fears, false expectations, and a sizable backlash, have been Presidents Roosevelt, Bush, and Clinton. There has never been any realistic possibility of the UN's being able to prevent or solve all or even most of the world's conflicts, since its more powerful members have never agreed that it should or given it the political, financial, and military resources to do so. Nor can it solve the world's economic, social, environmental, refugee, human rights, humanitarian, and other problems. Indeed, as former secretary-general U Thant wrote, "Great problems usually come to the United Nations because governments have been unable to think of anything else to do about them. The

UN is a last-ditch, last-resort affair and it is not surprising that the organization should often be blamed for failing to solve problems that have already been found to be insoluble by governments."[8]

The UN can play and has played a modestly positive role in helping with international issues, including peacekeeping and peacemaking operations for some inter- and intrastate conflicts, when it has had the necessary support. That support must include a realistic mandate from the Security Council, adequate material resources to carry out the mission, skilled military and political leadership on the ground, and active political help from major and regional powers. The UN cannot carry out a peacekeeping operation without Security Council approval, and that means a "yes" vote by the United States. However, there have been occasions when the vote was there but real support was not. Again, that is not the fault of the UN. The members of the Security Council, starting with the United States, must carefully analyze a crisis to determine what would be required to contain or resolve it and whether the requisite political, material, and financial support of member states is rapidly available and can realistically be expected to continue until success. The members must then decide whether the best "manager" of a peace operation would be the UN or a regional organization (e.g., NATO) or a powerful state (e.g., the United States). Only then should the members of the Security Council decide whether to proceed.

Almost always, successful UN peacekeeping and peacemaking activities have supplemented or complemented those of individual members, especially the United States. They have been part of a larger effort, not a derogation of responsibility or authority or sovereignty, and should be seen in that light. The UN as a complementary or supplementary actor can be and has been very much in U.S. interests over the past 50 years. In Haiti, for example, the United States took the leading role but was able to reduce its involvement and expenses within six months by having a successor UN-led operation take over, as well as by using the UN to help obtain participation and contributions by other governments.

Similarly, the UN can play and has played an important role in generating political, financial, and military support for actions undertaken by the United States and its coalition partners outside the formal UN structure, starting with the Korean crisis in 1950. Without the legitimizing action of the UN, many countries will not join U.S. efforts. If one is looking for evidence, there is no need to look any further than the success that the United States had in organizing and employing a cohesive coalition against Saddam Hussein in 1990–91 when it used the Security Council to complement its bilateral approaches to coalition partners. Contrast that with the events of September 1996 when the United States ignored the Security Council, attempted to reactivate the coalition on its own, and found that only Kuwait responded favorably while Saudi Arabia, Egypt, France, and other major military participants in the coalition of 1990–91 refused to allow U.S. aircraft to overfly their territory or to use their facilities.

Although sanctions are not normally seen as part of peacekeeping, there are similarities. If anything, even more international support is needed for sanctions to be effective than for peacekeeping. And U.S. attempts to mobilize international support without the Security Council have not been as successful as when there was a Security Council resolution calling for sanctions. It is questionable whether sanctions are an adequate or appropriate means of obtaining the objectives for which they are usually applied. However, the impact on Libya, Iraq, and Haiti, where U.S.-inspired sanctions were based on a binding Security Council resolution, has been much greater than the impact of sanctions on Iran and Cuba, where there are no such resolutions. In the latter cases, the United States has relied on ad hoc diplomacy or tried to extend U.S. domestic laws abroad in order to convince other countries to support the sanctions, but with little success. Moreover, the extraterritorial application of U.S. law is generating a growing backlash rather than increasing the pressure of sanctions.[9]

It is a fact of international life that other countries, even Russia and China, often need or want formal UN action as justification or cover for cooperating with the United States in efforts to prevent, contain, or resolve conflicts. Likewise, other countries often find UN diplomatic activities useful as an adjunct to direct U.S. action on issues of more interest to us than to them; if the UN is involved, they are less likely to be perceived as being strong-armed by the world's superpower. Ironically, since the end of the Cold War, the absence of the Soviet threat and the advent of greater democracy and freedom of information mean that, to get its way, the United States must place greater reliance on diplomacy of all kinds, including UN peacemaking and peacekeeping.

Another useful supporting role for UN peacekeeping has been to mount an operation following that of a U.S.-led multinational force. That allows the United States to reduce its involvement more rapidly and share the burden more broadly, as it did in Haiti.[10]

This principle of enhanced burden sharing applies, of course, to all UN peacekeeping operations, not only those that follow a U.S.-led multinational coalition outside the UN. However, many in Congress seem unable to understand the potential savings. Rather, they complain that the United States is spending too much for UN peacekeeping. By refusing to pay legally binding peacekeeping assessments, the United States complicates its own efforts to reduce its share of peacekeeping costs, weakens the capability of the UN, discourages participation in new operations by other countries that are still owed for past operations, and makes it more expensive for the United States when it comes to the sort of operations the UN can conduct effectively *and* the United States wishes to see take place.

Similarly, by following the general precept of either taking command and deploying large numbers of its own forces when it participates militarily, or of not participating at all except to provide transportation and perhaps equipment and logistics support for other countries that might participate in UN peace operations, the United States creates problems for itself. Other countries are much more reluctant to participate when the United States refuses to do so. A small number of U.S. forces in key places as part of a bigger operation—but one within the limited capabilities of the UN—can convince others to provide the preponderance of forces and increase the effectiveness of the overall operation. Virulent U.S. criticism of the alleged weakness, if not cowardice, of UNPROFOR operations in Bosnia and our urging that UNPROFOR act more boldly were deeply resented by the political and military leaders of countries (e.g., the UK, France, and the Netherlands) whose forces were on the ground—in danger and actually being kidnapped and killed—while the U.S. fear of casualties and other considerations meant our forces were absent, out of harm's way.[11] (Think about the firestorm of criticism there would have been in this country had it been UNPROFOR, rather than the U.S.-led IFOR, that refused to arrest indicted war criminals Radovan Karadjic and Radtko Mladic.) However, this concept should not be carried too far, because UN peace forces are not as capable of dealing effectively with situations where there is the risk or reality of serious conflict. We have seen that point confirmed in Somalia, Haiti, Bosnia, and elsewhere. Since the initial period of overoptimism in 1991–93 about UN military capabilities, expectations of the United States, the secretary-general, and the members of the UN generally have been significantly scaled back. At the same time, the capabilities of the UN Department of Peacekeeping Operations (DPKO) have been substantially improved. There were three military officers on the DPKO staff in May 1993, when the UN assumed responsibility for Somalia and Bosnia; by the fall of 1994, when the UN prepared to assume responsibility for Haiti, there were some 115 officers, including a dozen U.S. officers, led by a German lieutenant general on the DPKO staff. A number of other improvements have also been made, including better training, better communications, better coordination, better logistics, and better planning. The U.S. military has provided direct, hands-on assistance to bring about those improvements.

Thus, the UN is better equipped to undertake carefully selected and realistically conceived medium-sized peace operations than it was at the time of its difficulties with large, overly ambitious operations in Somalia and Bosnia. When the United States believes that its interests warrant a peacekeeping response to a crisis, it should look carefully at the UN as a potential manager of such a response. It should not automatically reject the possibility, since there are often significant additional benefits to using the United Nations.

Notes

1. The most interesting and relevant books on this important chapter in UN peacekeeping and the U.S.-USSR struggle in Africa are Brian Urquhart, *Hammarskjold* (New York: Harper & Row, 1977); Brian Urquhart, *Ralph Bunche* (New York: W. W. Norton, 1993); Madeline G. Kalb, *The Congo Cables* (New York: Macmillan, 1993); and Indar Rikhye, *Military Adviser to the Secretary General* (New York: St. Martins, 1993).

2. Personal communications with an official in the Office of the Spokesman for the Secretary-General, January 17, 1997, and March 17, 1997. See also United Nations Department of Public Information, "Frequently Asked Questions: United Nations Peace-Keeping," at http://www.un.org/ Depts/dpko/faq.htm.

3. CEDAR RAPIDS, Iowa—Ed Dolan, 44, works days as a computer programmer for the MCI long-distance phone company and moonlights as director of the Iowa Sportsmen's Federation, which opposes gun controls. He also spends a lot of time worrying that the United States is menaced by a shadowy plot to take over the world.

"I consider the United Nations the greatest threat to our personal liberty and to this republic," Dolan says. "Those who promote the United Nations have a plan to make it the center of a world government with unlimited power over the whole world."

Loras Schulte, 46, who was a manager of Patrick J. Buchanan's winning campaign in Iowa's Republican presidential caucuses earlier this year, agrees. "You don't have to believe in conspiracy theories to know what the U.N. is trying to do," Schulte said. "It wants the power to tax American citizens, to have its own central bank and treasury, to regulate trade between us and other countries. It's a blueprint for a socialist government spanning the world."

Such talk typifies a trend among many right-wing Americans to demonize the United Nations and portray it as a central player in a global effort to strip away U.S. national rights and liberties. Deep suspicions of the United Nations are evident in frequent alarms—including repeated but unsubstantiated reports of U.N. "black helicopters" on mysterious missions on U.S. territory—that spread through right-wing computer and fax networks and radio talk shows. John M. Goshko, "U.N. Becomes Lightning Rod for Rightist Fears; Criticism of World Body Resonates in GOP Themes," *Washington Post*, September 23, 1996, p. A1.

4. That criticism was notable in speeches at the 1996 Republican National Convention, including those of Robert Dole and Jeane Kirkpatrick. *Washington Post* correspondent John Goshko observed that Republicans in Congress, "especially House Freshmen have joined . . . conservatives in calling for U.S. withdrawal from the United Nations if it does not undergo major reform." Goshko also noted criticism of the UN by Republican presidential candidates Pat Buchanan and Robert Dole. Dole emphasized in his acceptance speech at the Republican convention, "When I am President, every man and woman in our armed forces will know the President is commander in chief, not the UN Secretary General." Goshko.

5. Further discussion of this change in U.S. and UN policies, and in the level of military force available, can be found in Robert Oakley and John Hirsch, *Somalia and Operation Restore Hope* (Washington: U.S. Institute of Peace, 1995).

6. On May 4, 1993, command of the operation was formally turned over from the United States to the United Nations Force Commander for UNOSOM II. The U.N. Force Commander was a Turkish general and the United States provided the deputy force commander, Major General Thomas Montgomery. The United States also provided approximately 2,800 logisticians who were under the operational control of the UN Force Commander, Turkish Lieutenant General Bir, and approximately 1,300 combat troops in a Quick Reaction Force (QRF) who remained entirely under U.S. command and control under Major General Montgomery in his role as Commander of U.S. Forces. . . .

On August 24, 1993, the United States deployed approximately 440 troops as part of Joint Task Force Ranger, whose mission was to apprehend General Aideed and his senior lieutenants. Joint Task Force Ranger was under the command of Major General William Garrison. General Garrison reported directly to General Joseph Hoar, Commander in Chief, U.S. Central Command. The Task Force was not under the operational control of the UN Force Commander and was not under the operational control of Commander U.S. Forces, Somalia. Task Force Ranger conducted seven raids. . . . On the seventh and last raid, . . . the Ranger Task Force tragically sustained 16 killed in action and the relief force which went to the assistance of the Ranger Task Force sustained 2 killed in action. A total of 84 were wounded in the operation.

Sens. John W. Warner and Carl Levin, "Review of the Circumstances Surrounding the Ranger Raid on October 3–4, 1993, in Mogadishu, Somalia," Memorandum to Sens. Strom Thurmond and Sam Nunn, September 29, 1995, pp. 14–15. Senator Nunn said similar things in U.S. Senate Committee on Armed Services, *U.S. Military Operations in Somalia: Hearings before the Committee on Armed Services,* 103d Cong., 2d sess., May 12, 1994, Opening Statement, p. 17.

7. "The Commander in Chief, U.S. Central Command . . . exercised combatant control over all U.S. forces in Somalia and the region." Ibid., p. 18.

8. U Thant, *View from the UN* (Garden City, N.Y.: Doubleday, 1978), p. 32.

9. The Canadian corporation, Sherwitt International, against which action was taken under the Helms-Burton amendment held its annual board meeting in Havana for the first time as a response to the unilateral U.S. action. The European Union has taken action to establish a watch list of U.S. firms for possible retaliation and lodged a formal complaint with the World Trade Organization. Steven Lee Myers, "One Key Element in Anti-Cuba Law Postponed Again," *New York Times,* January 4, 1997, p. A1.

10. The U.S. share of total expenditures for the multinational force operation in Haiti, which the United States led outside the UN, was roughly three times that of the UN Mission in Haiti, and the number of U.S. forces was reduced by 60 percent of what it had been.

11. On July 14, 1995, French president Jacques Chirac "called upon the U.S. to pull itself together in saving the West's honor by taking military action to protect Muslim enclaves in Bosnia (as already approved by the UNSC)." "French President Lashes Out at Allies, UN's 'Impotence,'" *Chicago Tribune,* July 15, 1995, p. A1. At the time, France had troops on the ground; the United States had none.

6. UN Military Missions and the Imperial Presidency: Internationalism by the Back Door

Alan Tonelson

The Cold War's end has brought about not only great changes in relations among states but great changes within states. Not surprisingly, some of the biggest changes have involved policies or arrangements that were themselves products of Cold War conditions—for example, the reemergence of ethnic conflicts in former communist countries and the fragmentation of right-of-center political coalitions in the United States and Japan. More surprising is that one feature of American politics has been almost completely unaffected by the Cold War's passing—the imperial presidency.

The term "imperial presidency" refers to the executive branch's unprecedented expansion of the power—claimed overtly and often seized covertly throughout the Cold War—to conduct American foreign policy and deal with its domestic repercussions. Examples range from infringements on civil liberties during the McCarthy era and the Johnson and Nixon administrations to the growth of government secrecy. But no feature of the imperial presidency has been more important than the expansion of presidential power to use military force in foreign policy—whether in covert, paramilitary operations; security assistance for foreign insurgents; or large conflicts such as the Vietnam War.

No decision facing a nation is more important than the decision to use military force. Consequently, one of the hallmarks of American democracy has been the Constitution's delegation of effective warmaking powers to the Congress, save for situations involving sudden attacks or other emergencies in which Congress simply cannot be consulted in time to permit American success. The express aim was to prevent that momentous decision from being made by one

individual and to ensure that those leaders closest and most immediately accountable to the public would have the decisive influence
on any call on U.S. blood and treasure.[1]

During the Cold War, a period of intense ideological and geopolitical struggle, that principle was frequently compromised, but not in
a cavalier manner. Citing such sage observers as Tocqueville and
Alexander Hamilton on the advantages of speed and stealth enjoyed
by nondemocratic countries in the Hobbesian international sphere,
proponents of the imperial presidency earnestly grounded their
arguments in the force of necessity. They claimed that the circumstances of the Cold War—specifically the continual state of national
emergency they perceived—often required the short-circuiting of
cumbersome constitutional procedures. (President Franklin D. Roosevelt, of course, often justified his pro-British military policies before
Pearl Harbor with similar reasoning, and American history had
witnessed numerous previous examples of presidential military
actions unauthorized by Congress.)[2] In fact, as Peter Schweizer, formerly with Stanford University's Hoover Institution, makes clear in
Victory, his study of Ronald Reagan's foreign policy, the Reagan
administration considered U.S.-Soviet relations in the 1980s to be
an undeclared war, during which the standards of peacetime politics
and policymaking were completely inappropriate.[3]

Although the imperial presidency's intellectual underpinnings are
almost purely situational, its practices have largely survived the
drastic change of situation brought about by the Cold War's end.
Since the fall of the Berlin Wall, American presidents have taken
numerous foreign policy actions that have flouted or ignored public
or congressional opinion. Those have included passage of the North
American Free Trade Agreement and the Uruguay Round world
trade treaty; renewal of China's most-favored-nation trade status;
implementation of the Mexican peso bailout; and military interventions in Somalia, Haiti, Rwanda, and Bosnia.[4]

The military interventions, revealingly, all began as or became
connected with UN peacekeeping or peace-enforcement operations.
(In this chapter, both will be included in the term "peacekeeping.")
More than coincidence is involved, for participation in such operations is becoming an integral part of an unfolding effort to preserve
a highly activist, interventionist U.S. foreign policy despite clear
public opposition.

U.S. political leaders and other members of the foreign policy elite—especially the overlapping communities of academics, journalists, former government officials, and think tank analysts—understand that, with no adversary (including China) possessing global power-projection capabilities currently facing America or on the horizon, the public strongly favors staying out of most international conflicts and wants American political leaders to focus on domestic problems. As President Clinton acknowledged in his televised speech explaining his decision to invade Haiti, "I know that this is a time, with the Cold War over, that so many Americans are reluctant to commit military resources and our personnel beyond our borders."[5] U.S. involvement in UN peacekeeping operations is becoming one way around public opinion as well as the U.S. Constitution.

Yet that strategy of back-door interventionism is bound to fail for two important reasons. First, the public has not been sold on post–Cold War interventionism and therefore is unwilling to provide the strong, durable support that such risky, expensive policies ultimately require. Second, the public has not bought interventionism because it is based on a conception of national interests that is incoherent and thus incapable of providing sound guidance for policymaking. Indeed, many of the rationales put forward for a peacekeeping-oriented foreign policy either implicitly or explicitly define such fundamentals as cost and risk—and even any viable concept of national interest itself—out of existence.

Rationales for the Imperial Presidency

One of the most troubling features of Cold War era U.S. foreign policy was the executive branch's success at sending U.S. troops into combat without the express authorization of Congress. At least as disturbing was the consistent failure of Congress to resist that practice. Indeed, citing intense security imperatives, Congress in 1973 passed the War Powers Resolution. That act was widely interpreted as a significant restraint on presidential war-making ability—even though all recent presidents have not only ignored its critical provisions but vigorously rejected its constitutionality. In fact, however, the resolution is an explicit grant to the executive of unilateral war-making authority for 60 days. Of course, the unlikelihood of legislators' ever voting, short of an absolute military catastrophe, to undercut presidential authority in the middle of a combat situation meant that, whatever its supporters' intent, in practice the resolution was a virtual blank check.

Congress's Cold War era reluctance to challenge presidential authority was also made clear by its unwillingness to cut off or reduce funding for the Vietnam War until the conflict was nearly over—an action not at all precluded by the Gulf of Tonkin resolution. In Congress's apparent view, the Cold War bottom line on war powers was that the president had a right to send Americans into harm's way in all of the "grey area" conflicts generated by the superpowers' determination to conduct their rivalry without triggering nuclear war.[6]

Even leaving UN peacekeeping operations aside, post–Cold War presidents and Congresses seem to agree. President Bush consulted Congress only after the fact when he ordered the Desert Shield buildup in the fall of 1990 following Iraq's invasion of Kuwait. And although he recognized the value of securing a congressional endorsement of the Desert Storm military campaign, he denied any constitutional obligation to do so.

In September 1993 President Clinton promised to seek congressional approval for U.S. participation in a NATO (not UN) peacekeeping force in Bosnia following a negotiated end to the conflict. But a White House spokesman later specified that the president had in mind only informal support, not necessarily a formal vote. The following month, however, Clinton vigorously opposed talk in Congress of restricting his use of U.S. troops in both Haiti and Bosnia. Ultimately, no congressional effort to do so was ever made; indeed, then–Senate Minority Leader Bob Dole voiced the opinion that "the War Powers Act doesn't apply when you're talking about UN operations."[7]

Interestingly, Clinton and even more forceful interventionists have justified the post–Cold War carte blanche in terms reminiscent of Cold War powers controversies. Efforts to "improperly limit my constitutional duties as commander-in-chief," Clinton warned, "could weaken the confidence of our allies in the United States" and "would provide encouragement to aggressors and repressive rulers around the world." According to Dole, if a president has a national security requirement before he can seek action from Congress, he can proceed without congressional authorization. Columnist Max Lerner insisted, "In an era of the electronic battlefield," permitting congressional debate on a war declaration "would represent a surrender of secrecy and surprise."[8]

Despite the record, internationalists are still worried about their creed's future. In particular, they display no confidence that, in the absence of an easily understandable threat such as international communism, America's consent-based political system will continue to support global interventionism and other elements of 20th-century internationalism, such as indiscriminate trade liberalization. As they did during the Cold War, internationalism's supporters in elite media, academic, and government circles view public opposition to internationalism as evidence that the American people are incapable of judging their own interests.

Thus Edward C. Luck and Tobi Trister Gati (the latter now serving as assistant secretary of state for intelligence and research) warn that Americans are feeling "a false sense of security." *Washington Post* columnist Jessica Mathews attacks Americans who are "turning inward" as "ignorant" and "fearful." Theodore Sorensen, who penned President John F. Kennedy's fateful inaugural promise to "pay any price, bear any burden" to defend freedom around the world, chides those politicians who "turned against the United Nations after the tragic deaths in Somalia of 18 U.S. servicemen," even though they "supported the Vietnam War after 50,000 fatalities." MIT political scientist and former Carter administration National Security Council staff member Lincoln P. Bloomfield more caustically criticized "the reaction of risk-averse Americans to casualties [in Somalia] fewer than New York experiences in a slow week."[9]

Given that domestic political climate, and given Congress's refusal to play its constitutional war-making role, UN peacekeeping missions offer many potential advantages to internationalists. First, those missions can add to the number of possible missions for U.S. forces that can be placed on the public agenda, attracting attention simply by virtue of their intrinsically dramatic qualities. Second, the availability of the UN option can convey the impression that those missions can be carried out relatively cheaply and safely, with much of the burden being shouldered by other countries or by unspecified "UN forces." Third, peacekeeping operations can set tripwires for American military forces by sending troops from other lands into situations they cannot handle, under command structures practically designed to fail. Consequently, those operations can present American leaders—and a public with emotional, vestigial attachments to vague notions like "world leadership"—with a choice between escalation (with increased U.S. participation) and seeming national impotence. Interventionists assume that policymakers and the public will choose the former (Bosnia before the Croat offensive of the summer of 1995 was a perfect example—and may become one again). Finally, many left-of-center internationalists view peacekeeping operations as a way of strengthening a UN-centered system of international security and restraining America's ability to use force unilaterally.[10] Indeed, just before his name was sent to the Senate, Morton H. Halperin, President Clinton's unsuccessful nominee for assistant secretary of defense for democracy and peacekeeping, called on the United States to "explicitly surrender the right to intervene unilaterally in the internal affairs of other countries by overt military means or by covert operations." Instead, he favored developing internationally approved norms for multilateral intervention to protect threatened democracies.[11]

The UN–Imperial Presidency Connection

So far, presidents have been testing the UN back door gingerly but with increasing activism. President George Bush initially considered taking the position that UN Security Council resolutions gave him all the authority he needed to launch Operation Desert Storm but, as mentioned, ultimately sought congressional approval. In 1993 President Clinton cited another Security Council resolution to send 350 American troops to bolster the UN Protection Force aimed at deterring Serbian aggression against Macedonia.[12] Since 1994 he has cited the need to assist UN missions or enforce UN resolutions in Bosnia, and more recently Iraq, to justify use of military force. In one instance, Somalia, UN resolutions have led to a significant and ill-considered expansion of a mission originally undertaken by a U.S.-led non-UN international coalition.

The Somalia disaster of 1993 has calmed some of the early post–Cold War euphoria about U.S. participation in UN peacekeeping—especially, it seems, in the Clinton administration. Yet both the UN and the United States continue to spend hundreds of millions of dollars annually on peacekeeping operations. Indeed, in his speech before the UN General Assembly in October 1993, President Clinton advocated providing UN peacekeeping forces with more resources and more dependable sources of men and materiel.[13]

Just as disturbing, analysts from all points on the political spectrum have been arguing, explicitly or implicitly, the position that President Bush was apparently considering during the Desert Shield buildup—that UN resolutions could be all the authorization presidents need to send America to war. For example, former undersecretary of state for political affairs Arnold Kanter has suggested setting up a congressional consultation process modeled on that for covert operations. The president would send Congress a formal statement detailing the proposed mission, and in exchange "for these more meaningful consultations, Congress would be making an implicit commitment to pay the U.S. share of the bill except in those cases in which it had expressed strong objections." Yet, as in the case of covert operations, Congress would apparently have "no formal authority to block any specific operation."[14]

New York University's Thomas M. Franck, a leading U.S. authority on international law, and Faiza Patel of New York University Law School's Center for International Studies argue that when America signed the UN Charter, it signed away its legal right to sit out a Security Council–approved military action—and that the Senate expressly agreed. In fact, in an impressive piece of sophistry, the authors go on to argue that turning such authority over to the UN "also comports with the intent of the drafters of the Constitution. The purpose of the war-declaring clause was to ensure that this fateful decision did not rest with a single person. The new [UN-centered] system vests that responsibility in the Security Council, a body where the most divergent interests and perspectives of humanity are represented, and where five of fifteen members have a veto power."[15] Franck and Patel cite neither the passage in the Constitution that enables American leaders to delegate war-making powers to foreign government representatives or international bureaucrats nor evidence from the Constitutional Convention debates, *The Federalist Papers*, or any other sources supporting the view that such was the intent of the Framers.

The concepts of national interest underlying those interventionist views and proposals fail the most basic tests of sound strategy and policymaking. In the first place, they are internally contradictory. Internationalists invariably portray UN peacekeeping operations as

103

valuable "force multipliers," which enable the United States to achieve important national security goals with less cost and risk than unilateral operations would entail.[16] Some influential analysts also argue that American participation in UN operations provides U.S. policies with international legitimacy—without which they ostensibly could not or would not be pursued.[17]

At the same time, internationalists just as vigorously insist that the United States must remain capable of acting unilaterally in a wide range of situations. As stated in the Clinton administration's 1994 blueprint for UN peace operations, "When our interests dictate, the United States must be willing and able to fight and win wars, unilaterally wherever necessary. To do so, we must create the required capabilities and maintain them ready to use. UN peace operations cannot substitute for this requirement." Vowed then UN Ambassador Madeleine Albright several months earlier, "We want a stronger UN, but we are not about to substitute elusive notions of global collective security for battle-proven and time-tested concepts of unilateral and allied defense."[18]

Such positions sound prudent until examined closely. If the United States is going to depend for the most part on its own resources to ensure its own security, how can participation in UN peacekeeping play anything more than a marginal role? And if the interests to be secured through UN peacekeeping are marginal, why incur any costs and risks to secure them at all?

Internationalist Fallacies

Internationalists tend to respond by pointing to portentous-sounding consequences of inaction, seemingly content to assume that the importance of those consequences is self-evident. It is not. Sorensen, for example, warns that "without the United Nations . . . the United States would be required to put out threatening brush fires on its own or not at all"—never bothering to explain why our unilateral capacity would not be adequate or why many such conflicts merit any attention. Albright similarly argues, "If we do not wish to assume responsibility for containing these conflicts ourselves, we must either enhance the UN's capability to do so or accept a future ruled not by the law of nations, but by no law at all."[19] But what makes her suppose that international affairs are strongly influenced by the law of nations now? What makes her suppose that international law can become so influential? And why does she believe that the security of a powerful country such as the United States depends so heavily on international law?

Without "generally applicable rules of intervention," specifying when Security Council action would be "automatically triggered," ask Luck and Gati, "how will the security interests of developing countries that are not deemed strategically important get addressed?"[20] If those countries are not strategic, however, why should the United States care whether their problems get addressed or not? Internationalists are understandably reluctant to face up to the bottom line, expressed nicely by the staff of the National Defense University's Institute for National Strategic Studies: "The most likely conflicts in the emerging world system are the least dangerous to the U.S."[21]

In other instances, internationalists retreat into tightly circular reasoning. Sorensen, for example, warns that if the United States decides that participating in UN peacekeeping is not in its interests, "other countries could do the same, ending UN peacekeeping altogether." Luck and Gati criticize the Bush administration for "excluding the world body completely" from the prosecution of the gulf war, arguing that its exclusion produced "a loss of credibility for the United Nations and for the concept of a 'new world order.'"[22]

Nearly as often, internationalists will support participating in UN peacekeeping simply by assuming that no viable alternative U.S. policies or positions exist—much as the economist in a well-known joke deals with a problem by assuming the solution. In the words of Columbia University political scientist John Gerard Ruggie, "Let us assume . . . that sooner or later the United States will be drawn into seeking to counter particularly egregious acts of aggression or violations of civility." Former senior U.S. diplomat Richard N. Gardner has offered another version of that proposition. Citing numerous statements by American presidents about the importance of creating a just, peaceful world, he concludes, "If statements like these . . . are more than meaningless historical flourishes, it must be because we consider that the construction of a global security system that protects all nations is something that serves the interest of the United States."[23]

Yet when internationalists do explain the consequences of inaction, they reveal themselves to be driven by concepts of national interest so vast and expandable as to be open-ended. The Clinton peacekeeping blueprint acknowledged that many conflicts potentially preventable by UN peacekeeping "may not directly threaten American interests." But the document maintained that "their cumulative effect is significant." Ambassador Albright specified some of the costs of that cumulation: "economic dislocation, terrorism and other forms of international lawlessness, regional political instability and the rise of leaders and societies that do not share our values."[24]

Internationalists outside government make similar points. Janne Nolan of the Brookings Institution has written, "The combination of economic austerity, ethnic conflict, and political disintegration is now so widespread that civil violence could become a general conflagration if tolerance remains the only realistic international option." And former under-secretary of the air force and historian Townsend Hoopes, who turned publicly against the pursuit of Wilsonianism in Vietnam in the late 1960s, has recently warned that if America "held aloof" from "the continued eruption of local and regional disorders . . . we would risk a progressive unraveling of the international fabric. In the worst case scenario, this might cause the world to drift—as in the 1930s, toward uncontrollable general conflict."[25]

Those concerns might all be valid—it is, of course, impossible to know for certain. But the approach favored by internationalists is incapable either of addressing such concerns or of protecting the United States from the consequences of their spread, except at increased levels of cost and risk. Logically, the "cumulation" theory turns every one of the world's countries into a potential domino, whose troubles could spill over into neighboring lands, and so on, and so on. Logically, America's only internationalist option must therefore be to do whatever is necessary to ensure the long-term security, prosperity, and stability of all countries. Indeed, Albright's fear of societies that do not share American values would seem to require that America remake the entire world in its own image.

That globalist policy led America to the brink of insolvency during the Cold War. Today, internationalists in the Clinton administration and elsewhere insist that they can make "disciplined and coherent choices about which peace operations to support" by imposing "increasingly rigorous standards of review" on the decision to intervene. Above all, the administration insists that peace operations "should not be open-ended commitments."[26] Yet, as it did during the Cold War, the absolute stake claimed by the administration in "international security" will make discipline and selectivity excruciatingly difficult, at best, and obviate any ongoing considerations of cost and risk.

Worse, internationalists sometimes argue that the very concept of national interest is rapidly becoming obsolete—at least in the sense that it has been understood throughout recorded history (i.e., that by virtue of their differing circumstances and experiences, sovereign states inevitably will see the world in significantly different ways and consequently pursue different and periodically clashing objectives).[27] According to international law specialist David Scheffer of the Carnegie Endowment, "The 'national interest' has become a somewhat misleading term, given the criteria and requirements of the post–Cold War world. We should begin to focus on what is in this country's global interests, as well as our national interests, which typically focus on the requirement for national defense of our territory." More subtly, former national security advisor Brent Scowcroft has criticized "the new unilateralism" in U.S. foreign policy, "which holds that we will deal with the world when we must, but only in our own way, in our time and on our own terms."[28] The "country's global interests," however, is a concept that can too easily undergird the view that anything threatening the political, economic, social, or ecological interests of any other state is ipso facto a threat to U.S. interests. Scheffer himself has offered a classic example. Humanitarian calamities, he argues, are

> not necessarily threats to the borders of the United States, nor are they necessarily threats to most of our major allies. Humanitarian calamities are not necessarily "regional conflicts." . . . Rather, humanitarian problems are internal conflicts in which the interest is the survival of large civilian populations, the preservation of whole national economies that, if destroyed, will have a costly impact for decades to come. Such destruction ultimately may affect the United States, the ecosystem (which can be severely endangered when humanitarian calamities occur), and the larger goal of international peace and security.[29]

Scowcroft, meanwhile, fails to understand that the only alternative to engaging the world on the United States' own terms (which would presumably reflect its own distinctive interests) is for the United States to engage the world on other nations' terms (which would presumably reflect their own distinctive interests). In fact, that is one of the main choices facing U.S. foreign policy today. The principal alternatives are

- to amass the power to set or decisively influence the terms of America's engagement in the world;
- to assume that surrogates such as international organizations or other countries will be as devoted to distinctively American interests as Americans are; or
- to assume international conflicts of interest out of the picture.

Scowcroft, widely regarded as a realist, seems to be hovering between utopian choices two and three.

The fairy tale "The Princess and the Pea" tells of a young girl so physically sensitive that she is able to feel a pea set beneath a tall pile of mattresses that serves as her bed. Internationalist arguments suggest that the United States is hypersensitive as well, with its security and well-being acutely, and usually vitally, dependent on a staggering variety of events and developments in every part of the world.

In fact, America's position is more nearly the opposite—a strong, geopolitically secure, wealthy, dynamic country amply capable of shaping the terms of its international engagement in favorable ways and insulating itself satisfactorily from much global turmoil. American internationalists, facing a public instinctively aware of the country's power and potential, have been working overtime with instruments such as UN peacekeeping to keep a cautious public out of foreign policy decisionmaking. Given the internationalists' record, it is far likelier that future American success in foreign policy depends on bringing the public in.

Notes

1. For a recent, documented statement of this still controversial view, see John Hart Ely, *War and Responsibility: Constitutional Lessons of Vietnam and Its Aftermath* (Princeton, N.J.: Princeton University Press, 1993).

2. See, for example, Louis Henkin, *Foreign Affairs and the Constitution* (Mineola, N.Y.: Foundation Press, 1972).

3. Peter Schweizer, *Victory: The Reagan Administration's Secret Strategy That Hastened the Collapse of the Soviet Union* (New York: Atlantic Monthly Press, 1994).

4. For some representative survey results on NAFTA, see Times-Mirror poll cited in "Listen to What the American People Say about NAFTA Now," Dear Colleague letter from Reps. Marcy Kaptur, Duncan Hunter, Peter DeFazio, Bob Barr, Bernie Sanders, and Helen Chenoweth, November 27, 1994. On the Uruguay Round, see "New Yankelovich Poll Finds: Majority of Americans Oppose GATT," memorandum, Yankelovich Partners, November 28, 1994. On China, see Albert R. Hunt, "Clinton's High-Stakes China Gambit," *Wall Street Journal*, December 16, 1993, p. A17; and Albert R. Hunt, "Dole High Ground Helps Dicey Relations with China," *Wall Street Journal*, May 23, 1996, p. A15. On the peso bailout, see John Maggs, "Clinton's 2nd Mexico Aid Plan Meets with Mixed Reaction," *Journal of Commerce*, February 1, 1995. On public caution on Somalia, see Andrew Kohut and Robert C. Toth, "Arms and the People," *Foreign Affairs* 73, no. 6 (November–December 1994): 50–53. On Haiti, see "Opinion Outlook," *National Journal*, July 30, 1994, p. 1822; and "In Speech's Wake: Majority of Americans Remain Opposed to Haiti Invasion but Those Familiar with Clinton Speech Less Opposed," *ABC News Nightline Poll*, September 19, 1994. On Bosnia, see Kohut and Toth, pp. 53–55.

Even more impressive than those findings have been the numerous surveys showing how little Americans have focused on these crises, and on foreign policy in general. See, for example, "Opinion Outlook," *National Journal*, August 1, 1992, p. 1806; Kohut and Toth, pp. 51, 53–54; and Peter Grier, "Why Americans Spurn U.S Playing the Role of World Policeman," *Christian Science Monitor*, December 14, 1994.

For contrasting evidence of public opinion on foreign policy, see, for example, Catherine M. Kelleher, "Soldiering On," *Brookings Review* 12, no. 2 (Spring 1994): 26–29; and Stephen S. Rosenfeld, "When the Public's Ahead of the Experts," *Washington Post*, July 19, 1996.

5. "Clinton's Speech: The Reasons Why," *New York Times*, September 16, 1994.

6. Ely, p. ix.

7. "Interview with Senator Bob Dole . . .," *Face the Nation*, Federal News Service, October 17, 1993. p. 2.

8. For Clinton's statements, see Frank. J. Murray, "Clinton Conditions Guarantees in Bosnia on Congress," *Washington Times*, September 9, 1993, p. A3; and Ruth Marcus and Helen Dewar, "Clinton Tells Congress to Back Off," *Washington Post*, October 19, 1993. For Dole's statement, see "Interview with Senator Bob Dole . . ." For Lerner's statement, see Max Lerner, "At the Caution Light," *Washington Times*, November 5, 1990.

9. Edward C. Luck and Tobi Trister Gati, "Whose Collective Security?" *Washington Quarterly* 15 (Spring 1992), excerpted in *America's National Interest in a Post–Cold War World: Issues and Dilemmas*, ed. Alvin Z. Rubinstein (New York: McGraw-Hill, 1994), p. 276; Jessica Mathews, "The New Isolationism," *Washington Post*, February 5, 1996; Theodore C. Sorensen, "The Star Spangled Shrug," *Washington Post*, July 2, 1995, p. C1; Lincoln P. Bloomfield, "The Premature Burial of Global Law and Order: Looking beyond the Three Cases from Hell," in *Order and Disorder after the Cold War*, ed. Brad Roberts (Cambridge, Mass.: MIT Press, 1995), p. 161.

10. See, for example, Luck and Gati, pp. 267–69; and Thomas M. Franck and Faiza Patel, "UN Police Action in Lieu of War: 'The Old Order Changeth,'" *American Journal of International Law* 85, no. 1 (January 1991), reprinted in *Taking Sides: Clashing Views on Controversial Issues in World Politics*, 5th ed., ed. John T. Rourke (Guilford, Conn.: Dushkin, 1994), pp. 334–39.

11. Morton H. Halperin, "Guaranteeing Democracy," *Foreign Policy* 91 (Summer 1993): 120.

12. Ely, p. 50; and Jeremy Rabkin, "Threats to U.S. Sovereignty," *Commentary*, March 1994, p. 44.

13. Cited in "Testimony, Ambassador Madeleine K. Albright, U.S. Permanent Representative to the United Nations before the Committee on Foreign Relations, United States Senate," October 20, 1993, p. 5. These proposals were presented in more detail in Presidential Decision Directive 25 (PDD-25), *The Clinton Administration's Policy on Reforming Multilateral Peace Operations* (Washington: White House, May 3, 1994). For a long list of other official and unofficial foreign and domestic proposals to strengthen and expand UN peacekeeping, see Doug Bandow, "Avoiding War," *Foreign Policy* 89 (Winter 1992–93): 162–63.

14. Arnold Kanter, "The U.S. and the UN," Forum for International Policy Issue Brief no. 95–8, Washington, June 1995, p. 3.

15. Franck and Patel, p. 338.

16. See *The Clinton Administration's Policy*, p. 1, for use of the term "force multiplier." For other versions of this argument, see Albright, p. 9; Carnegie Endowment National Commission on America and the New World, *Changing Our Ways* (Washington: Carnegie Endowment for International Peace, 1992), p. 12; and Paul Kennedy and Bruce Russett, "Reforming the United Nations," *Foreign Affairs* 74 no. 5 (September–October 1995): 58.

17. See Janne E. Nolan, "Cooperative Security in the United States," in *Global Engagement: Cooperation and Security in the 21st Century*, ed. Janne E. Nolan (Washington: Brookings Institution, 1994), pp. 507, 514.

18. *The Clinton Administration's Policy*, p. 1; and Albright, p. 4. For other examples, see *Changing Our Ways*, pp. 12, 65; and Edward C. Luck, "Making Peace," *Foreign Policy* 89 (Winter 1992–93): 147.

19. Sorensen; and Albright, p. 5.

20. Luck and Gati, p. 273.

21. Institute for National Strategic Studies, *Strategic Assessment 1995: U.S. Security Challenges in Transition* (Washington: Government Printing Office, 1995), p. 4.

22. Sorensen; and Luck and Gati, p. 270.

23. John Gerard Ruggie, "Peacekeeping and U.S. Interests," in *Order and Disorder after the Cold War*, p. 212; Richard N. Gardner, "Practical Internationalism," in *Rethinking America's Security: Beyond Cold War to New World Order*, ed. Graham Allison and Gregory Treverton (New York: W. W. Norton, 1992), p. 272.

24. *The Clinton Administration's Policy*, p. 1; and Albright, p. 5.

25. Nolan, p. 45; and Townsend Hoopes, "Whither U.N. Peacekeeping?" Center for International and Security Studies, University of Maryland School of Public Affairs, CISSM Paper 3, March 1994, p. 15.

26. *The Clinton Administration's Policy*, Executive Summary, p. 3.

27. For a more detailed discussion of the idea of national interest, see Alan Tonelson, "What Is the National Interest?" *Atlantic Monthly*, July 1991, pp. 35–52.

28. David Scheffer, "Humanitarian Intervention versus State Sovereignty," in *Peacemaking and Peacekeeping: Implications for the United States Military* (Washington: United States Institute of Peace), May 1993, p. 10; and Brent Scowcroft and Arnold Kanter, "The Perils of Going It Alone," *Washington Post*, February 3, 1995.

29. Scheffer, p. 16.

7. Getting UN Military Operations Back to Basics

John Hillen

A funny thing happened to the United Nations on the way to the post–Cold War world—it became a major player in global security affairs. Although the UN has been involved in organizing and running military operations since 1948, only recently has the organization assumed a global military posture that goes well beyond its traditional peacekeeping role.

At the height of UN military operations in 1993, the world organization was running 18 such operations around the globe involving some 80,000 troops at the cost of some $3.6 billion per year (with the United States paying almost one-third of the total cost). Moreover, several of those operations were complex military enterprises involving coercive mandates that required sophisticated air, sea, and land combat units on loan from major powers.

In contrast to those recent military ambitions, most of the UN's earlier experience was in putting together small quasi-military operations that were more quasi than military. In 1990, for instance, the UN controlled fewer than 10,000 blue helmets (peacekeeping troops) in eight small missions that cost only approximately $400 million.

The Cold War era UN missions generally consisted of unarmed observers or a few thousand lightly armed troops policing an already concluded peace settlement. The troops usually came from states such as Fiji, Austria, Ireland, Canada, Chile, Ghana, and other UN members noted more for their neutrality than for their military prowess. For 40-odd years UN missions were small, innocuous, painstakingly impartial, and unambitious by military standards. Occasionally, if the political environment was conducive to their use, UN peacekeeping missions even worked.

Only once during the Cold War did the UN stray from that formula. Between 1960 and 1964 the UN launched in the Congo a massive operation that involved almost 20,000 troops. The blue helmets were deployed while the situation was very unstable and, as a result, became embroiled in the decolonization process and civil war there. Some 234 UN troops were killed—making the Congo mission the most costly UN military operation to date in terms of casualties. The death toll even included Secretary-General Dag Hammarskjold, who perished in an air crash while inspecting the progress of the UN mission. Moreover, the Congo adventure almost split the UN asunder, causing major rifts between the United States, France, and Britain and greatly exacerbating the Cold War tensions between America and the Soviet Union.

Soon after the Congo intervention, the UN returned to its small and more traditional peacekeeping operations with emphasis on consent, impartiality, and simple, passive military operations. The experience of the Congo, both in New York and in the field, was so traumatic for the UN that many UN hands later referred to it as "the UN's Vietnam." Peacekeeping scholar William Durch noted that "the UN operation in the Congo lacked every element that history now says is necessary for a successful peacekeeping mission; namely, effective support from the Great Powers, consistent support of all local parties, a clear mandate, stable and adequate funding, and sufficiently good command, control, communications, and logistics."[1] Durch, writing in 1992, went on to forecast that, given the enduring effect of the Congo debacle, "the Security Council is unlikely to ever again dispatch such a sizable force under UN command with such a similarly undefined initial mandate."[2]

Unfortunately, Durch's sensible prediction was proven tragically and spectacularly wrong only a year later when the UN undertook two large and complex military missions—in the former Yugoslavia and Somalia. Both missions involved the world organization in the tasks of recruiting, forming, deploying, and commanding large (over 38,000 UN troops in the Balkan mission) combat formations with ambitious objectives that were to be accomplished in the middle of civil wars. The results of both operations were predictably bad—hundreds of peacekeepers killed and billions of dollars wasted in failing efforts to foster local reconciliation.[3] Because it once again abandoned the preconditions of successful peacekeeping for a more robust approach, the UN failed.

It is pertinent to ask how the UN managed to become twice trapped in a cycle that led it to undertake ambitious military projects

112

that vastly outpaced the intrinsic capabilities of the institution. It is equally relevant to wonder about the factors that motivated the UN and its influential member states to think that the end of the Cold War represented such a fundamental shift in the structure of the international system that the UN suddenly had the political legitimacy and military authority to command and control large, complex, and ambitious military operations.

The answers to those questions are like the autopsy of tragedy. Moreover, an examination of the Somalia and Bosnia episodes leads to an inescapable conclusion: the UN, a multinational organization predicated on the sovereignty of the nation-state, can never be a competent manager of large and complex military operations. The UN, like all political entities, is constrained by its nature—in this case, a diplomatic orientation that lends itself to small, passive, and impartial peacekeeping missions but not to ambitious peace-enforcement operations. The political and military challenges of large and complex military missions require a management capability that is antithetical to an organization composed of 185 voluntary participants whose sovereign powers are guaranteed by the organization itself.

Escaping History's Cycles

Between 1948 and 1996 the UN experienced two similar cycles involving its role in sponsoring and managing military operations. The first cycle began with the creation of the first UN military observation mission in Palestine in 1948 and ended with the Congo mission discussed above. The second cycle started in 1973 with the creation of the second UN peacekeeping force in the Sinai and ended recently with the failure of the missions in Somalia and the former Yugoslavia. In each of those cycles, the UN, encouraged by moderate success in missions involving small, impartial, and passive peacekeeping measures, attempted more active approaches to peacekeeping that strayed into the realm of coercive enforcement.

The first UN military operations consisted of no more than a few hundred military observers deployed to monitor a previously concluded peace settlement or cease-fire. Those missions were an improvised attempt to provide some sort of military response to crises that fell between cracks in the UN Charter. Chapter 6 of the charter provides for the peaceful settlement of disputes. Chapter 7

113

provides for more forceful actions, including economic sanctions and collective military action. The latter course was envisaged as a continuation of the allied collaboration in World War II.

Because Cold War tensions on the Security Council effectively negated the possibility of collective military action as provided for in chapter 7, the UN improvised a set of operations that were more than the diplomatic means outlined in chapter 6 but fell short of the coercive actions implied in chapter 7. The use of UN-sponsored military observers and lightly armed peacekeepers was an ad hoc arrangement jokingly referred to as "chapter 6½."

Almost 50 years after the first of those missions, improvisation remains their principal characteristic, in terms of both functional efficacy and political legitimacy. UN military missions, large and small, are put together on the fly and under the very transient conditions of short-term political expediency and media-generated urgency. Functionally, the ad hoc procedures and mechanisms used to set up and run UN military missions have to be invented and reinvented for almost every mission.

Politically, UN military operations as undertaken between 1948 and the present are not clearly rooted in the charter or the architecture of the UN established by the founders of the organization. Consequently, international legal scholars have been debating the basis of legitimacy of such operations for decades. However, as UN official Shashi Tharoor recently noted, the only thing that has been made clear by this dispute is that "in the debate about Chapter VI and Chapter VII, all we know is that we're still at sixes and sevens."[4]

Nonetheless, the UN pressed forward with its improvised operations in the early days of the Cold War. Two observation missions that seemed to work (although both are still running today—the UN observers in Palestine are in their 48th year and the blue helmets in Kashmir are in their 47th year of continuous operations) gave way to the first peacekeeping mission. In 1956 the UN deployed some 6,000 lightly armed peacekeepers to the Sinai to man zones separating the British, French, Egyptian, and Israeli armies that were confronting each other after a cease-fire in the Suez crisis. The operation succeeded in forestalling a resumption of the crisis and was judged a success (although Egyptian president Gamal Nasser rudely booted the UN out of Egypt in 1967 so he could prepare for war against Israel).

From those early experiences the UN evolved a peacekeeping doctrine that suited not only the nature of the operations in the field but the capabilities of the organization to manage small, impartial, and passive forces. The UN's capacity for managing military operations was small and improvised—reflecting the organization's diplomatic and passive nature. Ironically, those functional weaknesses were the UN's political strengths. The principles that would undergird UN peacekeeping were drawn, not from political authority, but from the moral authority of the organization. The UN was an honest broker providing support, not a supergovernment providing solutions. Consequently, the UN developed principles of peacekeeping—five tenets that were meant to guide the organization's military operations:

1. Unlike the U.S.-led multinational operation in the Korean War, peacekeeping operations would be truly UN operations. They would be formed and commanded by the UN under the authority of the secretary-general.

2. UN troops would be deployed only with the consent of all parties involved in the conflict and only after a fairly solid political settlement had been reached between warring factions.

3. UN forces would be strictly impartial in their actions.

4. Troops acceptable to all belligerents would be provided to the UN by "neutral" member states to reinforce their impartiality. There would rarely be direct participation by a great power or a permanent member of the Security Council.

5. UN forces would undertake only passive operations—the use of force would be limited to self-defense, including self-defense of their mandate if under attack by an armed force.

Despite the success of those tenets in the early UN observation and peacekeeping missions, they were abandoned in the Congo mission. In what Professor Alan James of the University of Keele has called a "double departure from the basic values of peacekeeping,"[5] the UN authorized limited enforcement measures for the Congo mission, entered the fighting, and squandered its status as an impartial actor. Its fingers burned in the Congo, the UN authorized only three new observation missions and four peacekeeping operations over the next 25 years. All of those missions closely adhered to the principles of peacekeeping. It appeared that the UN

115

had found its niche in the global security environment, a small but fairly comfortable and low-risk role as an occasional peacekeeper.

The End of the Cold War and the Resumption of the Cycle

The UN's admirable restraint lasted until the end of the Cold War when the international arena saw momentous changes. The advent of glasnost and the thawing of tensions on the Security Council produced an atmosphere of unprecedented cooperation that was most strikingly evident in the conduct of the Persian Gulf War of 1991. Nonetheless, while increased political cooperation made the gulf war coalition possible, the UN was not at all involved in the functional management of the 31-state, 750,000-troop military force. That burden fell to the United States, a military superpower that supplied 70 percent of the ground forces and even higher percentages of the advanced air and sea forces that made up the multinational coalition.

Soon after the conclusion of the gulf campaign, however, post–Cold War political cooperation on the Security Council began to produce real functional challenges for the UN as an institution that would sometimes be in the business of recruiting, forming, deploying, and controlling military forces under its command. Most notably, in 1992 the Security Council began to consider authorizing UN military operations in more belligerent and unsupportive environments. The old political prerequisite of a previously concluded peace settlement might not be present in a post–Cold War crisis. In addition, the new missions would need to be considerably more complex than inert buffer-zone peacekeeping.

Naturally, more ambitious missions that were expected to operate in more unstable environments would require larger and more robust UN forces than had traditional UN missions. Secretary-General Boutros Boutros-Ghali forecast the coming changes in his 1992 book, *An Agenda for Peace*, when he redefined peacekeeping as "the deployment of a UN presence in the field, *hitherto* with the consent of all the parties concerned."[6] That foreboding observation, that the UN was now free to launch peacekeeping missions without the full consent of the belligerents, was the conceptual seed for the UN peace-enforcement missions in Bosnia and Somalia.

Those missions, as well as other large peacekeeping operations, such as the 15,000-troop mission to Cambodia in 1992–93, were qualitatively and quantitatively different from traditional peace-keeping. The new missions were much more comprehensive, with the UN attempting the nearly simultaneous management of political, social, economic, humanitarian, electoral, diplomatic, and military initiatives within a troubled state. Moreover, the UN was attempting to do that in several large and complex operations at the same time in 1992 and 1993.

In those missions, UN military forces were no longer "alert, but inert" in buffer zones. They were instead spread out among mixed pockets of still-warring belligerents. The blue helmets attempted actively to protect the delivery of humanitarian aid, disarm and demobilize local factions, maintain and protect safe areas, enforce weapons-exclusion zones, monitor borders, monitor violations of human rights, repatriate refugees, assume temporary control of many government functions, and provide secure environments for elections and other nation-building activities.

In Somalia the nation-building ambitions of the UN mission caused resentment among several Somali factions, and the inevitable backlash occurred in June 1993 with the massacre of 24 Pakistani peacekeepers. Under U.S. pressure, the UN then authorized the use of active military force to capture Mohamed Farah Aideed after UN leaders had deemed his faction responsible for the killings. The UN and additional U.S. forces became fully embroiled in the local politics of Mogadishu street fighting, and in October 1993, 18 American soldiers were killed. That action prompted the withdrawal of the American contingent and, eventually, all UN forces.

In Bosnia the UN enlisted NATO as a "subcontractor" for coercive enforcement while the UN troops on the ground attempted to main-tain their passive impartiality. NATO planes enforced no-fly zones in the sky and threatened bombardment in the defense of safe areas on the ground while UN peacekeepers went about the business of delivering humanitarian aid and fostering political reconciliation. The results speak for themselves. As peacekeeping authority Mats Berdal noted, the missions obfuscated "the basic distinction between peacekeeping and enforcement action . . . [and] highlighted the par-ticular risks of attempting to combine the coercive use of force with peacekeeping objectives."[7]

The UN as Peace Enforcer

The inefficacy of peace enforcement as a technique of conflict resolution is not the principal lesson of the Somalia and Bosnia crises, however. The more profound lesson is the ineffectiveness of the United Nations as a political entity attempting to manage complex operations. The method may indeed be suspect, but the congenital frailties of the manager are the more relevant story. Unfortunately for the UN, it was thrust into the ambitious ventures of 1992–93 by a series of unrealistic expectations on the part of member states (the United States very much included) reinforced by Boutros-Ghali and a host of globalist thinkers and writers.

The globalist vein of thinking about a new role for the UN in international peace and security was unbounded in the initial period after the Cold War. Thomas Weiss, one of the scholars involved in the many projects of the post–Cold War UN, wrote in late 1992 that Boutros-Ghali's *An Agenda for Peace* "is perhaps the most spectacular indication of just how significant the UN's role could be in international peace and security as the twenty-first century dawns. . . . The United Nations is the logical convener of future international military operations. Rhetoric about regional organizations risks slowing down or even making impossible more timely and vigorous actions by the UN, the one organization most likely to fulfill adequately the role of regional conflict manager."[8] Professor David Hendrickson of Colorado College noted that the end of Cold War tensions "persuaded many observers that we stand today at a critical juncture, one at which the promise of collective security, working through the mechanism of the United Nations, might at last be realized."[9]

The UN itself was captive to that school of thought and, believing much of its own publicity, made structural and procedure changes to implement its enhanced role in the world's security affairs. The Department of Peacekeeping Operations was created, with its own under secretary-general, in 1993. The staff rapidly grew from a handful to almost 400 personnel, including many professional military officers on loan from member states. The UN also set up a round-the-clock situation center, installed a management information system, reorganized to bring the administrative and logistics staff into the same department as the operational planners, and established a registry of stand-by forces volunteered by member states. The idea of stand-by forces, meant to speed up reaction time, proved to be of little value. When the 1994 slaughter in Rwanda drew the world's attention, not a single state of the 19 committed to the stand-by force would volunteer its troops for an intervention in that unhappy country.

Nonetheless, the reinforced UN carried on with the tasks of recruiting, forming, deploying, and commanding new missions. Despite the new staff and improvements, the UN struggled under the burdens of managing almost 80,000 troops in 18 missions, some of which were extremely complicated military enterprises that required the heavy participation of the major military powers (who all brought their own agendas to the missions). In the end, the challenges of managing those operations far outweighed the slight improvements in management capability. The belligerency of the operational environment, the size of the operations involved, and the ambitious objectives of the missions themselves all proved to be too much for the UN (and, as Bosnia has shown, are a considerable challenge even for a credible military alliance with adequate resources, such as NATO).

Ultimately, the UN could not overcome its intrinsic character—a diplomatic character that served it well in traditional missions but could not be translated into the legitimacy and authority needed to manage more complex military operations. Jonathan Howe, the special representative of the secretary-general in Somalia, summed up his frustrations in a mission postmortem.

> The UN has all the disadvantages of a volunteer organization. Troop contributors rotate units at short intervals and withdraw them altogether with little notice. Nations want to dictate where their contingents will serve and what duties they will perform. The UN does not have the authority to hold individual nations to a fixed contract. The result in Somalia was a significant loss of time due to constant reassignment and readjustment of forces.[10]

Being Realistic about UN Capabilities

In the euphoric aftermath of the Cold War, many sophisticated observers of the international scene felt that the UN could free itself from Cold War bonds that had rendered it stymied and ineffective. However, the UN's institutional characteristics will always constrain its forays into the military realm. In a world of nation-states or smaller political entities, the nature of the UN is somewhat of a constant—it supersedes the current global environment. As Professor Innis Claude of the University of Virginia recognized many years ago, as long as sovereignty is inherent in states, the UN cannot be a "government of governments" regardless of whether the general structure of the international system is bipolar, unipolar, or multipolar.[11]

The functional military capabilities of any political entity cannot be separated from its inherent political character. That rudimentary and profound feature of the UN was not fundamentally altered by either Cold War tensions or post–Cold War cooperation. Managing complex military operations in bellicose environments requires more than cooperation on the Security Council. It requires the relationships of legitimacy, authority, and accountability that allow a political entity to mobilize military resources, send them into harm's way, and hold a steady course during times of casualties and the threat of mission failure. Throughout the existence of the UN, the nation-state has been the highest entity in which this relationship exists by law and tradition.

Some observers feel that the only answer to this fundamental dilemma of collective security is to give the UN the resources it would need to have such a relationship: permanent forces under UN authority, strategic independence from the unilateral decisions of member states, and the mechanisms and procedures to forcefully apply the collective will of the international community in matters of peace and security. Two authors at Cambridge University recently wrote, "It is a cornerstone of political legitimacy that both individual nations and regional organizations should possess mechanisms for exercising political control over the military operations which they authorize. That the United Nations is without such means is not only ironic, but deeply inimical to its credibility."[12]

Yet other observers feel that the lack of politico-military legitimacy is precisely what gives the UN its strength as an organization that is not a "world government."[13] Former assistant secretary-general Giandomenico Picco writes that the UN can be a strong and effective international force precisely because the "institution does not carry with it those basic tools of states. . . . The more the institution tries to resemble a state, the more it will fade away and, most seriously perhaps, the UN will become no more than the sum of its members."[14]

The functional difficulties experienced by the UN in its attempts to manage military operations are legion. However, through a process of trial and error, there "evolved" a system of limited military operations that was well suited for the inherent political and military constraints of a unique institution such as the UN. A workable UN military doctrine reflected in the principles of peacekeeping was the result. In many ways those principles can be considered, not just a means to an end, but an end in themselves. They accurately reflect the immutable and unique nature (and constraints) of a disparate multinational body.

Recent attempts to deviate from those principles, greatly expand the size and nature of UN military operations, and develop more "professional" UN management have overwhelmed the organization and resulted in expensive failures. Ironically, those failures not only undermined an enhanced UN role but now threaten the organization's very existence.[15] That warning is not voiced only by critics of the UN. Internationalists Paul Kennedy and Bruce Russett recently wrote that "these operations, hopes, and expectations far exceed the capabilities of the system as it is now constituted, and they threaten to overwhelm the United Nations and discredit it, perhaps forever, even in the eyes of its warmest supporters."[16]

In addition, attempts to deal with difficult security issues through the UN have led to many states' using the organization as a "policy cop-out." Knowing that the UN is one of the least effective means of managing complex military challenges, member states use the option anyway. Madeleine Albright is far more responsible for the UN failure in Somalia than is Boutros-Ghali, for it was the United States that pushed the ambitious mission on a reluctant UN in the first place.[17] Indeed, the UN is the ideal scapegoat. Its operations are protracted, its credibility is already damaged, and the stakes for member states are low; thus, there is always the UN to blame for policy failures. Working through the UN allows some member states to make half-hearted contributions to efforts that would ordinarily require a more serious commitment of resources and greater political will to competently address the problem (and simultaneously sets up a convenient whipping boy).[18]

That cynical ploy is quite evident in the conduct of the major European powers toward the former Yugoslavia and in the actions of the entire international community toward Rwanda. In true "let's ask Mikey; he'll try anything" fashion, the great powers fobbed off Bosnia and Somalia on the United Nations. Using the UN as a way to dodge more substantive policy options could be called the "politics of being seen to do something" or, even more apropos in the information age, "virtual reality politics."

By going "back to basics" in its military ambitions, the UN would restore its credibility and its role as an honest broker in international affairs. This counsel should not necessarily discourage the UN from attempting multifunctional efforts that have been successful in places such as Namibia, El Salvador, and Mozambique. Back to basics applies only to the military aspect of UN operations, especially those UN missions that require large and sophisticated combat formations employed in a coercive capacity. In managing those operations, the UN must recognize that it cannot overcome its inherent political constraints without a fundamental change in the structure of the international arena. The UN's attempts to undertake complex military operations are antithetical to its political nature and are ultimately futile—hurting both the UN and the mission. More realistic expectations about both the unique politico-military strengths of the nation-state and the diplomatic nature of the UN would better serve all members of the international community.

Notes

1. William Durch, *The Evolution of UN Peacekeeping* (London: Macmillan, 1993), p. 345.

2. Ibid., p. 28.

3. Those who dispute that billions of dollars were wasted and argue that "at least some humanitarian good was accomplished" are urged to consult John Hillen, "Killing with Kindness: The UN Peacekeeping Mission in Bosnia," Cato Foreign Policy Briefing no. 34, June 30, 1995.

4. Conversation with the author, September 1995.

5. Alan James, *Peacekeeping in International Politics* (London: Macmillan, 1990), p. 296.

6. Boutros Boutros-Ghali, *An Agenda for Peace* (New York: United Nations, 1992), p. 11. Emphasis added.

7. Mats Berdal, *Whither UN Peacekeeping?* (London: International Institute of Strategic Studies, 1993), p. 76.

8. Thomas G. Weiss, "New Challenges for UN Military Operations: Implementing an Agenda for Peace," *Washington Quarterly* 16, no. 1 (Winter 1993): 51, 63.

9. David Hendrickson, "The Ethics of Collective Security," *Ethics and International Affairs* 7, no. 3 (1993): 2–3.

10. Jonathan Howe, "The United States and the United Nations in Somalia," *Washington Quarterly* 18, no. 3 (Summer 1995): 54.

11. Innis Claude, *Swords into Plowshares: The Problems and Process of International Organization*, 4th ed. (New York: Random House, 1971), p. 14.

12. Jim Whitman and Ian Bartholomew, "UN Peace Support Operations: Political-Military Considerations," in *Beyond Traditional Peacekeeping*, ed. Don Daniel and Bradd Hayes (New York: St. Martins, 1995), p. 184.

13. In yet another market/corporate analogy, Professor Ronald Steel of the University of Southern California states the classic realist argument when he writes that "the UN was not designed to be a world government, nor the collective conscience of mankind. Rather, it is a marketplace where deals are struck and interests protected." Ronald Steel, *Temptations of a Superpower* (Cambridge, Mass.: Harvard University Press, 1995), p. 86.

14. Giandomenico Picco, "The UN and the Use of Force: Leave the Secretary-General Out of It," *Foreign Affairs* 73, no. 5 (September–October 1994): 16, 18.

15. See Jesse Helms, "Saving the UN: A Challenge to the Next Secretary-General," *Foreign Affairs* 75, no. 5 (September–October 1996): 2–8.

16. Paul Kennedy and Bruce Russett, "Reforming the United Nations," *Foreign Affairs* 74, no. 5 (September–October 1995): 57.

17. See Robert Oakley and John Hirsch, *Somalia and Operation Restore Hope* (Washington: U.S. Institute of Peace Press, 1995), especially pp. 45, 111. Foreign Policy Research Institute president Harvey Sicherman wrote that "the assertive multilateralists of 1993–94 placed more weight on the UN than it could bear, while ignoring NATO and other regional coalitions." Harvey Sicherman, "Revenge of Geopolitics," *Orbis* 41, no. 1 (Winter 1997): 11.

18. Steel writes that "the current enthusiasm for multilateralism results in large part from the *unwillingness* of states to make serious sacrifices to establish order." Steel, p. 135, emphasis added.

PART III

FUNDING, BUREAUCRACY, AND CORRUPTION

8. Systemic Corruption at the United Nations

Stefan Halper

The United Nations has become a Kafkaesque bureaucracy beset by inefficiency, systemic corruption, and misconceived programs. Numerous diplomatic efforts to encourage UN reform have failed. It is now obvious that the United States must use its financial leverage to force the UN bureaucracy and the misguided General Assembly to reexamine their practices. The bottom line is that the UN will either be fundamentally reorganized, or, in a relatively short time, it may cease to exist. Support for the organization in the United States (and ultimately other Western countries) will continue to ebb unless meaningful reforms are forthcoming soon.

A potent symbol of the UN's problems was the controversy over Secretary-General Boutros Boutros-Ghali's bid for a second term. Even without apparent alternative candidates, resistance to Boutros-Ghali became evident in the autumn of 1996. Washington announced its opposition and vetoed his nomination in the Security Council. For his part, Boutros-Ghali defiantly insisted, "I'm still a candidate and still the only candidate for Africa."[1] He also implied that there might be a tinge of racism in the U.S. position, since the first secretary-general from an African nation would also be the first secretary-general to be denied a second term.

The controversy facilitated a major confrontation among the United States, many of its allies, and most of the Third World. Moreover, the controversy demonstrated that underlying tensions, which surfaced over Boutros-Ghali's reelection, have the potential to severely damage and perhaps destroy the United Nations— although that is the last thing the Clinton administration intended when it assumed office in 1993.

Resistance to Boutros-Ghali arose because he failed to gain consensus on a number of policy and administrative areas and persisted in using UN resources in ways that were at odds with the views of the major contributors, especially the United States. Much of the problem derived from a clash of worldviews and vested interests in which Boutros-Ghali implied that the era of Western big-power dominance had passed. Equally important, the secretary-general failed to take meaningful steps to extinguish the culture of corruption and mismanagement that had become the norm at the United Nations.

The Problem of Mismanagement

Now in the UN's 52nd year, the jury's verdict is in. The data on reform, or lack thereof, are available for all to see—and they do not paint a pretty picture. There is abundant evidence that the familiar "unholy trinity" of waste, fraud, and abuse exists throughout the UN system.

The UN's astronomical personnel costs are one manifestation of the problem. Incredibly lucrative salaries are paid at the New York offices where, according to *Money* magazine, the average salary of a midlevel accountant was $84,000 in 1995; the comparable level of compensation among non-UN accountants was $41,964. A UN computer analyst could expect to receive $111,500 compared with $56,835 outside the UN bureaucracy. An assistant secretary-general received $140,256; the mayor of New York City got $130,000.[2]

Those raw figures do not reflect the full disparity, however, since salaries for UN diplomats are tax-free, and most salaries for non-American administrative staff include an "assessment" used to offset tax liability. In addition, non-American UN employees receive monthly rent subsidies of up to $3,800 and annual education grants of up to $12,675 per child. Yet, in a stunning report by the *Washington Post*, Boutros-Ghali estimated that "perhaps half of the UN work force does nothing useful."[3]

Nearly $4 million in cash was stolen outright from UN offices in Mogadishu, Somalia, and the *New York Times* reported that "nearly $457,000 earmarked for a two week conference on the Sustainable Development of Small Island States included $15,000 to fly representatives of a national liberation movement recognized by the Organization of African Unity. In fact, the movement was the Polisario from the Western Sahara, a desert region conspicuously short of small islands."[4]

Although some problems of that kind predate Boutros-Ghali, the above examples occurred on his watch, and his inability to rectify those problems over time belied the hopes of internationalists—the aspirations of Woodrow Wilson, Franklin Roosevelt, Harry Truman, and John F. Kennedy—and brought the organization to its current low ebb.

Small wonder the U.S. Congress is averse to paying the $1.5 billion in dues that the UN contends is still owed.[5] But Congress has concluded, and it is correct, that no avenue other than the threat to withhold payment is available to force the UN bureaucracy and the hallucinogenic salon that passes for the General Assembly to reexamine their practices.

At the heart of the UN's burgeoning management problems is an almost total lack of accountability. Former U.S. attorney general Richard Thornburgh's 1993 report on UN mismanagement, along with subsequent investigations, charged that UN budgets, formed behind closed doors, are shrouded in secrecy. In addition, the actual performance of the myriad bureaucracies is rarely measured against criteria established at program inception.[6] There is no way to tell whether the various, often overlapping, agencies—for example, at least two dozen are involved in food and agriculture programs—are reaching their stated objectives.

Although some of the organizational disarray could be addressed, and possibly cleared, by a comprehensive audit, Boutros-Ghali was reluctant to do so and, reportedly, had the Thornburgh report shredded. Not until April 1994, when an impatient U.S. Congress demanded reform or else (the "or else" was a threat to withhold $420 million of the U.S. assessment from the UN coffers), was an independent inspector general—German diplomat Karl Paschke—appointed. (Unfortunately, his independence was later compromised when Boutros-Ghali inserted a "service at the pleasure of the secretary-general" clause in his contract, which meant that the inspector general could be dismissed for virtually any reason.) Short on funds, staff, and time, Paschke nevertheless produced an interim report in seven months. That report, the first attempt at cost accounting in 50 years, produced little surprise, much less shock.

The new inspector general's initial swipe at the Augean stables revealed some $16.8 million in outright fraud and egregious waste.

- In Somalia $369,000 was paid for fuel distribution services the contractor never provided.

- A project director of the UN Relief and Works Agency, which helps Palestinian refugees, kept $100,000 of agency money in his private bank account and failed to disclose a personal stake in the irrigation project under way.
- In Nairobi, Kenya, a member of the UN Center for Human Settlements arranged loans worth $98,000 for a company where she had been a partner and with whose director she was "closely associated."[7]

By the time his report was out, however, Paschke had become part of the problem instead of part of the solution. His report contained the usual critique of poor management practices and incoherent personnel policy. But Paschke's overall conclusions proved more disturbing to the cause of real reform than any of his velvet glove criticisms. In perhaps the most troubling passage in the report, he said, "I have not found the UN to be a more corrupt organization, an organization that shows more fraud than any other comparable public organization."[8]

But what is a comparable organization? Certainly not the old League of Nations, whose standards of honesty and efficiency were very high.[9] The statement, in short, had a ring of self-serving complacency, precisely what the United Nations does not need if it intends to survive. Members of Congress had hoped for an inspector general who would prove to be a junk yard dog, but U.S. Ambassador to the United Nations Madeleine Albright—no UN buster—summed it up when she said that Paschke had thus far proved to be a "junk-yard puppy."[10]

The inspector general's effort, in short, devolved into another typical UN exercise designed to deflect criticism without addressing the central problem. And the result, at least on Capitol Hill, has been ongoing controversy and intensifying attempts to make the UN responsible and responsive to its major contributors.

From U.S. Preeminence to Third World Domination

Until the mid-1950s the United States enjoyed the support of a majority of the 51-member General Assembly. That margin vanished forever in the mid-1950s when a momentary thaw in U.S.-Soviet relations after Stalin's death allowed the admission of 20 new members. Five years later the General Assembly had 82 members, nearly all former colonies of the European powers. By 1970 the number had jumped to 108; by 1980 it was 136; and by 1995 the General Assembly had a total of 185 member states, each with one vote. The vastly expanded General Assembly was soon dominated by non-Western states whose elites seldom shared the political culture of the democratic West. The new majority felt free to exercise its power by passing resolutions favorable to the Third World and its member states' various pet projects.

Although the Third World was hardly homogeneous—operating with an identical agenda—a mutually convenient system of logrolling soon came into being. For example, Arab states would vote for resolutions against South Africa, provided that the black African states voted against Israel when called upon to do so. Arab votes supporting the Organization of African Unity's position on resolution of the civil wars in Angola and Mozambique were examples of the former; and black African votes supporting the infamous Arab-sponsored "Zionism is racism" resolution, which passed the General Assembly, illustrated the latter. All factions frequently condemned and voted against the United States and its democratic allies for an assortment of alleged sins, while they were noticeably less harsh with the Soviet Union.[11]

Nowhere was the power of the new majority in the General Assembly more evident than in the critical area of finance. While the United States was assessed 25 percent of the general UN budget—down from an original 39.98 percent—in 1992, 79 members each paid one one-hundredth (0.01) of the budget—the minimum allowed. And another 9 each chipped in a meager two one-hundredths (0.02).[12] The situation has not improved since 1992.

That means that a majority of the voting members of the General Assembly contribute less than 1 percent of the UN's general budget, while 14 members contribute 84 percent. (The situation is similar with regard to the peacekeeping budget—except that until recently the United States paid 31 percent.) That fundamental disconnect between power and purse is the central factor in the corruption of the UN. It has led to a proliferation of agencies, an oversized bureaucracy, and general irresponsibility.

The Third World and the General Assembly

Much of that is the consequence of Third World domination of the General Assembly and the UN bureaucracy. There is no need

131

for romanticism about the Third World. Westerners who persist in seeing those nations as poor and exploited—and therefore virtuous—are hopelessly out of touch with reality. Third World countries may be poor, but the elites that run them are decidedly not. Nor does their rule very often rest on the consent of the governed, even in theory. Although democratic rule has spread a bit in the post–Cold War era, the most dramatic gains for democracy have been in the former communist "second" world and in Latin America, which never quite fit into the Third World where Asian warlords feel comfortable rubbing shoulders with Middle Eastern and African dictators at meeting of the Non-Aligned Movement and the UN General Assembly.

A kleptocratic culture of nonaccountability at home was easily transferred to the world body—creating a patronage system unequaled anywhere. Since the Third World voting bloc took control of the UN and its budget, total UN employment has ballooned from 1,500 to more than 50,000 worldwide. That figure does not include nearly 10,000 consultants. Nor does it include peacekeeping forces, which at their height in 1993 totaled nearly 80,000.

Even though there has been some progress in downsizing in recent months, personnel costs still consume some 70 percent of the operating budget, leaving meager financial resources for the actual missions of the United Nations and its specialized agencies, including the much-touted humanitarian programs.

In fairness, the UN does some good work in the humanitarian assistance areas. The UN Children's Fund, for example, is a strong program. The UN's provision of shelter and medicine to so many refugees from the fighting in Rwanda—and in Burundi and Cambodia before that and in Angola and Mozambique even earlier—was worthwhile.

Moreover, the UN has successfully monitored cease-fire lines between hostile parties in Cyprus, the Sinai, the Korean peninsula, and now the Balkans—so let us not conclude that the organization has done nothing of value. In fact, it is likely that the U.S. Department of State would support the continuation of those programs—as would many American voters.

The problem is that Boutros-Ghali, in effect, made the wrong mistake. He went far beyond what the UN can and should be doing. His attempt to impose a military peace in Somalia, for example, was a disaster, given momentary credence only by the U.S. military. And the widely broadcast initiative to build representative government in that shattered country was pathetic. The same mistake was repeated in Bosnia, which proved even more disastrous in terms of displaced persons and loss of life.[13]

The UN cannot act as a coercive peacemaker. The UN does not have a general military staff and therefore is incapable of integrating command/control/communications and intelligence, with a planning function. There is no unified command. Military action, if there is to be any, depends on the United States or NATO. And there is great reluctance among the American people to have U.S. military personnel serve under UN officers who may or may not reflect U.S. training, standards, and judgment when it comes to putting people's lives in danger.

Boutros-Ghali's bulldozing effort to fashion a UN military peacemaking force came at the same time as sharpening concern in the United States about the issues raised earlier—bloated bureaucracy, fraud, and waste. His timing could not have been worse. In addition, Boutros-Ghali displayed an arrogance, a dismissiveness, based on his calculation that he controlled a majority of the General Assembly's votes and that the United States would be very hesitant to confront him. That assumption may have been correct in the short term, but the secretary-general ultimately miscalculated, and it cost him his job.

Toward Constructive Internationalism

The events of Boutros-Ghali's tenure were especially poignant for the Clinton administration, which entered office committed to the idea of a foreign policy based on multilateralism. That is to say, administration leaders believed that international problems could and should be solved in concert with organizations like the UN, the European Union, the World Bank, and the International Monetary Fund. They believed that the United States had a responsibility to support those organizations and, if possible, to let them take the lead in addressing international problems.

That idea fit nicely with the Clinton administration's initial reluctance to use American power in the international arena. Somewhere deep in their experience—rooted in the Vietnam War and other traumas—was the idea that the exercise of power invited a descent into immoral and unethical realms that had best be avoided.

They did not recognize, for example, that the UN had nothing to do with the fall of the Soviet Union and that, if we had relied on it to bring freedom to the USSR and to the nations of Central and Eastern Europe, we would be waiting still. In fact, the administration looked the other way for a very long time while the UN did next to nothing in Bosnia and then reluctantly concluded that only the large powerful nations, acting in concert on the basis of their bilateral relationships, mutual interest, and commitments, could close down the fighting there.

And Washington arrived at that conclusion only after some 2 million people were displaced and some 200,000 killed. So it was with some hesitation that the Clinton administration dug in its heels against Boutros-Ghali—and it was truly a last resort. Much credit in this regard goes to Madeleine Albright, who had seen Boutros-Ghali firsthand and had little positive to say about him.

The administration had, ironically, done the right thing but had defeated its purpose through a riot of errors in the way the decision was handled and then made public. Washington's veto in the Security Council underscored the isolation of the United States—to the horror of its allies, who feared that they too might end up isolated from the Third World. The election controversy turned into something of a crisis for the UN, generating pressures and factions that could, in time, lead to collapse. Nevertheless, the United States was right not to retreat on the issue.

Even with the replacement of Boutros-Ghali by Kofi Annan, Washington should make clear that it will refuse to make further payments, given the evidence of fraud and inadequate financial controls at the United Nations. Senate Foreign Relations Committee chairman Jesse Helms is correct in arguing that the UN must produce a plan for reform with specific targets and dates for the elimination of redundant bureaucracies; unnecessary personnel; and a strengthened, independent inspector general before the United States makes payment of arrears. The administration must reverse its call for Congress to release UN funds now and argue with the UN later. Instead, it should state that it is prepared to put the UN into bankruptcy, if necessary, to achieve reforms.

With management and mission in continuing disarray, the UN must initiate a zero-sum audit taking nothing for granted and placing all of its programs and agencies on the block. Confidence and consensus must be rebuilt if the organization is to continue—and that is the essential task that Kofi Annan will have to undertake. In addition to that essential change, the UN needs to concentrate on those missions it can perform well and abandon the temptation to engage in bureaucratic empire building. There are all too many conferences, declarations, and agreements. Humanitarian assistance programs should be retained, although executed more efficiently. Military operations—except the monitoring of tense borders—should be abandoned. Those changes, if joined with a Herculean effort to finish cleansing the Augean stables of mismanagement and corruption, would provide the foundation for a return to productive internationalism.

Notes

1. Quoted in Craig Turner, "U.N. Chief Suspends His Bid for Reelection," *Los Angeles Times*, December 5, 1996.
2. Karen Cheney, "It's the U.N.'s 50th Birthday, But Its Employees Get the Gifts," *Money*, November 1995, p. 27.
3. Quoted in John M. Goshko, "U.N. Chief: Political Will, Money Needed," *Washington Post*, November 22, 1992, p. A1.
4. Christopher S. Wren, "Mismanagement and Waste Erode U.N.'s Best Intentions," *New York Times*, June 23, 1995, p. A1.
5. The amount owed is a matter of considerable dispute. Many critics of the UN contend that the United States should receive a financial credit for its military activities on behalf of the UN missions in Somalia, the former Yugoslavia, and elsewhere. If that credit were granted, the sum owed to the UN would be far less than $1.5 billion. Indeed, one analyst contends that the UN would owe the United States several hundred million dollars. Cliff Kincaid, "Who's Soaking Whom?" *Washington Post*, January 19, 1997, p. C2. See also John M. Goshko, "Republicans, U.N. Differ on How Much U.S. Owes," *Washington Post*, January 25, 1997, p. A4.
6. Richard Thornburgh, "Report to the Secretary General of the United Nations," March 1, 1993, reprinted in *Management and Mismanagement at the United Nations: Hearing before the Subcommittee on International Security, International Organizations and Human Rights of the House Committee on Foreign Affairs*, 103d Cong., 1st sess., March 5, 1993 (Washington: Government Printing Office, 1993), pp. 100–101.
7. Christopher Wren, "Surprise! U.N. Auditors of Peacekeeping Missions Find Waste," *New York Times*, October 22, 1995, p. A18.
8. Quoted in ibid. See also Catherine Toups, "UN Critics Call Report on Fraud a Prescription for Action," *Washington Times*, October 31, 1995, p. A13.
9. See James Avery Joyce, *Broken Star: The Story of the League of Nations, 1919–1939* (Swansea: Christopher Davies, 1979), pp. 78–79; and Jack C. Plano and Robert E. Riggs, *Forging World Order: The Politics of International Organization* (New York: Macmillan, 1967), pp. 22–23, 172–73.
10. Quoted in Wren, "Surprise!"

11. See "Report on Voting Practices at the United Nations 42nd General Asssembly," Heritage Foundation Backgrounder no. 703, May 10, 1989, pp. 4, 5, 22–26, 26–32; and "Report on Voting Practices at the United Nations 43rd General Assembly," Heritage Foundation Backgrounder no. 775, May 20, 1990, pp. 10–13.

12. Simon Duke, "The U.N. Finance Crisis: A History and Analysis," *International Relations*, August 1992, pp. 133–37.

13. See John F. Hillen III, "Killing with Kindness: The UN Peacekeeping Mission in Bosnia," Cato Institute Foreign Policy Briefing no. 34, June 30, 1995.

9. Should the United Nations Have the Authority to Levy Taxes?

Daniel Gouré

The states are disunited. Social, cultural, regional, and sectarian divisions threaten to upset the peace only recently established after a long and exhausting struggle against a great foe. Many observers see a coming war between rich and poor that will tear society apart. Economic growth is rapid but appears only to contribute to inequalities of income distribution. Much needs to be done to facilitate trade among the states. In addition, new threats abound, yet the states cannot readily agree among themselves on the relative priority to accord those threats and the proper response to them. Even when all are in agreement, the absence of a standing army means that the availability of force is dependent on the willingness of the states to provide it. Finally, the absence of authority to levy taxes means there are few resources that can be devoted to civil, security, or humanitarian purposes.

A familiar situation? Certainly it is for those who have studied the history of America between 1781 and 1789. Then the complaints were about the inherent weakness of the new American government, fractionalized and held in disrepute, unable to raise funds except at the sufferance of the member states, and without a standing army. Those were the problems that confronted the delegates at the Constitutional Convention in Philadelphia in 1787.

It was the genius of the leading men of that age in America, the Founding Fathers, to have recognized that reform of the existing Confederation was inadequate to meet the needs of the new nation. In their wisdom they also recognized that circumstances required a radical solution, a new compact, one that created a union both federal and indivisible. It was a testament to their faith not merely in themselves but in the American people that they were willing to forgo the narrow republican virtues embodied in the Articles of Confederation, thereby risking the tyranny of the majority, in favor of a greater idea.

It may seem a little odd that I would choose to address the question of the UN's authority to levy taxes by speaking of the drafting of the Constitution of the United States of America. There are, however, some obvious similarities in the practical situations that confronted the nascent American government two centuries ago and those that face the UN and its member nations today. And there are some similarities between the responses to those difficulties. There is, most notably, a growing movement not merely to reform the UN but to see it metamorphose into a body that is representative of and the agent for a so-called civic culture.[1] I believe that there is an important lesson in the American experience for those who seek to expand the power and purview of the UN, to transform it from an agency of its member states to something more—a body that represents the people of the world. The effort to acquire for the UN an independent source of funding, to permit it the power to levy taxes, is but one step—and not the first, although by far the most significant—in that process of change.

I do not intend to play Cato to any pro-taxation Publius, for I think that the latter had the better of the argument then and does now. The essential and proven lessons of the American experience are these: first, that the power to govern free peoples rests on a recognition of their sovereignty and hence on the consent of the governed; and, second, that what is required in the way of political organization, if the loyalty and consent of the governed are to be achieved and retained, is representation and justice. The well-worn line from the American revolution still holds true: "No taxation without representation." Those who advocate new powers for the UN of such magnitude as the right to levy taxes globally cannot do so solely on the basis of references to the exigencies of the times or assertions regarding the goodness of the works performed by that organization.[2]

No statement on the subject of UN taxation could be as wrong as that made by a very senior British official when he said, "It is not sustainable for the member states to enjoy representation without taxation."[3] There may have been a bit of hyperbole in that utterance. Nevertheless, it is an idea that has apparently gained wide currency in UN circles of late.[4]

The UN and the Concept of Representation

It seems to me that the taxation proposals do a serious disservice to the very idea of representation. What Alexander Hamilton, James Madison, and the rest of the Federalists understood as representative government is far from what prevails at the UN. The structure of the UN and its organizations is intended to allow propinquity and common endeavors while also permitting factionalism to remain. That was a central tenet in the construct of the Security Council. It is intended to give the widest possibly play in a neutral setting to states as factions, not merely interests. Yet, such factionalism is truly anathema to any possibility of democratic representative government. Madison noted that "among the advantages of a well-constructed Union, none deserves to be more accurately developed than the tendency to break and control the violence of faction."[5]

One should observe that nations, not people, are the principal sovereign entities represented at the UN. Some of the subordinated agencies and organizations also represent nongovernmental organizations, interest groups, and even sects. Nowhere are people, the citizens of the members nations, represented. Therefore, as constituted, the UN does not meet the test of representation required to engender popular support and loyalty.

Moreover, in more than a few instances, the nations that occupy seats in the General Assembly and even the Security Council cannot reasonably be said to represent their own peoples. One need only cite the presence of China as a permanent Security Council member. In recent times so-called pariah states such as Libya, Syria, and Iraq have held nonpermanent seats on the Security Council. What kind of justice can a minority of democratic peoples expect from an institution in which the majority of the population encompassed is "represented" by non- or only quasi-democratic governments? One historian of the American Constitutional debates characterized them as a battle between men of faith and those of little faith.[6] What faith could the American people possibly place in an institution that must represent equally the United States, Britain, France, Germany, and Japan on the one hand and Nigeria, Iran, China, and Serbia on the other? The answer is none.

In the minds of the Federalists, true representation could only be achieved by the willing grant of power by the individual to representatives with whom he had some direct contact, presumably through the electoral process, and over whom he could exercise both direct and indirect controls. The indirect controls were a function of both the federal nature of the American system and the separation of powers between the branches of government that provided the checks and balances necessary to prevent any one branch, and the narrow interests they might come to represent, from dominating the entire polity. As Hamilton argued, the only true check against coercive power of the state is that the whole powers of the state are placed in the hands of representatives of the people.[7]

To grant the UN the power to levy taxes of any kind is to begin a process that will ultimately lead to the destruction of that institution. No matter how worthy its causes, no matter how successful its efforts, and no matter how efficient and cost-effective its operations, people will resist taxation without representation. They will closely measure each expenditure with an eye toward any hint of inequity. They will constantly criticize UN activities while seeking to turn decisions and programs to their benefit. Whereas at present the people of the rich nations allow the benefits of the Economic and Social Council (ECOSOC), for example, to flow disproportionately to the developing world, it would not long remain so once they understood that dissimilar services were being rendered to peoples of similar need on the sole basis of their nationality. Some 200 years ago, Alexander Hamilton, in his defense of the efforts then under way to form a more perfect union, warned of the corrosive effect of that human tendency:

> It is a known fact in human nature, that its affections are commonly weak in proportion to the distance or diffusiveness of the subject. Upon that same principle that a man is more attached to his family than to the community at large, the people of each State would be apt to feel a stronger bias towards their local governments than towards the government of the Union; *unless the force of that principle should be destroyed by a much better administration of the latter.*[8]

Even if such a bold approach were put forward, one can imagine the howls of protest that would arise from all corners. The well-off few would see in such a proposal the specter of the tyranny of the many poor. The poor would see in that same proposal an effort by the rich to deny them access to needed resources and opportunities. Democratic and authoritarian governments alike, with more than a little justification, would see in the idea of a global union of all peoples, however constituted, a threat to themselves.

Nothing in current plans for reforming the UN would address the central issue of adequate and proper representation as a precursor to taxation.[9] Indeed, if anything, many of the proposals seek to broaden the reach and responsibility of the UN. That would only add to the problem. One such proposal is to create an economic security council to address, inter alia, the promotion of stable, balanced, and sustainable development and to secure constancy among the policy goals of the major international economic bodies. Another scheme would be to empower the several thousand nongovernmental organizations (NGOs) that now populate the international environment by creating a special forum of civil society that would allow them to directly influence the workings of the UN's other agencies and councils. Yet a third idea would be to create a council for petitions, a body of eminent persons that would receive petitions from individuals and NGOs on matters concerning the security of peoples.[10]

Power to Tax, Power to Coerce

Even were the UN to be reformed in a manner consistent with reasonable notions of representation and justice, the question of the character and extent of its power to tax would remain. Advocates of a UN tax have looked longingly at various aspects of international commerce as a source of new funds. Airline travel has been proposed as one possible source, with a small tax added to the price of each ticket. Foreign exchange transactions have been discussed as a source of international tax revenue. A fossil fuels tax has also been proposed. In suggesting the idea of taxing international business, UN secretary-general Boutros-Ghali, displaying all the instincts of Willie Sutton, stated that "globalization is diminishing the role of the member states. . . . Multinationals are ten times richer than the majority of member states. We have to obtain their assistance."[11]

We should recall how gingerly the Founding Fathers approached the grant of the taxing authority to the national government they advocated. The Constitution gave Congress the right to lay and collect taxes, duties, imposts, and excises, as well as to borrow money. Generally, it was believed that while government should be able to tax commerce it could do so only at the edges, as import and excise taxes. Income taxes or collections on investments and the like were viewed as interfering with property rights. Against the argument that the national government should be allowed to levy only excise taxes, the Federalists responded with references to possible national exigencies that would require extraordinary measures. Nevertheless, the idea of direct taxation was considered so extreme at the time and for over 100 years thereafter that it took the Sixteenth Amendment in 1913 to permit levying of a personal income tax.

The power to tax implies the power to coerce. It is clear from their proposals that advocates of a UN tax understand that to openly address the issue of the power to enforce compliance would ensure that the idea of such a tax would be dead on arrival. Therefore, the various proposals attempt to make the tax as inconspicuous, if not covert, as possible. It might be imposed on activities that already sustain a high degree of indirect taxation, such as airline tickets. It is hoped that, as is the case with a value-added tax (pervasive in the nations of Western Europe), taxpayers will not notice the small amounts taken from their pockets with each transaction. In addition, such indirect taxation would leave the power to coerce with the member states. In that way the UN would be able to receive all of the benefits from a tax with none of the problems: no public scrutiny, no unhappy taxpayers, no need to spend money on collection services, and only limited accountability.

The arguments set forth here logically could open the door for a UN tax. But the organization would have to transform itself in accordance with the principles of representative government. Only a transformed UN, with vices eliminated, could be granted any of the powers sought by Boutros-Ghali, the right to levy taxes among them. Empowering the UN, as currently organized and operated, to levy taxes of any kind is not only a bad idea but an impossible one.

The Potential for Alienation

Even were restructuring feasible, I do not believe it would be desirable. With the power of representation in the sense of Hamilton and Madison goes accountability. There is something to be said for having UN funding provided by member nations. That feature makes the UN principally a subject of foreign and not domestic policy. Would those who advocate broadening the powers of the UN and allowing it to levy taxes truly wish to subject the organization to the kind of scrutiny that would inevitably arise once it was clear to the people that it was their money that was going to places with which they had no emotional or political connection and to fund activities that had only the most indirect relationship to their own lives?

Currently, many of the UN's agencies and subordinated authorities are allowed amazing latitude in their activities. Let me provide just one example of the relative freedom the current system affords the UN. The October 7, 1996, issue of *U.S. News & World Report* noted that ECOSOC had decided to admit as a member the International Rastafarian Development Society. The story goes on to note that two years earlier ECOSOC, under pressure from Washington, suspended the membership of the International Gay and Lesbian Society "after it was reported that an affiliate—the North American Man-Boy Love Association or NAMBLA—promoted pedophilia."[12] Clearly, the only reason that antics such as those are not a politically hot issue is that UN activities—and funding—are the province of foreign and not domestic politics.

That story and many like it passed almost unnoticed in the West, indeed the entire world. However, imagine what would have been the reaction if the headline to the story had started with the words "Your Tax Dollars at Work!" Questions would have begun immediately to fly: What right has the Rastafarian Society, or the Gay and Lesbian Alliance or NAMBLA, to representation in ECOSOC? Why does the UN permit such nonstate groups access to its functions? What groups are receiving or have in the past received funding from the UN, and why? What benefits have resulted from the disbursement of funds to such groups? The UN is already under assault from numerous quarters for management irregularities. It is not certain that the UN as a whole could stand the degree of scrutiny that would inevitably result if the scenario described above should come about.

There are numerous similar examples of what might charitably be termed a laissez-faire attitude toward the activities of some of the UN's subordinate operations. The UN has already suffered from the accusation of being politicized. The United States withdrew from the International Labor Organization after the ILO admitted the Palestine Liberation Organization, then not the recognized representative of the Palestinian people but a terrorist organization. The United States also withdrew from the United Nations Economic,

Social and Cultural Organization accusing it of exceeding its mandate, advocating collective economic rights, and seeking to create norms for intrastate behavior. The critiques that led to those actions by the United States would only intensify and broaden in scope in the event the UN were allowed to levy a tax.

In addition to a "relaxed managerial style" in UN organs and operations there are numerous cases of outright fraud, abuse, and mismanagement.[13] Such cases are sufficiently blatant, and efforts to reform the management and fiscal behavior of the UN so minimal, that it is difficult on these grounds alone to see merit in the argument for expanding that organization's access to funds, particularly any independent source of revenues.

The UN was not meant to represent the people of the world. It was and is a forum in which the nations that adhere to its charter can come together to address problems of mutual concern. The member states and their populations can tolerate a great deal of mismanagement, malfeasance, and sheer silliness. They also can support the range of experimentation in economic and social investments necessary if the developing countries are to achieve their hoped-for progress toward enrichment and enlightenment. But such latitude for UN operations will only be possible if the organization remains protected from the vicissitudes of ordinary politics.

In the end, the power to tax will be the power that destroys. It will destroy the UN.

Notes

1. See Independent Working Group on the Future of the UN, *The UN in Its Second Half-Century: The Report of the Independent Working Group on the Future of the UN* (New Haven, Conn.: Yale University Press, 1995).

2. Former Australian foreign minister Gareth Evans, British prime minister John Major, and others have asserted, at least implicitly, the *right* of the UN to levy taxes.

3. John Major, "Can the UN Find the Money?" *Tech* 115 (September 16, 1996).

4. Former UN secretary-general Boutros Boutros-Ghali suggested that taxation of international transactions or a form of business tax might be in order.

5. James Madison, "Federalist no. 10," in *The Federalist Papers*, ed. Garry Wills (New York: Bantam Books, 1982), p. 42.

6. Cecilia Kenyon, "The Thought of the Anti-Federalists," in *The Anti-Federalists*, ed. Cecilia Kenyon (Indianapolis: Bobbs-Merrill, 1966), p. xcvii.

7. Alexander Hamilton, "Federalist no. 28," in *The Federalist Papers*, pp. 135–36.

8. Alexander Hamilton, "Federalist no. 17," in ibid., p. 81. Emphasis added.

9. On efforts to reform the UN, see U.S. Department of State, "U.S. Views on Reform Measures Necessary for Strengthening the United Nations System," Presentation to

the Open-Ended, High-Level Working Group on the Strengthening of the United Nations System, February 1996.

10. Ingvar Carlsson, "The U.N. at Fifty: A Time to Reform," *Foreign Policy* 100 (Fall 1995): 3–18.

11. Colum Lynch, "U.N. Strikes Again: United Nations Proposes World Tax to Fund Itself," *Boston Globe*, September 11, 1996, p. 2. See also, for example, "A Call for Action on the U.N. Financial Crisis," Global Policy Forum, New York, September 16, 1996.

12. "A Seat for NAMBLA at the UN?" *U.S. News & World Report*, October 7, 1996, p. 24.

13. See, for example, "The United Nations," in *Issues 1996* (Washington: Heritage Foundation, 1996), pp. 528–30.

10. Reforming the United Nations

Edward Luck

UN reform has many meanings, just as the United Nations represents different things to different people. Probably no other human institution in history has embodied such disparate expectations, aspirations, and apprehensions. The United Nations, as a result, is a complex and little-understood institution, too often praised or dismissed with sweeping generalizations. So it is understandable that, while almost everyone agrees that the UN is in need of a substantial overhaul, there persist many competing visions of what form and shape the revitalization of the organization should take. Should the reform effort focus on achieving organizational economies, on enhancing performance, or on realigning priorities? Reform is a process, not an event, and until there is a more widely shared understanding of what needs fixing and what the ultimate goals are, many member states will be reluctant to hop onto the reform bandwagon.

What Is Wrong with the UN?

It is said that the UN simply spends too much money.[1] But a judgment about whether an organization is too expensive should be based on an assessment of the value and importance of what it does. When an institution's purposes and programs are generally seen as valuable—whether the institution is the U.S. military, the Salvation Army, or the United Nations Children's Fund—there tends to be less public questioning of its management or expenditures. It is hard to believe that saving money, while hardly a trivial issue, is the heart of the matter when U.S. contributions to the UN system (about $1.5 billion in fiscal year 1996) amount to 1/1,000 of the federal budget and when peacekeeping payments ($359 million in FY96) are less than 1/700 of U.S. defense spending. The emotions

---

The views presented here are personal ones and do not necessarily represent those of any organization with which the author is affiliated.

generated for and against the UN suggest that much more is at stake, that the real debate is about what the UN is and what it does or does not do.

Some say that the UN's fundamental flaw lies in its nature as a grouping of nation-state governments. The only thing wrong with the UN, the old saying goes, is its member states. Those who are suspicious of government, whether from the political right or left, are never going to be enthusiastic about an assemblage of 185 sovereign national governments, no matter how efficiently it operates. When the role of government is shrinking in many parts of the world, the allegedly statist bias of the UN appears from this perspective to be out of date as well as wrong-headed. Others, claiming that diversity immobilizes the UN, dampens its moral fervor, and compromises American interests for the sake of consensus, would prefer an organization of "like-minded" states with similar values and interests.[2]

To advocates of world government, on the other hand, the UN is little more than a service organization for member states that acts to reinforce the antiquated nation-state system. Those people warn that the will of the peoples of the world could be thwarted by the competitive and short-sighted policies of individual nation-states as those policies are played out at the UN. Their preference would be for a stronger, more assertive, and independently funded body that could pursue the larger interests of humanity as a whole.[3] International civil servants similarly tend to believe that their task is to serve global and human interests that transcend national boundaries. They chafe when national delegations pursue narrow aims, project domestic politics onto the world scene, or confuse micromanagement with oversight. Some nongovernmental organizations claim that, in any case, they represent the interests of humanity better than governments do and that they should be given a bigger voice, greater transparency, fuller access to UN deliberations, and perhaps even a "people's assembly" to parallel the General Assembly.[4]

Others charge the UN with developing a will of its own, beyond the control of the member states. It is said that the UN Secretariat, personified by the secretary-general, has its own interests and agenda and manipulates the intergovernmental organs to protect its programs, priorities, and jobs in typical bureaucratic, empire-building fashion. Some say that the Secretariat's outlook is inherently interventionist, plunging the UN into humanitarian crises and civil strife that were once considered to be within the exclusive domain of sovereign nation-states.

From each of those perspectives, the goal of reform looks different. Is the UN too large or too small, does it employ too many or too few staff, and is its budget excessive or too modest? Where some see a bloated bureaucracy, others see a structure that is painfully inadequate to the tasks at hand and should be reinforced to meet the expectations of the peoples of the world. Should the reform focus be on aggregate numbers of staff and spending, on the proliferation of mandates and activities, or on the decisionmaking structure? Is the UN system too centralized or too decentralized, and should it be funded primarily through assessed or voluntary contributions? Is the UN reformable?

What Is Correctable, What Is Not?

It is true that change does not come easily to the UN. But it is also true that, over the past half century, the UN has undergone a metamorphosis. As the collective security machinery of chapter 7 of the UN Charter waned with the emergence of the Cold War, the collection of affiliated agencies and programs devoted to functional, humanitarian, and development tasks expanded rapidly. Decolonization, peacekeeping, environmental, human rights, and election-monitoring efforts over time assumed a prominence unanticipated by the UN's founders. The charter was amended once to expand the Security Council and twice to enlarge the Economic and Social Council as UN membership more than tripled.

A consensus rule has applied to the adoption of the budget for the past decade, more than three-quarters of General Assembly resolutions are now adopted by consensus, and vetoes in the Security Council have become rare. Nonstate actors have gained a foothold both in advising intergovernmental forums on issues such as sustainable development, human rights, and disarmament and in helping to carry out humanitarian missions, development operations, and election monitoring. The UN has slowly come to recognize the need for transparency in its budgets and its bureaucracy, and a spokesman for Secretary-General Kofi Annan has promised that the UN building from now on will "breathe with information."[5]

At the same time, the UN's core—its decisionmaking structure and the principles of universality and sovereign equality—has largely remained intact (though the operations of the Trusteeship Council, its work completed, have been suspended by the General Assembly). Change has come more through evolution than revolution. The UN is never going to become a tidy body of like-minded states. But do we want it to shed the virtual universality that makes it uniquely valuable as a forum, a consensus builder, a norm setter, and a source of political and legal legitimacy? As a sort of continuous global political convention, the UN is a messy, uncertain, and occasionally obnoxious place to do business. At times, however, the results both serve U.S. national interests and help to build a larger sense of shared values and respect for international norms, laws, and institutions.

If the UN is always going to be the UN, albeit an evolving one, how far can reform go? To understand the possibilities, it is essential to make distinctions about who has control over what, because the UN is a complex and decentralized amalgam with several layers of decisionmaking. The member states are the key to structural or system-wide reforms. They control, financially and politically, both the UN proper (the central UN and the programs covered by the regular budget) and the much wider universe of the specialized agencies and the loosely affiliated Bretton Woods institutions. Too often, the policies of member states are internally inconsistent, giving different signals to different parts of the UN system. Among the powers of the member states are those to choose the secretary-general and the heads of agencies and set the terms of their employment, approve the budgets, decide assessment levels and what should be funded through assessments or voluntary contributions, establish new programs and abolish old ones, define mandates, launch or suspend peacekeeping and humanitarian missions, authorize chapter 7 enforcement action, manage the working relationships among the principal organs, and exercise quite detailed oversight over the Secretariat's implementation efforts. Member states, by the ratification action of two-thirds of their governments, can also amend the UN Charter.

The secretary-general's span of control, on the other hand, is largely limited to the UN proper, which includes only a fraction of the staff and outlays of the whole system of affiliated institutions. Though he engages in system-wide consultations and tends to be an advocate for greater coordination among the disparate parts of the system, he has little leverage over the independently funded and administered specialized agencies and financial institutions. As the UN's chief administrative officer, the secretary-general has line authority within the central UN over staff appointments, promotions, and terminations, though member states frequently bring acute political pressure to bear in specific cases. The secretary-general has no authority to interfere with the inspector general's reports to the General Assembly, and he is discouraged from attempting to shift people or funds from one area to another. Though a skillful secretary-general can try to influence the UN's programmatic priorities through use of his unique bully pulpit, his advisory and reporting functions, and his preparation of the central budget, he clearly can have much greater influence over administrative than over structural reform. Even at that level, he needs the backing of influential member states if he is to make major changes stick, especially if they have system-wide implications.

Over the 45-year history of UN reform efforts, the charter has been amended on three occasions. Each involved expanding a principal organ. Member states have been far readier to add mandates or tasks than to terminate existing ones, though the mix of UN priorities has evolved quite dramatically over time as international conditions and interests have changed. At different points, reform efforts have focused—often with significant results—on individual programs or agencies or on the UN proper, but attempts to achieve system-wide reforms have been few and their yield has been modest, as one would expect in such a decentralized system. While the process of building broad international support for deep reforms has tended to be slow and cumbersome, in part because of the differing visions noted above, budgetary restraint and staff reductions in the UN proper were attained in a wave of reform in the late 1980s and are now under way again, repeating the 10-year cycle that has tended to characterize UN reform efforts through the years.

Ongoing Reform Efforts

The current wave of reform is far broader and more ambitious than its predecessors, though whether it will succeed in producing deeper structural change remains to be seen. It is unfolding on two levels—one within the Secretariat and the other through an unprecedented series of five working groups of the General Assembly—with numerous points of interaction between the two parallel tracks. Predictably, the work within the Secretariat has produced more visible and immediate results, while the member state dialogue is still laying the conceptual, factual, and political foundation for the next round of the continuing negotiations.

Recent trends in the number of posts, established and temporary, included in the regular budget suggest that a significant downsizing is under way in the central UN. Whereas from 1974–75 to 1984–85 the number of posts grew 27 percent (9,586 to 12,207), it declined by 16 percent over the next decade (to 10,275 in 1994–95).[6] Under the current streamlining, another 10 percent were cut in 1996, down to a current low of 9,000 staff, and a further staff reduction of 500 (6 percent) is being proposed for the 1998–99 biennium (down to 8,500). High-level posts—under secretaries-general and assistant secretaries-general—have been pared 37 percent (from 63 to 40) between 1986–87 and 1996–97. As the Security Council has scaled back its ambitions, the UN now deploys less than one-third the number of peacekeepers it did just three years ago. The regular budget has been capped at $2.608 billion for the 1996–97 biennium ($1.304 billion per year), $117 million less than the previous biennium, and an additional $250 million in cost reductions is expected by the end of 1997. Another 7 percent real contraction in spending below current levels is reflected in the budget outline for 1998–99 that has been submitted to the General Assembly.

The inspector general system—embodied in the Office of Internal Oversight Services—is now well established and beginning to show results. In its first year, through mid-1995, the office identified about $17 million in savings and, more important in the long run, encouraged a more transparent and responsive style of management. Since he cannot be dismissed by the secretary-general without cause and without the approval of the General Assembly and his reports are to be transmitted to the General Assembly unchanged,[7] the inspector general has been able to exercise his duties with considerable independence. The Efficiency Board, established in November 1995, has called on all UN offices and departments to carry out efficiency reviews and to identify ways that better performance and cost savings can be achieved. In its first report to the secretary-general, released in September 1996, the board identified 400 such projects, most of which had been volunteered by the relevant program managers.[8]

On the political level, the member states are addressing a deeper and more comprehensive series of reform questions, but—as one would expect—their deliberations remain a work in progress. The five working groups are considering, respectively, the composition and working methods of the Security Council; financing and assessment; the functioning of the General Assembly and the Secretariat, the budgeting process, and the UN's relationship to civil society; the content and structure of the organization's work on development questions; and the range of issues raised in Secretary-General Boutros Boutros-Ghali's *Agenda for Peace*. For the most part, the deliberations have been both serious and specific, though the pace of such open-ended forums would be deliberate under the best of circumstances. Some topics have of course proven more stubborn than others, and there is a growing feeling that any final package could well require a set of tradeoffs among working groups and among different clusters of issues. In the absence of anything approaching a common vision of the UN for the 21st century, those deliberations are a most ungainly and complex task, which has been made even more difficult by America's go-it-alone financial withholdings.

Self-Defeating Tactics

For more than a decade Congress has been employing unilateral financial withholdings to try to compel various changes in the way the UN operates. The results have been mixed at best. Now two factors—the inability of the Clinton administration and Congress to agree on a credible plan for paying U.S. arrearages ($1.3 billion as of December 31, 1996, according to UN figures) and additional unilateral restrictions and conditions Congress has imposed on dues payments to the UN—have combined to put a damper on efforts to negotiate a far-reaching reform package among the member states. Financial pressures may at times encourage financial restraint at the Secretariat level, but such unilateral tactics are decidedly counterproductive when it comes to trying to build an effective reform coalition among the member states. America's closest allies have been among the most vociferous in rejecting what they describe as unilateral financial blackmail.[9] Many nations, developed and developing, would like to see significant administrative and financial reforms enacted, but the unilateralism of the congressional approach has tended to isolate the United States and to spark resistance to its demands, whatever their merits. Going it alone in the UN has a way of becoming a self-fulfilling prophecy.

Too often, critics of the UN take an excessively negative approach, treating reform as a kind of distasteful punishment for bad behavior rather than as a normal component of an institution's life cycle. When their complaints about UN management are embedded in what appears to be wholesale rejection of what the UN does and stands for, from a UN perspective, it appears that no amount of reform will satisfy those critics because of their deeper and more political concerns.[10] Moreover, repeated financial threats lose their credibility when congressional critics fail to acknowledge the steps the UN has taken to meet their concerns. It would be more persuasive to offer at least a few carrots along with the sticks. Over time, the power of the purse is becoming a dwindling asset as U.S. withholdings make it a less significant factor in the UN's financial picture.

From the standpoint of sound management and sensible decision-making, it makes little sense to focus on aggregate indicators such as total staff and spending. A decade ago a similar but less severe crisis led to across-the-board staff and budget cuts that failed to address the fundamental problems of the UN, given its 185-member board of directors, in setting priorities and making choices. Reducing all programs equally simply exacerbates performance problems by spreading fewer resources over an undiminished range of programs and by treating high performers and low performers the same. Both critics and supporters of the UN have the same challenge: to make a sober assessment of where UN programs have a comparative advantage or disadvantage and to act accordingly. That is the essence of good management.

Also, it would be enormously helpful if the U.S. government could learn to speak with one voice about these issues. Other member states are frequently puzzled as we play out our domestic political disputes on the global stage. Our message gets garbled by the frequent struggles between the executive and legislative branches of the U.S. government and by endless partisan bickering. The U.S. effort is further undermined when key positions on the American team remain open for long periods because of confirmation problems.[11] UN reform need not be a partisan issue. Independents,

Republicans, and Democrats should be able to rally around a common reform agenda that could appeal to like-minded member states and provide the basis for a broad transnational reform coalition.

Where Do We Go from Here?

It has been said that the UN's critics are too unloving and its supporters too uncritical. No one should excuse waste, duplication, inefficiency, or corruption just because it is associated with a good cause. Supporters of the UN, in fact, should be doubly vigilant both because of the harm such things could do—and have done—to the credibility of the institution and because those who believe in the importance of the organization's work should be concerned that its inevitably modest resources are used as efficiently and effectively as possible. Some of the UN's harshest critics, on the other hand, are giving reform a bad name. The launching of anti-UN broadsides that are poorly researched or clearly one-sided, or both, in the name of management reform makes the task of building political support for deep and durable reform among the member states and within the Secretariat that much more difficult.[12] Reform should aim to strengthen the UN, not weaken it, and to enhance the possibilities for effective multilateral cooperation. Neither those who feel that the UN can do no wrong nor those who claim it does next to nothing right have a place in a serious reform effort.

Perhaps those calling for sweeping cuts in the UN budget and staff should specify what functions and programs they find most valuable, while those prone to defending the status quo should indicate which areas they consider expendable. Such an exercise might identify some common ground, or it might suggest that the arguments about management mask deeper and more fundamental differences over the organization's nature, purposes, and programs, as well as over America's interests and place in a changing world. Would the world body's severest critics really want to see a highly efficient and effective UN? From their perspective, why would a well-oiled UN machine serve U.S. interests so much better? Are some UN supporters, on the other hand, simply giving lip service to UN reform in order to placate congressional critics? While most member states speak of the need to overhaul the UN, how many are willing to make a major political investment in the effort when even an inefficient UN serves their national interests?

In the end, the impetus for deep, structural reform is most likely to come from those individuals and member states most committed to the organization and its principles, who believe that they have a stake in its success. Through the years, in fact, it has been the so-called middle powers that have been in the vanguard of the reform movement. Most member states, and certainly the other major contributors, share Washington's concerns about keeping spending in check and maintaining close oversight of UN management. Among the developing countries there is also widespread concern about the UN's structure, programs, and management. Their answers in terms of program priorities and the balance of power in UN decisionmaking bodies, however, are strikingly different from those voiced by Congress.

Since there is no single, take-it-or-leave-it reform agenda, a number of tradeoffs will be required to negotiate a consensus reform package. The end product—if it can be achieved at all—is likely to look a bit different from any of the proposals currently on the table. Those interested in moving the process forward need to give serious thought to what they would be prepared to give up as well as to what they hope to get. For the General Assembly working groups, the 51st session is likely to be the make-it or break-it point on key questions such as the composition of the Security Council, assessments, the workings of the General Assembly and the Economic and Social Council, and system-wide coordination on development issues. U.S. leadership will be essential to building a broad-based reform coalition. But that, in turn, will entail speaking with a single voice and developing the kind of forward-looking and positive reform agenda that can indeed unite the nations in a common effort to reinvigorate their collective organization.

Notes

1. For more than a decade, since the Kassebaum-Solomon amendment, it has been U.S. government policy to oppose any growth in the regular budget of the United Nations. When there is inflation, of course, zero growth in nominal terms means a real decrease in UN spending. Such aggregate quantitative measures do not take into account whether the member states are mandating the organization to do more or less or whether the UN is or is not cost-effective in specific spheres of activity.

2. As Robert Dole has argued, international organizations "will not protect American interests. Only Americans can do that. International organizations will, at best, practice policymaking at the lowest common denominator—finding a course that is

the least objectionable to the most members. Too often, they reflect a consensus that opposes American interests or does not reflect American principles and ideals. Even gaining support for an American position can involve deals or tradeoffs that are not in America's long-term interests." Robert Dole, "Shaping America's Global Future," *Foreign Policy*, 98 (Spring 1995): 36–37.

3. See, for example, Harlan Cleveland, *Birth of a New World: An Open Moment for International Leadership* (San Francisco: Jossey-Bass, 1993); Harlan Cleveland, *The Global Commons: Policy for the Planet* (Lanham, Md.: University Press of America, 1990); Benjamin Ferencz, *New Legal Foundations for Global Survival: Security through the Security Council* (New York: Oceana, 1994); Benjamin Ferencz, *A Common Sense Guide to World Peace* (New York: Oceana, 1985); Benjamin Ferencz, *An International Criminal Court, A Step toward World Peace: A Documentary History and Analysis* (New York: Oceana, 1980); Hazel Henderson, *Building a Win-Win World: Life beyond Global Economic Warfare* (San Francisco: Berrett Koehler, 1996); and Harlan Cleveland, Hazel Henderson, and Inge Kaul, eds., *The United Nations: Policy and Financing Alternatives* (Washington: Global Commission to Fund the United Nations, 1995). See also the writings of Walter Hoffman, Richard Hudson, and John Loque.

4. Among the many authors urging a greater role for nongovernmental organizations in the United Nations are Barbara Adams, Erskine Childers, Gareth Evans, Leon Gordenker, Peter and Ernest Haas, Brian Urquhart, and Thomas Weiss. Also see reports by the United States Commission on Improving the Effectiveness of the United Nations, the Stanley Foundation, and the UN's Joint Inspection Unit. Erskine Childers Brian Urquhart, Thomas Franck, Tatsuro Kunugi, Makato Iokibe, Takahiro Shinyo, and Kohei Hashimoto have called for a people's or parliamentary assembly, while the Commission on Global Governance suggested a civil society forum as a first step.

5. Quoted in Barbara Crossette, "How UN Chief Discovered U.S. and Earmuffs," *New York Times*, January 7, 1997.

6. These numbers are drawn from the proposed program budgets of the United Nations for each biennium (see Official Records of the General Assembly for each of these sessions).

7. Both of these points are clearly stipulated in General Assembly Resolution 48/218B, which established the post and the office.

8. See *Progress Report of the Efficiency Board to the Secretary-General* (New York: United Nations, September 1996).

9. See statements made at the 50th and 51st sessions of the General Assembly and the October 1995 Special Commemorative Meeting, *Provisional Verbatim Records of the General Assembly*. The European Union has also put forward a plan to provide incentives for early payment and penalties, including interest payments, for arrearages. See "Statement on Behalf of the European Union by the Deputy Permanent Representative of Italy to the United Nations," Italian Mission to the United Nations, New York, January 24, 1996.

10. In his recent *Foreign Affairs* article, Senator Helms states that "the time has come for the United States to deliver an ultimatum: Either the United Nations reforms, quickly and dramatically, or the United States will end its participation." Noting that the sweeping changes and downsizing he is calling for represent "a gargantuan, and perhaps impossible task," he concludes that "if it cannot be done, then the United Nations is not worth saving." To many at the United Nations, it sounded as if the senator expected the organization to fail his test and would shed few tears if the

United States left as a result. Jesse Helms, "Saving the UN: A Challenge to the Next Secretary-General," *Foreign Affairs* 75, no. 5 (September–October 1996): 7.

11. Douglas Bennet stepped down as assistant secretary of state for international organization affairs on May 31, 1995; Princeton Lyman was nominated to be his successor in December 1995; hearings on his nomination were held in April 1996, but he is yet to be confirmed in the post. David Birenbaum was nominated to be U.S. ambassador for UN reform and budgetary matters on December 13, 1993, and was confirmed seven months later; he stepped down from the post on April 4, 1996, and a successor had not been nominated as of January 1997.

12. See, for example, Stefan Halper, "A Miasma of Corruption: The United Nations at 50," Cato Institute Policy Analysis no. 253, April 30, 1996; and Burton Yale Pines, ed., *A World without a UN: What Would Happen if the United Nations Shut Down* (Washington: Heritage Foundation, 1984).

PART IV

THE UN's SOCIAL AND ENVIRONMENTAL AGENDA

11. The United Nations and the Myth of Overpopulation

Sheldon Richman

The United Nations Population Fund (known as UNFPA) was established in 1969, shortly after the contemporary hysteria about overpopulation was launched with Paul Ehrlich's book *The Population Bomb*.[1] Since that time, UNFPA has propagandized the world with the fallacies that the world is becoming overburdened with people, that the developed world's population is depleting natural resources, and that the developing world is doomed to poverty unless it can curtail its population growth.

As Nafis Sadik, executive director of UNFPA, wrote recently, when the fund began,

> population concerns were at, or near, the bottom of the agendas of most countries and international organizations. . . . A marked change has taken place in the way population issues are viewed today. Far from being ignored, population issues are, it is generally agreed, inextricably linked with development and the quality of life for millions all over the planet. . . . Today, it is clear that it is the balance between numbers of people, resources and development that will determine whether and how countries and individuals can forge a better life for themselves and generations to come.[2]

In the last 25 years, writes Sadik, governments and UN officials have learned that "the problems of rapid growth, uneven distribution and runaway urbanization can be addressed effectively through timely and comprehensive population policies and programmes."[3] UNFPA sees its role as assisting nations in the planning and carrying out of such policies and programs. Accordingly, the fund has spent almost $2.5 billion on its various activities, which range from collecting data to sponsoring family-planning programs.[4]

The Cairo Program

In 1974 UNFPA began to hold decennial international conferences on population. The 1994 conference in Cairo marked a shift in focus. The appearance of both "population" and "development" in the title of the conference was intended to indicate the newly fashionable view that "sustainable development" could be produced only if it was built around population control. The International Conference on Population and Development (ICPD) adopted a Program of Action that called for policies integrating population "objectives" (the word "control" was eschewed) with virtually all other objectives, particularly those of economic development, women's health, and education. In the past, UN-sponsored population activities were sometimes criticized for demeaning women. The new focus on women's health and role in development was designed to blunt that criticism.

Governments in the developing world were urged to combine their concern about their citizens' reproductive activities with almost all other policies. The taxpayers of both the developed and the developing world will pick up the tab to the tune of $17 billion in the year 2000, $18.5 billion in 2005, $20 billion in 2010, and $21.7 billion in 2015.[5]

The new UNFPA approach, as embodied in the Program of Action, assumes that empowerment of women will lower fertility rates. That is not necessarily true, and there is an element of condescension in that principle: it assumes that no educated woman would want a large family. That is a dubious assumption—unless by "educated" women the UN means women who have been force-fed propaganda designed to make them feel guilty about having more than one or two children. That seems to be what the Cairo delegates had in mind when they approved their program. As Sadik writes, "The Fund will pursue awareness-creation activities underscoring the value of the girl child and the need to eliminate all discriminatory practices— for example, prenatal sex selection, differential access to the resources of the household, and harmful traditional practices."[6]

That sounds like a recipe for major interference by the UN in the internal affairs of member nations. The program, for example, called on governments to "raise the minimum age at [sic] marriage where necessary."[7] Sadik also writes that the "UNFPA is firmly committed to expanding the involvement of women in sustainable development and will provide assistance to enable women's groups to better participate in monitoring the implementation of the ICPD."[8]

Despite the benign language, the Cairo program is inherently flawed. It calls for comprehensive development and women's education and reproductive health programs, all aimed at spurring economic progress and curtailing population growth. Although those sound like laudable goals, in the past such programs have perpetuated poverty and led to violations of women's rights and freedom of choice. The poor record of government-guided development was well documented by the late economist David Osterfeld.[9] The evidence on the treatment of women by population programs is horrifying. For example, China for years has had an official program of compulsory contraception, sterilization, and even abortion.[10] Even ostensibly "voluntary" sterilization programs, such as India has run, are suspect. During India's sterilization season, desperate and destitute women are bribed by bounty-seeking civil servants to submit to tubal ligation under horrendously unsanitary conditions.[11]

The women's health policies recommended in the Cairo program have a central contradiction: they attempt to serve two masters. Although the program expressly opposes coercion and claims to support complete freedom for people to determine their family size, that position is compromised by the call for policies that incorporate "demographic goals." What if freedom of choice and those demographic goals conflict? Which will get priority? Considering the urgency with which the Cairo conference called for the achievement of demographic goals, it is hard to believe that freedom of choice would prevail. In China and elsewhere, freedom is casually cast aside for the sake of population control.[12]

People typically determine their family size by criteria other than the policy set by their government or the UN. After adjusting for such factors as availability of Western contraception, researchers at the World Bank found that "high fertility is explained almost completely by a high desire for children."[13] So a clash between population targets and free choice is almost inevitable.

Moreover, government-sponsored and UN-sponsored women's health facilities embody a fundamental breach of medical ethics. When a woman goes to a health clinic, she assumes that the personnel are acting in her interest, that she is the client. Yet a health clinic funded by government and the UNFPA has other considerations, most especially the achievement of demographic goals. That clinic has a client other than the woman. That is an inherent conflict of interest. Will women be informed? Or will they be propagandized about how their health and their nation's welfare depend on having fewer children than they may want?

State-Driven Development

The Cairo program envisions development strategies that are entirely government driven—as if the failure of centrally planned economies in the Soviet bloc had never occurred. Indeed, the program sounds like it was written in the 1950s. It attributes poverty in the developing world to inequitable distribution of natural resources, trade imbalances, lack of education, and so on. That explanation of poverty has been debunked repeatedly by such scholars as Peter Bauer, Julian Simon, and David Osterfeld. The authors of the program seem not to have noticed that wealthy Hong Kong has nearly the highest population density in the world and is so "resource poor" that it has to import drinking water. Suffice it to say that if the authors were correct, no country would be rich today.[14]

Nowhere in the program are the governments of the developing world urged to introduce market reforms by deregulating agriculture and industry. Instead, they are told to set up a host of centralized programs to manage and allocate resources. Yet the only way for the developing world to advance economically is for those governments to relinquish power and let people be free to pursue independent market activity under the rule of law. As traditional societies voluntarily and gradually adopt Western ideas and as incomes rise, people will reduce their own fertility rates without the need for government goals and pressure. That is the demographic transition that all developed societies have undergone.[15]

Thus, the Cairo program is a bad solution. Worse than that, it is a bad solution in search of a problem.

Is There a Population Problem?

How many people are too many? We know that more than 5.5 billion people walk the earth today. But that number itself says nothing. Maybe it is too few. How can we tell?

The prefix "over" implies a standard. For example, "overweight" implies a standard based on height. By what standard is the earth overpopulated? For overpopulation to be real, there must be indications of features that are undesirable and unmistakably caused by the presence of a certain number of people. If such indications cannot be found, we are entitled to dismiss the claim of overpopulation.

In arguing their case, the believers in overpopulation make vague, tautological references to "carrying capacity" colorfully illustrated with stories about gazelle herds in meadows and bacteria in test tubes (anything but human beings). When the verbiage is cleared away, what are adduced as the symptoms of overpopulation? Famine, deepening poverty, disease, environmental degradation, and resource depletion. Yet on no count does the evidence support the anti-population lobby's case. On the contrary, the long-term trend for each factor is positive and points to an even better future.

Television pictures of starving, emaciated Africans are heartbreaking, but they are not evidence of overpopulation. Since 1985 we have witnessed famines in Ethiopia, Sudan, Somalia, and elsewhere. Many of those nations are among the least densely populated areas on earth. (There are exceptions such as Rwanda.) Although their populations are growing, the people are not hungry because the world cannot produce enough food. They are hungry because civil war and primitive economies keep food from getting to them.

In the 20th century there has been no famine that has not been caused by civil war, irrational economic policies, deliberate retribution, or natural disaster such as an earthquake. Moreover, the number of people affected by famine compared to the number affected in the late 19th century has fallen—not just as a percentage of the world's population but in absolute numbers.

Food is abundant. According to Dennis Avery of the Hudson Institute, science and capital investment have brought dramatic increases in the production of food. Output has more than doubled in the last 30 years. Per capita food supplies rose 25 percent in the developing world, where the world's population growth is occurring. The real cost has declined. "The world could readily feed another billion people, right now, without stressing any fragile acres or putting on heavy doses of farm chemicals," writes Avery. That could be accomplished in part, he points out, by using over 100 million acres of prime farmland that have been taken out of production by the governments of the United States and Argentina.[16]

The most telling indication of the trend in food production is the presence of a farm lobby in every Western capital city. Those lobbies spend millions of dollars a year to persuade their governments to restrict food production and hold prices *up*. The farmers apparently don't expect help from nature.

What is true of food is also true of other resources. The claim that "uncontrolled" population growth depletes resources has no more foundation than the catastrophists' other arguments. For centuries resources of every kind, including energy, have been growing more plentiful and less expensive. The Cato Institute's Stephen Moore reports that the cost of resources relative to wages is today half what it was in 1980. Resources are three times cheaper than they were 50 years ago and eight times cheaper than they were in 1900.[17]

Proven reserves of nearly everything have increased dramatically. Nonrenewable energy sources are no exception. Proven reserves of oil and gas have increased by over 700 percent since the 1950s. That is about 500 years' worth of fuel.[18]

Mankind has expanded the supply of energy and other resources through technological innovation. Not only does technology enable us to find more resources; it also lets us use them more efficiently. Doubling the efficiency of our use of oil would be equivalent to doubling the available supply of oil. In terms of human purposes, the supply of natural resources is not fixed.

"If there is one characteristic that tends to define the world's commodity markets, it is overcapacity and oversupply," wrote Thomas R. De Gregori in 1987.[19] The story is the same today. Thus, the anti-natalists' prediction that uncontrolled population growth will deplete the earth's resources is just dead wrong.

But that tells only part of the story. "Natural resources" do not actually exist as a meaningful concept. Resources are manmade. Something is not a resource until it can accomplish a human purpose, and that requires the application of human intelligence to the world. Before Benjamin Silliman Jr., a Yale University chemist, discovered in 1855 that kerosene (a better illuminant than whale oil) could be distilled from crude oil, oil was not a resource. It was black gunk that ruined farmland and had to be removed at great expense. Silliman turned oil into a resource by discovering a worthwhile use for it. Nature does not provide resources, only "stuff." Stuff does not become a resource until it is stamped with a human purpose.

The latest evidence of that truth is the information revolution that swirls around us. That revolution runs on silicon computer chips, threads of glass (fiber-optic cables), and ideas. The first two are made from sand—one of the most abundant substances on the planet. Thanks to human ingenuity, however, a common substance that was merely part of the landscape has become a tool of revolutionary human advancement. People don't just use resources; they create them. And our undeniable material progress indicates that people generally are net producers of resources rather than net consumers, a fact utterly at odds with the anti-natalist line.

Increasing Longevity

The catastrophists' claim that the population explosion causes famine, poverty, disease, and environmental degradation founders on a single fact: the global plunge in the death rate. Nearly everywhere, people are living longer and more babies are surviving infancy than ever before. That is why the population grows. The World Health Organization (WHO) reports that "average life expectancy at birth globally in 1995 was more than 65 years, an increase of about 3 years since 1985." In the developed countries, life expectancy was over 75 years, compared to just 65 in the period 1950 to 1955. It was 64 years in developing countries and 52 years in the least developed countries, compared to 41 years in 1950–55.[20] Today at least 120 countries (with a total population of 4.9 billion) have a life expectancy at birth of over 60 years—up from some 98 countries (with a total population of 2.7 billion) in 1980.[21]

"The increase in average life expectancy during the twentieth century," Osterfeld noted, "equals or exceeds the gains made in all the preceding centuries combined."[22] The connection between affluence and longevity is well known; as the late University of California professor Aaron Wildavsky liked to say, wealthier is healthier.[23] The increasing life expectancy in the developing world is evidence that population growth cannot be increasing poverty.

Falling Fertility Rates

The world's population has actually been heading toward stabilization for more than 30 years. Worldwide, women today have an average of 3 children compared to 3.2 in 1990, 3.7 in 1980, and 5 in 1950.[24] (The replacement rate is 2.1.) In the developing world, total fertility rates dropped by 40 percent, from 6.2 in 1950–55 to 3.5 in 1990–95.[25] The population controllers credit their efforts (while

167

complaining that not enough is being done). But the fall in those rates preceded their campaign. Moreover, there is a simpler explanation: as economies develop and become richer, people tend to have fewer children. In preindustrial, agricultural economies, children produce wealth as farm workers, and later they provide retirement security for their parents. Children are economic assets in such societies. A large number of children correlates with wealth. In developed economies, however, children consume wealth, for education and other things. They are an expense. Thus people in industrial societies tend to have fewer children. A low fertility rate is an effect, not a cause, of development.

The UNFPA cliché that a growing population impedes development contradicts history. The West grew rich precisely when its population was increasing at an unprecedented rate. The world's population was essentially stable from before 8000 B.C. until the late 18th century, and those millennia were a period of miserable poverty for mankind. At the dawn of industrialization, the world's population was about 750 million. After that, it skyrocketed. The time it took for the population to double fell from 35,000 years up to 1650, to 243 years between 1650 and 1750, then to 116 between 1850 and 1900. By 1970 the doubling time reached a low of 35 years. Between 1776 and 1975, while world population increased 6-fold, real gross world product rose about 80-fold.[26]

The increases in population and productivity were not coincidental. They were mutually reinforcing phenomena. Today, with few exceptions, the most densely populated countries are the richest, while the least densely populated are the poorest. Any mystery in that is dispelled by the realization that people are the source of ideas, in Julian Simon's phrase, the "ultimate resource." Population growth geometrically increases the potential for combining ideas into new and better ideas that benefit the world.

The doomsayers at UNFPA respond that past success does not guarantee future success. On some simple level that is true. But since we understand the conditions that produced that past success— freedom, to put it most generally—there is no reason why we cannot duplicate those conditions and results in the future. The nonpolitical indicators up to the current moment warrant nothing but optimism. All we need to do to ensure a continuation of the benign trends is to undo current interference with free markets and entrepreneurship and prevent new ones.

Nothing written here implies that population growth does not bring problems and the need for adjustment. The rapid addition of people can cause crowding, short-run economic dislocation, and the spread of disease. But as Julian Simon says, it also brings problem solvers who apply their intelligence, discover and invent solutions, and leave human society better off than it was before the problems arose.[27] Doubters need only study the quality of life of the inhabitants of what is now the United States before the arrival of Europeans. A few million indigenous inhabitants barely scratched out subsistence amid the same "natural resources" that today enrich the lives of billions of people worldwide.

Human advancement is not automatic and cannot withstand complacency. The precondition is liberty, specifically, the individual's right to think, to produce, to trade, and to keep the resulting profits. In institutional terms, liberty means free markets, the rule of law protecting property and contracts, and strict limits on government power. Without those things, the doomsayers' predictions may indeed come true—but for far different reasons than those specified. Unfortunately, the planners at the United Nations Population Fund have yet to learn the main lesson of the 20th century.

Notes

1. The fund was originally called the United Nations Fund for Population Activities, hence the acronym. Paul R. Ehrlich, *The Population Bomb* (New York: Ballantine Books, 1968). I say "contemporary hysteria" because irrational concern about the size of the human race goes back to antiquity. Modern concern with population began with Thomas Malthus in the late 18th century.

2. Nafis Sadik, ed., *Making a Difference: Twenty-Five Years of UNFPA Experience* (London: Banson, 1994), p. 1.

3. Ibid.

4. Ibid., p. 9.

5. Ibid., p. 134.

6. Ibid., p. 137. Of course, the conference threw in the obligatory language: "Governments should respect the cultures of indigenous people. . . ." "Draft Programme of Action," International Conference on Population and Development, Cairo, Egypt, September 5–13, 1994, p. 38.

7. Ibid., p. 26.

8. Sadik, p. 137.

9. David Osterfeld, *Prosperity versus Planning: How Government Stifles Economic Growth* (New York: Oxford University Press, 1992).

10. See John S. Aird, *Slaughter of the Innocents: Coercive Birth Control in China* (Washington: AEI Press, 1990). Aird was the U.S. Census Bureau's long-time China expert.

11. Molly Moore, "Teeming India Engulfed by Soaring Birthrate: Sterilization Quotas Blasted as Inhuman and Coercive," *Washington Post*, August 21, 1994, p. A1.

12. Professor Betsy Hartmann of Hampshire College has pointed out how population control programs are contrary to the interests of women in the developing world. Regarding Bangladesh, which the UNFPA claims as an example of enlightened population control, see her "What Success Story?" *New York Times*, September 29, 1994, p. A25.

13. Lant H. Pritchett and Lawrence H. Summers, "Desired Fertility and the Impact of Population Policies," Policy Research Working Paper 1273, World Bank, Washington, March 1994, p. 8.

14. See, among others, Peter Bauer, *The Development Frontier: Essays in Applied Economics* (Cambridge, Mass.: Harvard University Press, 1991); Julian Simon, *The Ultimate Resource* (Princeton, N.J.: Princeton University Press, 1981); and Osterfeld.

15. See Osterfeld, pp. 108–24. The prediction of a fall in fertility is reasonable. But it does not follow that if fertility rates do not fall, serious problems will result. A nation should have whatever fertility rate results from the free choices of its people.

16. Dennis Avery, "The World's Rising Food Productivity," in *The State of Humanity*, ed. Julian L. Simon (Cambridge, Mass.: Blackwell, 1995), pp. 388–89.

17. Stephen Moore, "The Coming Abundance," in *The True State of the Planet*, ed. Ronald Bailey (New York: Free Press, 1995), p. 111.

18. Jerry Taylor, "Sustainable Development," *Regulation* 1 (1994): 37. "Proven reserves" is not a measure of the earth's physical inventory. It is an economic concept indicating how much of a resource is worth extracting at the current price. Falling reserves could indicate a falling price.

19. Thomas R. De Gregori, "Resources Are Not; They Become: An Institutional Theory," *Journal of Economic Issues* 21, no. 3 (September 1987): 1252.

20. These figures are available on the World Health Organization's site on the World Wide Web at http://www.who.ch/whr/1996/50facts.htm. See also Osterfeld, p. 121.

21. WHO Web site, http://www.who.ch/whr/1996/50facts.htm. The decline in life expectancy in the former Soviet Union and Eastern Europe is unrelated to population issues. See Osterfeld, p. 16.

22. Ibid., p. 130.

23. That was the theme of Aaron B. Wildavsky, *Searching for Safety* (New Brunswick, N.J.: Transaction Books, 1988).

24. WHO Web site, http://www.who.ch/whr/1996/exsume.htm. See also Osterfeld, p. 109.

25. Nicholas Eberstadt, "Population, Food, and Income: Global Trends in the Twentieth Century," in *The True State of the Planet*, p. 16.

26. Osterfeld, pp. 108, 116–17.

27. Julian L. Simon, *Population Matters* (New Brunswick, N.J.: Transaction, 1990).

12. A Clean and Comfortable Planet without Global Regulation

Ronald Bailey

I want to begin with the following proposition: "Anything that retards economic growth also retards ultimate environmental cleanup."[1] If one looks around, it is clear that the countries with the cleanest air, the purest water, rebounding forests, and declining fertility rates are the wealthiest ones. Many of the ideas and proposals being considered by the United Nations and associated global bureaucracies would significantly retard the creation of new wealth. That would, despite the best intentions, be bad for the natural world and especially bad for the poorest people on our planet. In what follows I will take stock of where humanity is today with regard to selected environmental issues and briefly indicate where global regulations could slow the progress humanity is making in cleaning up and protecting the natural environment.

Countries undergo a series of "environmental transitions" as they become wealthier and reach various points at which they start cleaning up parts of their natural environments. The opening proposition comes from Department of the Interior analyst Indur Goklany, who found that there are distinct thresholds of per capita wealth at which people begin to reduce given pollutants. The first such threshold is for waterborne pollutants.[2] Since safe drinking water is very important to good health, people begin to purchase that environmental amenity when annual per capita incomes reach $1,400. At that income level, people begin to invest in sewage treatment and other water pollution control measures, and levels of fecal coliform bacteria in rivers begin to decline. The next environmental transition occurs when per capita incomes reach $3,300. At that point, the amount of smoke and soot in the air begins to be reduced. The next transition is reached soon after; at $3,700 per capita, sulfur dioxide levels in the air begin to be reduced.

171

Imposing First World environmental standards on developing countries, as some have suggested, through the "harmonization" of environmental regulations, could easily have the paradoxical effect of slowing environmental cleanup. While it is true that a power plant might perhaps cut its sulfur dioxide emissions if it used relatively expensive First World technology, the higher price of the resulting electricity could encourage poor people to continue to use dirty fuels such as wood and coal for household cooking, making the air even dirtier as well as posing much higher health risks from indoor air pollution.

The Myth of Global Food Shortages

Let's consider next global food supplies. In November 1996 the UN's Food and Agriculture Organization held a global food summit in Rome at which the usual suspects peddled recycled warnings of impending mass starvation and made renewed calls for more population control measures. Between late 1995 and mid-1996, the historical downward trend in world prices for wheat and corn was briefly interrupted and prices spiked considerably, rising from $3.40 per bushel for wheat in early 1996 to $7.60 per bushel and from $2.40 per bushel for corn to $5.25. Please note that prices have since essentially dropped back to their earlier levels; wheat was going for a little over $3.84 and corn for $2.55 in late December 1996. (I should also note that rice prices barely budged during 1996.)

Naturally, the Worldwatch Institute's Lester Brown and Stanford University's Paul Ehrlich cite that jump in prices as heralding a new era of food scarcity. Brown warns, "Food scarcity will be the defining issue of the new era now unfolding, much as ideological conflict was the defining issue of the historical era that recently ended."[3] He continues, "Rising food prices will be the first major economic indicator to show that the world economy is on an environmentally unsustainable path."[4]

What does Brown want us to do? Free markets and expand free trade, so that farmers worldwide can respond to increased prices by planting more productive varieties of crops, using more inputs such as fertilizers, and finding better methods to protect harvests from pests and wastage? Just kidding—Brown, of course, has a very different "solution." The new era he predicts is dawning means that "governments may be forced to formulate a new strategy to achieve a humane balance between food and people. . . . At a minimum, this may mean stabilizing population size in many countries much sooner than political leaders have anticipated and much sooner than has been projected."[5] Stabilize populations? How? Brown does not say, though he cites with approval China's one-child policy and Iran's new policy to eliminate health and education benefits for any children beyond three per family.[6]

What is the real-world food situation? Have we finally run up against the infamous "limits to growth"? Absolutely not. If governments do not interfere too much with farmers, the price of humanity's daily bread should resume its steep decline, and less land should need to be cultivated as farm productivity increases.

But why did wheat and corn prices jump so high? The principal reason is changes in government policies, according to Dennis Avery, director of the Hudson Institute's Center for Global Food Issues. He argues that the grain shortage of 1996 was created when the U.S. and West European governments finally began cutting their farm price support programs. Because of those programs, the United States and the European Union ended up essentially holding the world's grain stocks at their taxpayers' expense for decades. While the United States and the EU were cutting their stocks, they were also idling farmland. So when the 1995 feed grain harvest was down 75 million tons from the year before, prices soared.[7] Predictably, higher prices have led to more production. The grain harvest in member countries of the Organization for Economic Cooperation and Development is expected to be up 15 percent for 1996, and world production will be up 7 percent.[8]

But what about the claims that we are running up against biophysical limits in farming? Paul and Anne Ehrlich admit that the recent declines in grain stocks are largely a result of government policies, but they assert in their new book, *Betrayal of Science and Reason* (which one wag suggested might be an autobiography), that "far more relevant to future food production are tightening constraints such as degradation and losses of land, limited water supplies, and biophysical barriers to increased yields, all of which are increasingly evident."[9] Evident? Not really.

Paul Waggoner, a distinguished scientist at the Connecticut Agricultural Experiment Station, presents a far different analysis. Waggoner demonstrates convincingly that farmers are nowhere near the biophysical limits of agriculture. He concludes, "The global totals of sun, CO2 [carbon dioxide], fertilizer, and even water could produce far more food than what ten billion people need."[10]

Waggoner also points out how important high-yield agriculture is to preserving the natural environment. Globally the area used to grow crops, about 6 million square miles, has barely budged in the last two decades, but rapidly rising yields have been more than a match for rapidly rising world population. Farmers today supply 11 percent more calories per capita than they did in 1975.[11] Estimates of how much additional wildlands would have been plowed under if farm productivity had not kept pace with population growth since 1950 range from 3.5 million square miles to 10 million square miles.[12] Just to give an idea of how much land that is, 10 million square miles is equal to the land area of North America.

The main threat to global biodiversity is deforestation. According to the Consultative Group on International Agricultural Research, deforestation is driven, not by commercial logging, but by "poor farmers who have no other option [for] feeding their families other than slashing and burning a patch of forest. . . . Slash-and-burn agriculture results in the loss or degradation of some 25 million acres of land per year."[13] By contrast, in countries that practice modern high-yield agriculture, forests are expanding.

Clearly, modern agriculture, spurred by free markets and expanding world trade in food, has already done much to protect and preserve the natural environment. Bad policies could, of course, have substantial effects on future food security. For example, in an attempt to keep domestic prices low, the European Union has begun taxing wheat exports and South Africa has halted all new grain export contracts.[14] Other examples of misguided policies include a striving by countries for self-sufficiency in food production and cuts in production resulting from government set-aside and subsidy programs. If such panicky responses can be avoided, the 50-year trend of producing more and cheaper food with less damage to the environment should resume. According to Waggoner, "If during the next sixty to seventy years the world farmer reaches the average yield of today's US corn grower, the ten billion [in projected population] will need only half of today's cropland while they eat today's American calories."[15]

The Specter of Global Warming

Probably the most contentious area of recent international environmental activity has been the science and politics of global warming. I will not cite the controversy that has erupted over the editing of the text of Chapter 8 of the report of the UN's Intergovernmental Panel on Climate Change. That editing significantly tilted its conclusions in favor of attributing global temperature increases to anthropogenic effects, especially the addition of carbon dioxide from the burning of fossil fuels. What that controversy shows is that the IPCC's scientific review process is far from objective and could well cause policymakers to adopt bad international policies. But before going on to policy, let's take a brief look at what is actually happening to the world's climate.

On January 4, 1996, the *New York Times* ran a front-page story with the headline "'95 Hottest Year on Record As the Global Trend Resumes."[16] That headline was based on data from the British Climate Research Unit at the University of East Anglia. There was only one problem: 1995 was not the hottest year on record. Very accurate satellite data say that 1995 was an average year temperature-wise—only the eighth warmest year in the satellite record. The East Anglia temperature record was for only 11 months—temperatures for December were "statistical estimates." Why didn't the scientists wait for the actual temperature data to come in? One climate scientist at the National Aeronautics and Space Administration speculated that the East Anglia group was afraid that if they waited, the temperature might plummet, depriving them of their opportunity for a sensational headline. And that is indeed what happened. Global temperatures nosedived in December for the biggest one-month drop in the last 17 years.

What has been going on with the climate? The computer models relied on by proponents of the global warming hypothesis say that the earth's temperature should have increased by an easily detectable 0.3 to 0.4 degree centigrade since 1979. However, the satellite data show that, instead, a slight cooling has occurred over that period of time.[17] On a longer time scale, it does appear that the average temperature of the globe has increased by about half a degree centigrade during the last 100 years. That increase, however, is well within the limits of natural climate variation.

What about the future? Climate researchers Roy Spencer and John Christy, using the satellite data, calculate that the earth may warm by about 1 degree centigrade over the next century.[18] As the global climate models have become more refined, their predictions of temperature increases have been cut in half, and now the lower boundary of the models' predictions conforms nicely with Spencer and Christy's warming calculations. A one-degree warming over the next century is not a big environmental problem. So, is the "warming crisis" dissipating? Hardly.

Here is what the Ehrlichs have to say: "Rapid climate change is a huge potential threat to agricultural productivity. Any significant disruption of food production could have catastrophic consequences in a world where the nutritional future of the still-growing human population seems less than secure in any case."[19] Please note that that is a basically contentless statement, but its portentous rhetoric is meant to frighten the public and policymakers into adopting certain policies.

At the UN's Earth Summit in Rio de Janeiro in 1992, the United States signed the Framework Convention on Climate Change. Under that convention, signatories agreed to adopt the goal of cutting their carbon emissions to 1990 levels by the year 2000. At a UN climate change meeting in Geneva in July 1996, the Clinton administration offered for the first time to set legally binding limits on the amount of greenhouse gases the United States can emit. Those mandatory limits on emissions are to be negotiated at a global UN meeting at Kyoto, Japan, in December 1997.[20]

Although that is all very vague, the way the UN process works is like being nibbled to death by ducks. First, negotiators agree to "voluntary" limits. Then when those do not "work," something stronger is needed, so vague "mandatory" limits are proposed— no deadlines, no specific amounts, but mandatory. Next, after the principle of mandatory limits has been accepted, the screws will be slowly tightened and, somewhere down the road, the limits on emissions will become increasingly stringent.

Since we do not know what the limits might be, let's look at a range of estimates for the costs of cutting carbon emissions. Taxing carbon is the most likely technique that the United States and other countries will use to try to limit emissions. One study for the Electric Power Research Institute estimates that annual losses of U.S. gross domestic product that would result from imposing $50, $100, and $200 per ton carbon taxes in 2010 would be $89 billion, $172 billion, and $311 billion, respectively.[21] A study conducted by Charles River Associates, DRI, and McGraw Hill concluded that taxes high enough to cut carbon emissions to 1990 levels by 2010 would result in the loss of 500,000 jobs per year between 1995 and 2010.[22] Another estimate suggests that a carbon tax could cut U.S. gross domestic product by $200 billion to $400 billion annually and cost 600,000 jobs a year.[23] Still another study, by Constad Research, Inc., estimates that 1.6 million jobs could be lost and 3.5 million jobs could be put at risk over the next nine years if certain emission limits were adopted.[24] And those numbers reflect only the impact that carbon taxes would have on the United States. Costs for implementing them globally would be proportionately greater.

For the moment, let us assume that significant warming will occur in the next century. Must we act now to prevent it? According to the original IPCC analysis, even fairly stringent reductions in emissions from its baseline estimates would result in sparing the earth only 0.3 degree centigrade of warming by the year 2050.[25] An important study published in the January 1996 issue of *Nature* concluded that it could well be less costly to allow emissions to continue to rise for a decade or more, because technological innovations and judicious capital investment will make it possible to reduce them much more easily in the future, yet well before they become a significant problem.[26] In other words, we need not take drastic and costly action now.

There is an interesting and more speculative analysis in the summer 1996 issue of *Daedalus*. That article suggests that the world's economy has been moving since the middle of the 19th century toward using fuels that contain less and less carbon—from wood, to coal, to oil, to natural gas, to nuclear, and perhaps eventually to hydrogen.[27] Please note that this process of decarbonization is a result of technological advances, consumer choices, and increased economic efficiencies, not pressures from global planning bureaucracies.

Given the uncertainties in climatology, especially the question of how much warming we can expect over the next century, and the great likelihood that improved technologies will make any reductions of carbon emissions that may be advisable in the future easier to achieve, it is premature for the United States to agree to, much less suggest any, binding limitations on carbon emissions at the 1997 UN Conference of the Parties in Kyoto.

Humanity has been making considerable progress in ameliorating environmental problems by building wealth and knowledge through that process of intelligent trial and error known as free markets. If the process is allowed to move forward without too much interference from national governments and UN agencies, planet earth will become progressively less polluted, famine will become a thing of the past, forests will rebound as less and less land is used for crops, and humanity will be better able to respond to any environmental concerns such as global warming, should they prove to be significant problems in the future.

Notes

1. Indur Goklany, "Richer Is Cleaner: Long-Term Trends in Global Air Quality," in *The True State of the Planet*, ed. Ronald Bailey (New York: Free Press, 1995), p. 340.

2. Ibid., p. 342.

3. Lester Brown, *Tough Choices: Facing the Challenge of Food Scarcity* (New York: Norton, 1996), p. 19.

4. Ibid., p. 1.

5. Ibid., p. 120.

6. Ibid., pp. 124–25.

7. Dennis Avery, "What Grain Prices Are Saying about U.S. Farm Policy," Knight-Ridder Financial News, June 14, 1996.

8. Don Mitchell, International Economics Department, World Bank, private communication, October 1, 1996.

9. Paul Ehrlich and Anne Ehrlich, *Betrayal of Science and Reason: How Anti-Environmental Rhetoric Threatens Our Future* (Washington: Island Press, 1996), p. 81.

10. Paul Waggoner, "How Much Land Can Ten Billion People Spare for Nature?" *Daedalus* 125, no. 3 (Summer 1996): 90.

11. Ibid., p. 85.

12. The estimate of 3.5 million square miles is from Indur Goklany, "Is It Premature to Take Measures to Adapt to the Impacts of Climate Change on Natural Resources?" Office of Policy Analysis, U.S. Department of the Interior, 1994, p. 3. The estimate of 10 million square miles is from Dennis Avery, private communication, October 1994.

13. Ismail Serageldin, Consultative Group on International Agricultural Research, Press release, August 4, 1996, p. 2.

14. Per Pinstrup-Andersen and James L. Garrett, "Rising Food Prices and Falling Grain Stocks: Short-Run Blips or New Trends?" International Food Policy Research Institute, 20/20 Brief, Washington, January 1996, p. 2.

15. Waggoner, p. 87.

16. William K. Stevens, "'95 Hottest Year on Record As the Global Trend Resumes," *New York Times*, January 4, 1996, p. A1.

17. See generally Ronald Bailey, "Fevers, Fires, Floods, Oh My!" *Weekly Standard*, February 5, 1996, pp. 12–13.

18. Roy Spencer and John Christy, personal communication, January 1996. See also John Christy and Richard T. McNider, "Satellite Greenhouse Signal," *Nature*, January 27, 1994, p. 325.

19. Ehrlich and Ehrlich, p. 126.

20. Naomi Freundlich, "The White House vs. the Greenhouse," *Business Week*, August 19, 1996, p. 75.

21. "Emissions Cap Prescription for Economic Disaster," Global Climate Coalition Climate Watch Brief 4, no. 3 (Fall 1996): 2.

22. Charles River Associates, DRI, and McGraw Hill, "Economic Impacts of Carbon Taxes: Overview," November 1994, p. 8-2.

23. William O'Keefe, "The Global Warming Debate," Letter to the editor, *Washington Post*, September 25, 1996, p. A22.

24. Quoted in H. Sterling Burnett, "Global Warming Treaty Costs for the U.S.," National Center for Policy Analysis Brief Analysis, September 6, 1996, p. 2.

25. Robert Balling, "Messy Models, Decent Data, and Pointless Policy," in *The True State of the Planet*, p. 102.

26. T. M. L. Wigley, R. Richels, and J. A. Edmonds, "Economic and Environmental Choices in the Stabilization of Atmospheric CO2 Concentrations," *Nature*, January 1996, pp. 240–43.

27. Nebojsa Nakicenovic, "Freeing Energy from Carbon," *Daedalus* 125, no. 3 (Summer 1996): 95–112.

13. Why We Need the United Nations to Protect the Global Environment

Gareth Porter

The economic activities of human societies have begun to bring about significant physical changes in the major environmental support systems (atmosphere, climate system, ozone layer, and oceans) and the key natural resources (forests, fisheries, biological diversity, and land) of the planet. Those changes could profoundly affect the quality of human life, and the global environmental threats they pose require coordinated action by nation-states to bring about timely changes in the human activities that have created the threats. UN institutions are needed to fulfill a number of functions related to global environmental policymaking that cannot be adequately carried out by nation-states alone.

Major Environmental Issues Facing the World's Nations

The environmental problems that have the greatest urgency or long-term potential impact on humankind include climate change, stratospheric ozone depletion, ocean pollution, depletion of fish stocks, deforestation, and biodiversity loss. This section briefly outlines the challenges four of those major global environmental issues will pose for the international community in the coming years.

Climate Change

Greenhouse gases are increasing in the atmosphere because of human activities, and the warming that has been observed over the past 100 years seems more likely to be due to human influence than to purely natural causes. Based on scientific findings on which there is now little international debate, the Conference of Parties (COP) to the United Nations Framework Convention on Climate Change agreed in July 1996 that stabilizing atmospheric concentrations of greenhouse gases at *twice* the pre-industrial levels will require that global emissions of those gases be cut by 50 percent. The COP further agreed to accelerate the negotiation of binding legal commitments by developed countries to reduce emissions significantly over the next 10 to 25 years.[1] To reduce greenhouse gas emissions sufficiently to stabilize concentrations in the atmosphere will require far-reaching international cooperation involving both developed and developing countries in the coming years.

Fish Stock Depletion

The UN's Food and Agriculture Organization (FAO) reports that all 17 major ocean fisheries are being fished either at or beyond their ability to regenerate themselves and that 9 of them are already in serious decline as a result of overfishing.[2] A 1995 agreement on straddling and migratory fish stocks failed to establish binding standards for sustainable management of fish stocks or to deal with problem of overcapitalization of fishing fleets worldwide. So pressures on fish stocks have not receded. It is now widely recognized by fisheries specialists that the common property–open access fishing regimes maintained by most nations within their economic zones lead inevitably to overcapitalization and overfishing and that assigning property rights to fishermen, in the form of individual tradeable quotas, is the only way of establishing economic incentives for conservation of fish stocks. Nonbinding guidelines for fisheries management refer to that fact, but so far there has been no move toward either a binding agreement or a detailed nonbinding global action plan that would involve such a shift.

Deforestation

The rate of global deforestation has continued to accelerate over the past two decades, and tropical rain forests are disappearing at an annual rate of 6.8 million acres, an area roughly the size of the state of Washington. Although conversion of forests to agricultural production is the leading cause of deforestation, commercial logging is linked directly or indirectly with most forest loss. But no real plan of action now exists to slow either commercial logging or conversion for other purposes. A first step would be systematic reform of logging concessions to ensure that they are secure and tradeable and to end trade-distorting subsidies of logging and wood-processing industries, especially in the countries that export the most timber and wood products. But some key forest countries, including Malaysia,

Indonesia, and Brazil, are determined to keep responsibility for forests in the UN forum that is least likely to reach meaningful agreement: the UN Commission on Sustainable Development.

Loss of Biological Diversity

The earth's wealth of biological diversity, defined as both variations in species and genetic diversity within species, is threatened by loss of habitat, overexploitation, and overfishing. The Convention on Biological Diversity (CBD) does not commit parties to any specific and measurable actions. The main challenges facing the COP are to reach agreement on what kinds of incentive measures should be adopted to promote biodiversity conservation and to negotiate protocols covering the major sectors in which biological diversity is threatened (forests, marine and coastal zones, and agriculture). Eliminating environmentally harmful subsidies to the agriculture, fishing, and forest sectors would be a major step forward, but that objective would be resisted by states that subsidize those sectors. The European Union has exercised its veto power on reform of agriculture subsidies, while Japan has tried to veto action on fisheries subsidies. Indonesia is certain to oppose any move to deal with subsidies to forest-based industries.

Is There a United Nations Environmental Agenda?

Those who see the United Nations as a reflection of an international political elite with ambitions for imposing binding international rules, or even world government, on nation-states believe that there is a "United Nations agenda" for the global environment. The reality is, however, that various UN bodies and multilateral bodies that have been created by UN-sponsored treaties have their own global environmental agendas. Those agendas are often marked by differences over goals to be achieved by the international community on global environmental issues or the means to be employed.

Among the UN agencies that have their own agendas are the FAO, the United Nations Environment Programme (UNEP), the United Nations Development Programme, the World Meteorological Organization (WMO), and the United Nations Commission on Sustainable Development (UNCSD). In addition, the conferences of parties to existing multilateral environmental treaties may play a role in determining how particular issues are dealt with in the international political arena.

Moreover, in each case, the global environmental agenda of the organization (i.e., the list of priority issues on which the organization intends to work in the next few years) is decided by a negotiated consensus among the nation-states that make up its governing body. In those governing bodies, of course, the United States has an influence on agenda setting far greater than that of any other single country. The United States has often been the key country in persuading UNEP to take on a new global environmental problem, as it was for the problems of the ozone layer and biodiversity. Not only does the United States have greater capacity to get an issue on the agenda of a UN body than does any other country, but it has greater ability to define the issue in a way that is most compatible with its interests and to prevent outcomes to which it objects. The U.S. power to lead in global environmental cooperation, as well as to veto such cooperation, is based on its scientific capabilities, financial resources, market power in trade, and diplomatic clout, as well as its capacity—far greater than that of either the European Union or Japan—to coordinate the positions of its various government agencies and pursue a unified policy.

Each of the UN organizations that deal with global environmental issues has its own set of actors, its own political dynamics, and therefore its own policy orientation on a given issue. Despite the fact that the same states are represented in all of the organizations, they do not necessarily approach a given issue in the same way in each organization, because different agencies of the member governments are represented in the organizations' meetings.

Thus two UN organizations (FAO and UNCSD) and the signatories to one multilateral treaty (the biodiversity convention) have shown interest in global forests, but each of them has had its own distinct approach, which is related to the government agencies that have been involved. The FAO, which was the lead international organization on forests until the 1990s, tended to emphasize the exploitation of forests, because its primary constituency was government forest departments, most of which see high levels of logging as a means of supporting their budgets and personnel.

The UNCSD, which was created by the UN General Assembly as a follow-up to the 1992 UN Conference on Environment and Development, is perhaps the most highly politicized of all UN organizations dealing with the environment. Many states, especially those in the developing world, are represented in the UNCSD by foreign ministry officials and others who have little knowledge or concern about environmental problems. The UNCSD meets only once a year for two weeks to discuss a wide range of issues related to the linkages between environment and development, but it has no mandate to take collective action on forests or any other environmental problem. Consequently, it has been essentially a "talk shop"—a forum that produces broad, carefully compromised language with no meaningful effect on environmental problems.

In 1995 the UNCSD created the Intergovernmental Panel on Forests (IPF), on which agriculture and forestry ministries are heavily represented. The IPF has produced a very long, heavily bracketed negotiating text on forests that fails to recommend any new policy initiatives aimed at curbing global deforestation. Moreover, the IPF is now contemplating the creation of yet another such forum for discussion of forest policy that could last three to five more years.

The CBD is not a UN agency but a multilateral institution with its own small secretariat and a conference of parties. Unlike the other institutions with an interest in the world's forests, it has a unique mandate to work on the role of forests as habitats for many of the earth's plants and animals. Moreover, environment ministries provide the leaders of many countries' delegations to the COP, thus giving greater urgency to its work on forests than exhibited by the FAO and UNCSD. For those reasons, nongovernmental organizations have viewed the CBD as the best hope for advancing a binding agreement on conserving biodiversity in the world's forests, and thus for meaningful action to slow global deforestation. But Brazil, Malaysia, and other tropical forest countries strongly oppose letting the CBD negotiate a binding agreement on forests.

Meanwhile, UNEP, the UN agency with the greatest environmental expertise and a mandate to address global environmental threats, has been cut out of the issue of the world's forests altogether. Those governments and agencies that do not want forest management subject to a strong international regime have worked to ensure that the issue of forest management remains in the safest arena of all.

The political reality, therefore, is that the UN system reflects the conflicting political forces that are in play with regard to global environmental issues. But that does not mean that individual UN agencies cannot play a useful role in promoting international environmental cooperation.

185

Why Do We Need UN Agencies?

Although the UN system often produces intergovernmental processes that are a waste of time and money at best, it also includes organizations and individuals that are dedicated to reversing global environmental threats and understand what needs to be done. UNEP in particular has played a key role in bringing about some of the major steps that have already been taken on environmental problems by the international community. But the FAO, whose role in forests and pesticides has been distorted by the bureaucratic and industry constituencies with which it has been linked, has been relatively independent and objective on fisheries management. And the role of WMO is crucial to progress on the climate change issue.

The leadership and staff of those UN agencies undertake functions that are indispensable to arriving at and carrying out global environmental agreements, especially those that cannot be undertaken as effectively by nation-states. Five such functions are discussed here.

Building and Publicizing Scientific Consensus on a Global Environmental Issue

On some global environmental issues, establishing that there is a scientific consensus has been a political precondition for effective action. That has been especially true of climate change and ozone depletion issues.

UNEP has undertaken the necessary scientific consensus—building on a number of global environmental issues—but its greatest contribution in that regard was on the issue of ozone depletion. In April 1987, just before the crucial round of negotiations on the Montreal Protocol, UNEP convened a meeting of leading atmospheric scientists to compare computer models of ozone depletion. The scientists were able to agree on estimates of total ozone depletion with no regulation of chlorofluorocarbons (CFCs) and with a 50 percent cut in CFC emissions.[3] That consensus helped weaken European resistance to cutting emissions by 50 percent and paved the way for the 1987 Montreal Protocol, the first binding agreement on regulating emission of ozone-depleting chemicals.

Convening Government Experts to "Depoliticize" an Issue and Establish a Common Factual Baseline

One of the processes that must take place in order to reach international consensus on a strong global environmental agreement is "fact finding," meaning that governments review together the scientific evidence, as well as the economic analyses and other data necessary to understand the implications of various courses of action. When that process is carried out only marginally or not at all, the chances are that the final agreement will be weaker and less effective, because it will be highly politicized.

Although the fact-finding function could in theory be carried out by a group of states on their own, an international organization provides more credible leadership in convening and facilitating the review of the facts by government experts, because it is not tied to the interests of any of the governments involved in the issue.

UNEP and WMO have made a major contribution to international cooperation on climate by organizing the Intergovernmental Panel on Climate Change, which was made up of government experts, including those from major developing countries. The 1990 report of the panel, approved by participating states after exhaustive review of the facts, affirmed that global warming is a serious threat. Without that degree of consensus on the facts, it would have been impossible to reach agreement on the climate convention in 1992.

UNEP also helped "depoliticize" the ozone issue by "disaggregating" it. In 1986 UNEP organized two informal workshops on regulatory regimes for ozone in which fact-finding by government experts focused on alternative regulatory strategies and their impacts on demand for CFCs, trade, equity, cost-effectiveness, and ease of implementation. The exercise was explicitly aimed at achieving consensus incrementally on relatively small points, and thus at increasing the open-mindedness of various governments on the issue. As a result of the workshops, Soviet and Japanese representatives indicated openness to international regulation of CFCs for the first time.[4]

Creatively Managing Negotiations to Overcome Political Obstacles

Negotiations on a global environmental agreement require a convening body whose director can effectively manage the negotiating process. Without a nonstate party that is regarded as independent of any of the key participating states, the chances of a negotiating impasse are much greater. Mostafa Tolba, the former UNEP executive director, helped steer negotiations on the Montreal Protocol and its amendments around such impasses by helping to persuade reluctant states to make concessions and by mediating differences among the major delegations. It was Tolba, for example, who convened informal meetings with 25 environmental ministers at the London COP meeting in 1990 to work out a compromise on the demand by India that its obligations to phase out CFCs be conditioned on transfer of technology from the industrialized countries.[5]

Developing International Support for Innovative Solutions to Global Environmental Problems

In certain instances, the international discourse on a global environmental threat has avoided dealing with a particular policy alternative that is crucial to addressing the threat effectively. In the case of fisheries management, for example, it is clear that agreement on allocating property rights to national fisheries and ending fisheries subsidies must be central components of a global regime. But only a few governments now support those approaches, and powerful domestic political forces have blocked their acceptance in most major fishing states. The FAO Fisheries Department, however, has been quietly advocating individual tradeable quotas and removal of subsidies through workshops on fisheries management and through the process of writing nonbinding guidelines to accompany the Code of Conduct for Responsible Fisheries adopted by the FAO in 1995.[6]

Providing Secretariat Functions and Support for Global Environmental Conventions

The secretariat of a global environmental convention is needed to assist the parties in a variety of functions, including reviewing progress on implementation, gathering and disseminating information on compliance with the agreement and providing legal interpretation of the agreement. UNEP is the main repository in the global political system of expertise for fulfilling those functions, and it has provided such expertise for the Montreal Protocol and the Basel convention on hazardous waste trade, among other agreements.

Conclusion

There is no common UN approach to global environmental protection. UN agencies and institutions involved in global environmental policymaking vary widely in their commitment to reducing global environmental threats. The UN system is certainly capable of producing time-consuming and ultimately meaningless documents. But the roles of certain UN agencies, such as UNEP, the WMO, and in the case of fisheries management the FAO, are indispensable to whatever progress the international community is capable of making in reducing global environmental threats.

Notes

1. Conference of Parties to the United Nations Framework Convention on Climate Change, Ministerial declaration, Geneva, July 18, 1996.

2. Food and Agriculture Organization, "Marine Fisheries and the Law of the Sea: A Decade of Change," Fisheries Circular no. 853, Rome, 1993.

3. See David Leonard Downie, "UNEP and the Montreal Protocol," in *International Organizations and Environmental Policy*, ed. Robert V. Bartlett, Priya A. Kurian, and Madhu Malik (Westport, Conn., and London: Greenwood, 1995), pp. 178–79.

4. Richard Elliott Benedick, *Ozone Diplomacy* (Cambridge, Mass.: Harvard University Press, 1991), pp. 47–50.

5. Gareth Porter, *Global Environmental Politics*, 2d ed. (Boulder, Colo.: Westview, 1996), p. 43.

6. See "Report of the Expert Consultation on Guidelines for Responsible Fisheries Management," Wellington, New Zealand, January 23–27, 1995, FAO Fisheries Report no. 519, Rome, 1995, pp. 67, 71–72.

14. Does the World Health Organization Return Good Value to American Taxpayers?

Richard E. Wagner

American taxpayers provide 25 percent of the budget of the World Health Organization. In this chapter I shall consider the performance of the WHO from the perspective of an average, or representative, American taxpayer. I start by asking on what grounds such a taxpayer might be willing to contribute to the support of the WHO. I then examine the WHO's budget for the 1994–95 biennium to assess the extent to which that budget represents a pattern of activity that would warrant taxpayer support. The examination shows that the WHO's pattern of activities matches poorly what would be required to justify taxpayer support. That divergence is then explained in terms of the WHO's being an organization that is run principally for the benefit of strong interest groups, particularly WHO officials and public health interest groups within the major donor nations.

External Cost, Health Assistance, and the WHO: A Framework for Assessment

There are two general considerations that can be reasonably used to justify the taxation of Americans to support the WHO. One involves the prospect that such contributions might be a cost-effective means of promoting the health of Americans. That is possible, though not necessary, if communicable diseases are present in other nations. The typical example in this context would involve a communicable disease that was present in Third World but not in First World nations. Through travel, however, inhabitants of the First World could be exposed to that disease and possibly even spread it at home. Some payment by First World nations to support the control of communicable diseases in the Third World might be a cost-effective means of promoting the health of inhabitants of the donor nations. For instance, First World nations might find some level of support for malaria control in Third World nations a cost-effective means of promoting the health of their own citizens.

To be sure, the mere statement of a principle of external cost does not guarantee that the principle applies in a particular case. There may be other, more effective options for dealing with the external cost. For example, an alternative to reducing the prevalence of a communicable disease in a Third World nation is to increase the extent of immunity to the disease among citizens of First World nations. An immunization program may in some cases be more economical for the representative American taxpayer than a program to combat the disease abroad. Regardless of the approach that might be taken to address claims of external cost in any particular case, the presence of the external cost that communicable diseases can involve provides one of the two main points of orientation from which the WHO's activities can be examined.

The second point of orientation arises out of a recognition that charitable motivation might also generate within a representative American taxpayer some willingness to contribute to the support of the WHO. Such motivation is responsible for a large volume of privately organized charity and no doubt explains some of the sup-port for public assistance as well. There is no necessary reason why such humanitarian impulses must stop at the U.S. borders. Individual Americans make charitable contributions to people and organizations in foreign lands, and there is no reason, in principle, why public assistance cannot similarly flow abroad. To say that charitable motivation might generate some support for the WHO on the part of a representative taxpayer is not to imply that such is actually the case, for such assistance may be given for very different reasons. Nonetheless, the prospect of charitable motivation also provides a point of orientation from which to assess the WHO.

Those two considerations, external cost and public assistance, can be used to create a reasonable framework within which the activities of the WHO can be assessed. Those two considerations are, in turn, illustrated effectively by the examples of smallpox and Mother Teresa. Smallpox, which was eradicated with major participation by the WHO, provides a textbook example of a communicable disease. Mother Teresa similarly provides a textbook example of assistance being rendered to the poorest people, who are least able to provide for themselves. Indeed, I would expect that if Americans who are aware of the WHO were asked to summarize their perception of it, they would respond by describing something like smallpox control and the work of Mother Teresa. If so, smallpox and Mother Teresa provide a good organizational framework for appraising the activities of the WHO.

Smallpox, Mother Teresa, and WHO Budgeting

The WHO's regular budget for the 1994–95 biennium was $872.5 million, of which the American contribution was 25 percent.[1] How effective is that contribution from the standpoint of the representative American taxpayer, as assessed against the standards of smallpox and Mother Teresa? Does the WHO's budget resemble that of an organization that is dedicated to the effective control of communicable diseases and to the granting of health assistance to those people who are least able to secure their own health?

One thing that becomes apparent from a reading of the WHO's budget is that it is not presented in a readily transparent fashion that facilitates quick and easy judgment. It is necessary to comb and sift through the budget and to reflect upon it before reasonable judgments can be offered. Once that is done, it becomes clear that the examples of smallpox control and Mother Teresa are reflected in some of the WHO's activities. The WHO does deal with the control of communicable diseases, and it does provide health assistance to people in the poorest lands. The first five entries in Table 14.1 provide a few illustrations from the WHO's 1994–95 budget. There is no specific category for malaria in the WHO's budget, and it is hard to say what besides malaria control is included in the category "integrated control of tropical diseases," which was allocated $36.6 million in 1994–95. Nonetheless, the WHO is engaged in combating malaria. Diarrheal diseases, mainly cholera, are not communicable, but they are primarily afflictions of the very poor. Entries 3–5 in Table 14.1 are likewise compatible with the touchstones of smallpox and Mother Teresa, in that they illustrate WHO activities that are consistent with the external cost and health assistance justifications.

The remaining entries in Table 14.1, however, show that there is another, larger side to the WHO. The remaining entries deal neither with the control of communicable diseases nor with the afflictions

Table 14.1
SELECTED SPENDING ITEMS, 1994–95 BUDGET

Item	Amount ($ millions)
1. Integrated control of tropical diseases	36.6
2. Diarrheal diseases	3.7
3. Tuberculosis	4.8
4. Acute respiratory diseases	2.5
5. Immunizations	13.6
6. Europe	55.3
7. Workers' health	4.3
8. Psychosocial health	4.0
9. Mental disorders	4.1
10. Health and social action	2.7
11. Elderly health	3.1
12. Alcohol and drug abuse	3.0
13. Toxic chemicals	3.9
14. Office supplies	5.6
15. Meetings	15.0
16. Budget meeting	2.5
17. WHO Executive Board	4.5

SOURCE: World Health Organization, *Proposed Programme Budget for the Financial Period 1994–1995* (Geneva: WHO, 1992), pp. A-33 through A-38.

of the poorest people. Entry 6 shows that however large the amount the WHO might spend on tropical diseases, it spends half as much again on programs in Europe, where neither poverty nor communicable diseases are much of a problem, particularly when viewed in a global context. Entries 7–13 illustrate the many kinds of programs that the WHO sponsors that have nothing to do with communicable disease or poverty. Such programs as workers' health, psychosocial health, mental disorders, elderly health, alcohol and drug abuse, toxic chemicals, and health and social action have nothing to do with external costs or health assistance. They have very much to do, however, with budgetary and regulatory controversies that are taking place within First World nations. So too, for that matter, are such WHO programs as Tobacco or Health and the Helmet Initiative.

The WHO's Helmet Initiative was, according to its Web posting, created in 1991 to promote the use of helmets by bicyclists and motorcyclists. The initial meeting, held in Paris in 1991, was attended

Table 14.2
SELECTION OF RECENT WHO CONFERENCES

Topic	Venue
Health for all leadership development	Geneva
Conference on safe communities	Stockholm
Nursing informatics	Washington
Congress on adolescent health	Montreaux
Conference on AIDS	Florence
Clean air at work	Luxembourg
Aging and working capacity	Helsinki

SOURCE: *Yearbook of the United Nations 1991*, no. 45 (1992): 953–59.

by 20 participants from 10 nations. Three additional meetings have been held since 1991. The Helmet Initiative is based at the Rollins School of Public Health at Emory University in Atlanta, and in 1994 programs at Reading in the United Kingdom and Linkoping in Sweden were selected as exemplary helmet promotion programs. The Helmet Initiative sponsors the collection and distribution of data, has developed programs to promote the use of helmets, and is ready to assist localities in promoting legislation to increase the use of helmets. Whatever the merits of helmet requirements in First World nations, it is quite obvious that the WHO's Helmet Initiative has nothing to do with smallpox or Mother Teresa and everything to do with the expansive agenda of health regulators in First World nations.

Items 14–17 in Table 14.1 reflect the high cost of bureaucracy. Office supplies were allocated $5.6 million. That sum exceeded the WHO's allocation for programs in all but nine nations.[2] Furthermore, though not included in Table 14.1, the WHO's budget contained a direct allocation of $455,000 for "hospitality," which exceeded its allocations for programs in 55 Third World nations.

Table 14.1 also shows that the WHO sponsors a lot of meetings. There is one general allocation of $15 million for meetings, but there are also allocations for special meetings. One such allocation was an award of $4.5 million for meetings of the WHO executive board, and there was an allocation of $2.5 million to discuss the WHO's budget.

Table 14.2 provides the titles and venues of some of the WHO's recent conferences. The venues are places to which few people would

Table 14.3
Distribution of the WHO's Budget by Bureaucratic Level,
1994–95

Level of Bureaucracy	Amount ($s)
Global and interregional	320,403,000
Regional	112,055,700
Intercountry	135,764,400
Country	304,272,900

Source: World Health Organization, *Proposed Programme Budget for the Financial Period 1994–1995* (Geneva: WHO, 1992), p. A-14.

object to having to travel. No shots are required, the water is drinkable, and fresh fruits can be eaten without fear. And the topics of discussion have next to nothing to do with communicable diseases or the health troubles of the very poor but everything to do with issues at the forefront of public health controversies in the First World.[3]

Another way of forming a picture of the WHO is by looking at where its money is spent. An organization that was combating the external costs of communicable disease and was providing health assistance to the poorest populations would spend most of its money in the field in poor lands. Table 14.3 shows the distribution of the WHO's expenditures by bureaucratic level. "Country" expenditures are made for programs in various nations; they are expenditures in the field, so to speak. To move up the table through "intercountry," "regional," and "global and interregional" is to rise in the level of bureaucracy, through the six regional headquarters (Washington, Copenhagen, Alexandria, Brazzaville, New Delhi, and Manila) to WHO headquarters at Geneva. Table 14.3 shows that barely one-third of the WHO's expenditures is made at the country level; the largest share is made at the global level. WHO officials are roughly divided into three categories: those in Geneva, those in the six regional headquarters, and those in the field. The Geneva posting is both rich and amenity laden, as Table 14.4 illustrates, with nearly two-thirds of the professional staff employed at an average salary of $149,200.

The WHO is clearly a large, conglomerate health organization. It is possible to find in that conglomerate programs that look like

196

Table 14.4
WHO EMPLOYMENT AND SALARIES, GENEVA HEADQUARTERS,
1994–95 ($s)

Item	Professional Level		
	P1–P3	P4–P5	P6–D2
Base salary	78,100	103,150	122,700
Other costs	37,850	46,050	52,000
Total compensation	115,950	149,200	174,700
Share of positions	23%	64%	13%

SOURCE: World Health Organization, *Proposed Programme Budget for the Financial Period 1994–1995* (Geneva: WHO, 1992), pp. C-37 through C-38, C-75.

variations on smallpox control and Mother Teresa. But an inspection of the WHO's budget shows that those programs occupy only the background of the portrait. The foreground is dominated by caviar and chardonnay, served in amenity-rich First World cities to well-paid professionals.

The Conflict between Reality and Justification

A portion of the WHO budget clearly goes to support activities that would resonate well with a representative American taxpayer. The WHO does act to control communicable diseases and to provide health assistance to poor people in poor countries. It is equally clear, however, that the major portion of the WHO's budget would have no such resonance. Most of what the WHO does concerns neither communicable diseases nor the health of poor populations. The WHO is a public health conglomerate whose activities reflect to a large extent the kinds of concerns that can be found in any of the public health agencies of the First World.

That should not be any cause for surprise. By now a large literature on bureaucracy has come to recognize that the performance of bureaus is governed largely by two things: the interests of the governmental sponsors of those bureaus and the interests of the bureaus' officials. That is true of both national and international bureaus, save perhaps that the interests of sponsors might be more diffuse for international bureaus, which in turn would give freer rein to bureau officials.[4]

The WHO receives one-quarter of its budget from the United States and more than two-thirds of its budget from seven nations:

the United States, Japan, Germany, Great Britain, France, Italy, and Russia. It is no surprise that so many of the WHO's activities reflect the predominant health concerns in the primary donor nations. Psychosocial health occupies a more prominent place on the public health agenda in the United States than does zoonosis, a disease that is transmitted from animals to humans in poor nations. The WHO is primarily a First World public health conglomerate that is involved in shifting budgetary priorities within First World nations in the directions favored by the national health-related regulatory agencies.

In many respects, the problems with the WHO are reflections of the problems with public health discourse in the social democracies of the First World. In a social democracy, as contrasted with a liberal democracy, government replaces the market as the arena in which health and medical care is organized.[5] The traditional, narrow public health agenda, rooted in communicable disease and poverty, gives way to an expansive agenda. In a social democracy, with the collective organization of health care, individual responsibility necessarily gives way to collective regulation. Such things as patterns of drinking, smoking, and eating; whether people wear bicycle helmets; and even mental states become objects of collective interest because collective financing is always present.

A good deal of public-choice scholarship recognizes that democratic political processes do not always serve the interests of representative taxpayers or citizens. In many cases, conflicts can arise between the desires of particular interest groups and bureaucracies on the one hand and taxpayers or citizens on the other. Public health is one of those cases. The WHO serves largely to reinforce the interests of public health agencies in the donor nations, thereby increasing the scope of regulatory authority and budgetary appropriations in matters relating to the health interests in the legislative committees and bureaucracies of the major donor nations. The WHO is financed by First World social democracies, and it is only natural to find the public health agendas of those donor nations dominating the activities of the organization. At the deepest level, reform of the WHO would follow naturally from a generalized movement away from the collectivization of health care that would accompany a return to more liberal democratic principles.

In the interim, and from the perspective of a representative American taxpayer, whose interest is reasonably characterized by the images of smallpox control and Mother Teresa, the choice would seem to be between abolition and banishment. To abolish the WHO would not, of course, be to abolish activities that were of genuine interest to the typical American taxpayer. What would happen to those activities would depend on the particular substitutions that arose in response to abolition. By banishment, I mean the end of all WHO activities and operations in the major donor and First World nations. Those nations are rich enough to tend to their own health concerns. There would undoubtedly still be some tendency within such a reformed WHO for officials to locate their activities in the nicest of places. That is probably unavoidable. Still, banishment and relocation would modify the constellation of interests and concerns that run through the WHO, and that would surely shift the pattern of activities in a direction that would lead the WHO to more success-fully emulate the record of smallpox control and Mother Teresa.

Notes

1. That budget also called for the expenditure of $967.5 million in extrabudgetary funds, through the Pan American Health Organization, the Voluntary Fund for Health Promotion, and various trust funds. The examination here is limited to the WHO's regular budget, because that is the part that is financed most directly by contributions from member nations and to which the perspective of the representative taxpayer is most directly applicable.

2. Those nine nations were Bangladesh, China, India, Indonesia, Nepal, Thailand, Pakistan, Sudan, and Vietnam.

3. A partial exception might be the conference on AIDS, which is commonly consid-ered a communicable disease. But it is a self-limiting disease, not one that can be communicated indiscriminately. See Thomas J. Philipson and Richard A. Posner, *Private Choices and Public Health: The AIDS Epidemic in an Economic Perspective* (Cam-bridge, Mass.: Harvard University Press, 1994).

4. For a general treatment of this topic, see Robert D. Tollison and Richard E. Wagner, "Self-Interest, Public Interest, and Public Health," *Public Choice* 69, no. 3 (1991): 323–43. For related treatments focused on the WHO, see Petr Skrabanek, Mike Gibney, and James Le Fanu, *Who Needs WHO?* (London: Social Affairs Unit, 1992); and Robert D. Tollison and Richard E. Wagner, *Who Benefits from WHO?* (London: Social Affairs Unit, 1993).

5. For a contrast between social and liberal democracy in terms of their respective property foundations (common property vs. private property), see Richard E. Wagner, *Economic Policy in a Liberal Democracy* (Cheltenham, UK: Edward Elgar, 1996).

PART V

THE UN'S ROLE IN ECONOMIC DEVELOPMENT

15. Using the United Nations to Advance Sustainable Growth with Equity

Roy D. Morey

A Framework for Development

Before assessing the UN's contribution to development in the past 50 years, I shall define the concepts of sustainable growth and equity and describe the relationship between the two (Figure 15.1). For growth to benefit present and future generations, it needs to be qualitative as well as quantitative. Economic growth measured by real income per capita is the engine behind economic and social development. But for economic growth to be truly successful, and to have a lasting, positive effect on people's livelihoods, it must be sustainable.

The concept of sustainable development combines a concern for the environment with sound economic, financial, and social policies. That means, first, that macroeconomic policies that will encourage continued growth must be adopted. Second, the recurrent costs of projects and public expenditures must be considered from the outset. Third, natural resources must be managed and used with the needs of future generations in mind. Fourth, access to some acceptable level of health care and educational opportunities must be made available regardless of race, gender, class, or religion.

But there is even more to development than sustainable economic growth. Equity is just as important. Equity is not only closely linked to economic progress; it is also a necessary condition for well-balanced development. Equity does not guarantee equality of incomes, nor does it imply equality of outcomes. Rather, it means that there are decent minimum standards for all and that those of equal competence have an equal chance for success. In short, equity means a level playing field.

Figure 15.1
RELATIONSHIP OF SUSTAINABLE GROWTH, EQUITY, AND STABILITY

Sustainable Economic Growth
Deepen macroeconomic reforms
leading to environmentally,
socially, and financially
sustainable growth.

**People-Centered and
People-Led Development**

Stability
Promote good governance,
macroeconomic stability,
and the rule of law.

Equity
Ensure decent minimum
standards and equal
opportunity
to succeed for all.

While equity is an essential ingredient of economic growth, the reverse also holds true. Without equity, the skills and talents of people are ignored and stunted. The growth potential of a nation is reduced, and a social burden is created. Hence being equitable is not just right, it is smart.

Not only are sustainable growth and equity interdependent, but they are also linked to stability. Stability is essential for economic growth because high levels of efficient investment require a stable legal structure and confidence that a government and its policies will increase in efficiency and endure. Stability is threatened by lack of equity when people conclude they are living in a system loaded against them.

Hence, lasting stability is best achieved through constant improvements in equity and economic growth; it really cannot be imposed. That point is well stated in the 1995 UN report, *Poverty Elimination in Viet Nam.*[1]

The Lessons of Development

A framework has been established for identifying the key components of sustainable development, which is the ultimate goal of UN and non-UN development assistance organizations. The question that now must be addressed is whether UN organizations have been allies in or obstacles to achieving that goal. I plan to answer that question by selecting several major lessons that have emerged in the last half century of development experience and determining whether or not the UN agencies learned those lessons and used the resulting knowledge to guide their work. There are many lessons great and small, but I shall focus on four.

Human Capital

Economic growth is not the end of development; it is one important means to development. The primary objective of development is to ensure that people enjoy long and healthy lives and have a growing range of alternatives from which to choose. That simple truth introduces the first lesson: development must be human centered. The concept of human development is based on the notion that government should foster an environment for expanding choices so that people can shape their own destinies. People need the opportunity to use their creativity, drive, and imagination to create better lives for themselves and their families. In short, successful development is people led, not state driven.

The UN agencies did not simply learn that lesson; they were responsible for taking the lead in promoting the concept. UN agencies learned from the start that it is empty rhetoric to talk about human development without recognizing the need to invest in human capital by promoting equal access to a basic level of health care and education. The importance of such policies is well documented in the World Bank report, *The East Asian Miracle*.[2] A common feature of the eight fastest growing economies in Asia examined in the study was the willingness to invest in human capital to achieve economic success. The study also noted that economic success goes hand in hand with eliminating the gender gap by providing educational opportunities.

Largely through the efforts of UN agencies, the adult literacy rate in developing countries has risen to 69 percent (a 50 percent increase during the past 25 years), and female literacy rates increased from 36 percent in 1970 to 60 percent in 1994. Through United Nations Children's Fund– and World Health Organization–sponsored health and nutrition programs, including oral rehydration therapy and improved sanitation, child mortality rates in the developing world have been cut in half since 1960, and life expectancy has increased during the same period from 37 years to 67 years.[3] Despite those achievements, there are still 1.5 billion people in the world who are desperately poor. Moreover, there are 120 million people officially unemployed and millions more underemployed. It is no wonder that poverty eradication is the central program focus of the United Nations Development Programme (UNDP) and the other UN agencies.

Basic to the concept of human development is the promotion of human rights. Since adopting the Universal Declaration of Human Rights in 1948, the United Nations has helped to negotiate more than 80 comprehensive agreements on political, civil, economic, social, and cultural rights. The UN Commission on Human Rights has focused world attention on cases of torture, disappearance, and arbitrary detention and has generated international pressure on governments to improve their human rights records. Sustainable growth is dependent on expanding human choice and encouraging people to use their drive and creativity within the rule of law and without fear of arbitrary state action. In short, sustainable development and human rights are interdependent, and that fact is recognized in the Preamble to the Charter of the United Nations.

Growth and Market Economy

The second and most fundamental lesson is described in the 1992 edition of the *Human Development Report* published by the UNDP.[4] The lesson is that economic growth is vital; no society has in the long run been able to sustain the welfare of its people without continuous economic growth. Most people now agree that applying the basic principles of a market economy is the most efficient and effective way of achieving economic growth. For example, as stated in the development strategy adopted by the government of Viet Nam, "A market oriented economy is considered best for ensuring rapid economic growth on a sustainable basis, and for achieving social goals."[5]

Fostering growth and a market economy requires a favorable enabling environment. In countries throughout the world, the UNDP has supported projects to promote private foreign direct investment and policies fostering competitiveness. Ten years ago in Viet Nam, the UNDP supported a major private investment project, including a consultant who helped to formulate the country's first foreign direct investment program. In the case of Singapore, the UNDP was a principal source of technical assistance. Starting as early as the 1960s, it helped devise a comprehensive industrial strategy and establish the country's Economic Development Board.

Another prerequisite for a market economy is the establishment of physical and intellectual infrastructure. Given the interdependence of economic growth and transport, it is not surprising that air transport is expanding more rapidly in Asia than in any other region of the world. If you are aboard an aircraft in Asia, especially in one of the seven member countries of the Association of Southeast Asian Nations, there is a good chance that the air traffic controller or other personnel vital to air transport were trained at one of the regional civil aviation training centers established by the International Civil Aviation Organization and funded by the UNDP. Those centers are now operated by the countries themselves.

Effective investment (foreign or domestic), to say nothing of world trade, is inconceivable today without a proper intellectual property system. While there are still major problems and unmet needs in that field, we can be grateful for the outstanding work of the World Intellectual Property Organization, which leads the world in providing protection for inventors, artists, composers, and authors and maintains a register of nearly 3 million national trademarks.

By definition, the major purpose of an international organization is to assist countries to better integrate into the global economy by facilitating the transfer of knowledge and skills and by promoting global standards in areas such as telecommunications, ocean transport, social and economic statistics, and postal services. UNDP-funded projects, carried out by the UN technical agencies, have been of enormous benefit to the private sector in all of those areas.

The question remains: did the UN agencies lead or follow in recognizing the value of competitive markets for growth to promote human development? Until the 1980s, frankly, the UN agencies did not play much of an advocacy role for a transition to a market economy. However, once countries saw the need for change, many UN agencies were quick to respond. The recognition of the importance of the private business sector in development emerged in most UN agencies about the same time the socialist countries started moving toward market-oriented economies. Such recognition also coincided with the enormous growth of private foreign investment in the developing world during the past decade. There was more official development assistance than private investment in those countries 10 years ago. Today there is roughly five times more private investment than official development assistance. In short, the private business sector is clearly the leader in funding development.

Governance

The third lesson is drawn from experience in both developing and developed countries, including the United States. You cannot have sustainable human development without a strong and vibrant nongovernmental sector. The much acclaimed book, *Reinventing Government*, presents a convincing argument that in today's world the public sector is successful when it establishes strategic alliances and partnerships with the private sector in pursuit of the larger goal of good governance.[6]

There are three dimensions of governance that I would like to touch on briefly. The first is the performance of public institutions. Even in the most market oriented of economies you will not have sustainable growth without public institutions that are effective, efficient, and honest. For the past three decades the UN has been at the forefront of promoting public institutional and civil service reform. That effort has been accelerated since the establishment of the Management Development Programme of the UNDP 10 years ago. That program has supported public administration reform projects throughout the world, especially in the transition countries of Eastern Europe, the Commonwealth of Independent States, Asia, and Africa.

The second aspect of governance is the link between the public and private sectors and the framework to be used to guard against abusive action by the state. Of special significance are promoting the rule of law and fostering democracy. In accordance with its charter, the UN and its various agencies have been promoting democracy by providing electoral advice and assistance, monitoring voting results, and helping to draft numerous national constitutions. The UN has helped citizens in over 45 countries participate in free and fair elections, including those held in Cambodia, El Salvador, Mozambique, Namibia, Nicaragua, South Africa, and Bangladesh.[7]

The third aspect of governance is the vital role of national and international nongovernmental organizations (NGOs) in the development process. That is a lesson the UN and its agencies have learned, though perhaps slowly. The UN agencies respond to needs and requests on a country level. For years, in many developing countries, development was regarded as a state-driven exercise and the importance of civil society was downplayed. Moreover, even in the industrialized countries it has only been in the last 30 years that the agenda for social and economic change has been heavily influenced by NGOs and private business. The best illustrations of leading public awareness include concern for the environment, issues of equality, and the HIV/AIDS pandemic.

Some UN organizations recognized the critical role of the nongovernment sector early on, but others still need to catch up. In any event, one can cite numerous examples of UN organizations working closely with NGOs in maternal and child health, rural development, environment, gender equality, and poverty eradication. It is interesting to note that the governing body of the new UNAIDS effort includes five representatives from NGOs who sit with representatives of the six UN cooperating agencies plus 20 government representatives from various countries.

Globalization

The fourth and final lesson is that many emerging issues are, by their very nature, transnational, indeed global, and they involve both developing countries and the industrialized world. Such issues require collective solutions and intercountry cooperation. When one looks at the critical role played by UN organizations in dealing with many types of transborder issues, it would be reasonable to conclude that if certain UN organizations did not already exist, they would have to be invented. I will illustrate the point by focusing on three diverse problem areas: the environment, refugees, and weather forecasting.

The implications of the mismanagement of our global resources are awesome. In the next 30 minutes two species of flora or fauna will be lost forever; 30,000 species are destroyed each year. Some 8 percent of existing species will disappear in the next 25 years. The disappearance of species means that the world could well be deprived of a new treatment for cancer or heart disease, or a plant species that might allow farmers to grow crops without pesticides or in dry or salty soils.

Our planet is threatened both by the local effects of environmental degradation and by the effects that tend to migrate. Polluted air, for example, drifts across borders. And the greenhouse gases produced in individual countries have global impact. To combat such transnational environmental problems, the UNDP joined with the World Bank and the UN Environment Programme in October 1991 to establish the Global Environment Facility (GEF). Focusing specifically on the problems of global warming, the depletion of the ozone layer, the global loss of biodiversity, and the pollution of international waters, the GEF had approved 153 projects in about 70 countries as of January 1996. The GEF is providing more than $900 million to fund those projects. In Viet Nam there is a $3 million GEF project carried out by the UNDP and the World Wildlife Fund that has helped the country strengthen its capacity to manage newly established protected areas. The project has trained 800 conservation officials nationwide to preserve some of the most exotic and endangered plants and animals found anywhere in the world.

The problem of refugees is, by definition, transnational, and it occupies the attention of the UN Office of High Commissioner for Refugees as well as other UN organizations. In 1996 the office assisted 26 million refugees, up from 10.7 million in 1995. The World Food Programme provided 1.6 million tonnes of emergency food to 25 million refugees in 1995. The mammoth job done by those organizations speaks for itself.

Just as the spread of disease (as well as HIV/AIDS and environmental problems) requires intercountry cooperation, so does weather forecasting. It would be impossible to maintain today's volume of air and sea transportation with even a modicum of safety and cost-effectiveness without a coordinated effort to link the nations' weather systems. That is exactly what is being done through the World Weather Watch program, which operates under the auspices of the World Meteorological Organization.

Conclusion

UN agencies have been not only helpful but often instrumental in promoting sustainable human development throughout the world. The success of the United Nations in economic and social development is not accidental. The UN Charter recognizes that enduring peace is built on the foundation of expanding prosperity and social justice. There are special strengths the UN brings to development work, which have been summarized by UNDP administrator James Gustave Speth as follows:

1. The United Nations provides a universal forum for raising public consciousness, defining the international development agenda, promoting international standards, and building the consensus needed for action.
2. The neutrality of the United Nations means that it does not represent any particular national or commercial interest and has the trust and confidence of the countries in which it works.
3. The UN's international presence means that it has the world's largest network of country offices. It does not overlook any country and has a unique delivery capability.
4. The UN emphasizes bottom-up, country-driven programming of development resources and is built on the principle of self-reliance.
5. The UN programs focus heavily on the neediest countries, the neediest people within those countries, and transition countries where building effective governance is critical.
6. The UN has a comprehensive mandate spanning social, economic, and political issues. It can thus support political and economic transition linked to development, such as the process of democratization and market development.[8]

Should we conclude that the UN economic and social development efforts have been so successful that there is no room for improvement? Certainly not. Given the momentous changes that have occurred in the world since the founding of the United Nations in 1945, there is an obvious need for reform and renovation. But as the late Chinese leader Deng Xiaoping once said, the fact that one recognizes a need for reform does not necessarily mean that what has been done in the past has been wrong. The UN has done well in the past, and changes are needed so that it can continue to do well in the future.

The United Nations is a patchwork of 10 departments, 5 regional economic commissions, 18 funds and programs, and 18 specialized agencies. The system is so complex that it is difficult to describe and to understand. There is need for improved coordination of UN development efforts at the country level; a more rational division of responsibilities; greater efficiency in management; improved savings through economies of scale; greater policy coherence in programs and resource mobilization; and more transparency, accountability, and collaboration with NGOs and the private business sector.

The need for such reform does not mean that less funding is required for development and humanitarian relief. Quite the contrary; more is required to face the challenges that already exist. Nonetheless, both those inside and those outside the UN system recognize that its efficiency and effectiveness should be enhanced. It is in recognition of that need that the United Nations as a whole and the UNDP in particular are currently undergoing the most serious review ever of their structure, organization, programs, and operations. The desire is to enhance the ability of the UN to carry out perhaps its most important function described in its charter, to "employ international machinery for the economic and social advancement of all people."[9]

Notes

1. UN Development Programme, UN Population Fund, and UN Children's Fund, *Poverty Elimination in Viet Nam* (Hanoi: United Nations, 1995), p. 1.

2. World Bank, *The East Asian Miracle* (New York: Oxford University Press, 1993).

3. For comprehensive statistics on human development, see United Nations Development Programme, *Human Development Report* (New York: Oxford University Press, 1996), chap. 1.

4. United Nations Development Programme, *Human Development Report* (New York: Oxford University Press, 1992).

5. Socialist Republic of Viet Nam, *Viet Nam: A Development Perspective* (English version) (Hanoi: Government publication, September 1993), p. 8.

6. David Osborne and Ted Gaebler, *Reinventing Government* (Reading, Mass.: Addison-Wesley, 1992).

7. United Nations, *Support by the United Nations System of the Efforts of Governments to Promote and Consolidate New or Restored Democracies: Report of the Secretary-General,* document no. A/51/512, October 18, 1996; and Boutros Boutros-Ghali, "Support by the United Nations System of the Efforts of Governments to Promote and Consolidate New or Restored Democracies," Letter from the secretary-general to the president of the General Assembly, December 17, 1996, document no. A/51/761, December 20, 1996.

8. James Gustave Speth, "Time for a Reunion: The UN, the US, and Development Cooperation," Address to the Foreign Policy Association, New York, September 19, 1996.

9. *Charter of the United Nations* (San Francisco: United Nations, June 26, 1945), Preamble, p. 1.

16. The Impact of the UN's "Development Activities" on Third World Development

Nicholas Eberstadt

The United Nations has played a critical—arguably a central—role in the globalization of what are now called "development assistance" policies. The idea of development assistance (foreign aid granted expressly to hasten material advance in the recipient country) was originally proposed by the United States in 1949, and the United Nations quickly endorsed that then-novel concept and introduced an international "technical assistance program" of its own in 1950. Not only was the UN "present at the creation" of that new instrument of diplomacy and finance; in the decades that followed, the UN system helped to secure worldwide acceptance of the proposition that massive state-to-state resource transfers in the name of growth and progress for low-income areas should be a regular feature of the modern international order. Moreover, though many bilateral programs and multilateral organizations have sprung up since the early 1950s to augment international flows of "development aid," the United Nations today remains a major purveyor of official development assistance (ODA) in its own right.

Pinpointing just how much the UN and its subsidiary institutions currently allocate for development assistance—or any other purpose—is more difficult than one might at first imagine. According to estimates by the Organization for Economic Cooperation and Development, however, net disbursements of concessional aid by the UN family of agencies averaged just under $6 billion a year for 1992–94 (the most recent years for which such figures are available). In absolute terms, by the OECD's estimates, concessional transfers from the UN agencies nearly match the total from the international financial institutions—the World Bank and all the other regional development banks *combined*. By that measure, in fact, only three governments in the world—those of France, Japan, and the United States—apparently maintain bilateral ODA programs that are larger than the UN's own multilateral one.[1] Where development assistance is concerned, the United Nations clearly qualifies as a great power.

Although it is not possible in this brief chapter to provide a comprehensive analysis of the impact of the UN's development efforts on patterns of economic development and prospects for development in the low-income regions—the so-called Third World—even a general overview leads to troubling conclusions.[2]

"Development Assistance" and Economic Development since World War II

To begin, one should recognize the obvious: the era of the "development assistance" policy has, in fact, been a time of tremendous worldwide economic development. Despite the obvious limitations of such statistics, available economic and social data point unambiguously to substantial increases in per capita output, dramatic expansion of trade volume, and meaningful improvements in life expectancy for the world as a whole and virtually every major region within it for the period since 1950. Material progress has completely transformed the economies and societies of some once-poor countries, and it has altered standards of living in countries still considered poor far more than is sometimes appreciated. In India, for example, per capita gross domestic product appears to have more than doubled and life expectancy at birth to have risen by over 20 years since 1950.[3]

Despite such welcome strides, however, we must recognize another obvious fact: all has been far from well in the collectivity of economies distinguished by long-term receipt of ODA. In many of those economies, anomalous, but common, patterns of severe structural distortions have emerged, the symptoms of which may be described as "industrialization without prosperity" and "investment without growth."[4] Economies afflicted by those syndromes appear strangely incapable of responding to the needs of their own consumers—or of arranging for their own sustained growth.

To judge by its output, for example, one could easily conclude that India's great hunger is for steel, not food; according to World Bank figures, industry accounts for a greater share of GDP today in India than in Hong Kong or the Netherlands. By the same token, although per capita growth rates for the whole of sub-Saharan Africa are thought to have been negative for the 1980s and (to date) the 1990s, World Bank numbers suggest that the investment ratio—investment as a proportion of GDP—was higher for that region than for the United States over the same period![5]

How such perverse and intrinsically unsustainable patterns have arisen, spread, and (in some places) continued for decades is one of the great puzzles facing modern development economics. Part of the answer to the puzzle, sadly, may lie in development assistance policy itself—more specifically, in the workings of those long-term transfer programs in actual practice. Ironically, the prospect of substantial and steady flows of concessional external finance from developed countries has permitted Third World governments (and not just a few of them) to pursue "development" policies that have been expensive, ill-conceived, and unproductive—or, in some instances, so positively destructive that they probably could not have been sustained without outside support.

In retrospect, the overall record of international postwar development assistance policies has been problematic and decidedly mixed. But where do the United Nations' development efforts fit into the greater picture?

Are UN Development Activities Distinctive?

Naturally, the impact of diverse projects and activities varies according to location and sponsoring UN agency—as well as over time. Pockets of excellence do exist within the UN development apparatus (in the UN Statistical Office, for example). Worthwhile, commendable, even outstanding development-related initiatives under the UN imprimatur can surely be identified.

But as much would be expected simply as a result of the law of large numbers—and increasingly, it may be the law of large numbers that accounts for any new "success stories" that the United Nations' development apparatus might wish to single out. As far as developmental impact is concerned, the quality and effectiveness of the UN's development activities appear to be, on the whole, distinctly *lower* today than those of either the World Bank group or the major bilateral Western ODA programs. Anyone familiar with the current state of the World Bank's international operations, or with, for example, the present condition of the programs of the U.S. Agency for International Development, will know that this does not speak well for the UN's development activities—and does not augur well for those societies they are meant to serve.[6]

The constant and inescapable hazards inherent in development assistance—a financial mechanism that enables every recipient government to pursue its own particular ambitions with less external constraint—seem to have been magnified by the UN's own distinctive approach to development assistance policy. In the UN's development agencies, as is by now well known, nothing like a culture of accountability can be said to pervade; instead, it is often extraordinarily difficult for donors to find out where their money has gone or what it has achieved.[7] Lack of transparency and accountability has predictably encouraged wastefulness, and perhaps corruption.

Yet as unattractive as such practices may be, they are hardly the worst features of development assistance policy. For waste and corruption are, in a sense, self-limiting. Under the very worst of circumstances, after all, development officials could only squander as much—or steal as much—as their development program had allotted in funding; and even in such an extreme hypothetical situation, a recipient country would be no worse off than before it had been awarded the diverted grant.

The great damage that development activities can wreak in recipient economies derives instead from the potential influence of those activities on the local policy environment. Adverse policies and malign practices by an ODA recipient can waste or destroy vast amounts of *local* wealth and prevent productive *domestic* enterprise from being undertaken. By contributing to the degradation of the local policy climate, aid transfers can pervert development, slowing the pace of economic growth or derailing growth altogether. In extreme cases, development assistance can actually impoverish its intended beneficiaries.

It is precisely the pernicious effects of so many UN development activities on policy formation in poor countries that are cause for the greatest concern. Even a summary review of the UN's record in development assistance will illustrate the disturbing degree to which the UN system's function in the postwar development process has been to offer unsound advice (sometimes spectacularly unsound advice) to low-income countries—and to make such unwise counsel respectable, authoritative, and financially enticing.

216

UN Agencies, Conferences, and Commissions for Development

If that judgment seems too harsh, we should reflect for a moment on the actual history of the major voices within the UN system on development issues.

Let us start with a few of the major specialized development agencies. First, there is the Food and Agriculture Organization. Forty-five years ago, in a prescient turn of phrase, *The Economist* described the FAO as "a permanent organization, devoted to proving that there is not enough food in the world, and that with the growth of population this state of affairs will get worse."[8] Since then, misdiagnosis of the world food situation has become something of an FAO institutional tradition.

For more than a generation, a succession of methodologically flawed FAO *World Food Surveys* seriously overstated the prevalence of malnutrition in developing countries.[9] By so doing, the FAO arguably impeded the advance against hunger, discouraging action by depicting the problem as almost insurmountably large and misdirecting available international resources away from the places where they might have made the most difference. In the early 1970s the FAO mistook the "world food crisis" (which was triggered principally by destabilizing governmental interventions in world food markets and which subsided as those distortions were relieved) for its long-awaited Malthusian reckoning. To the extent that FAO analyses and recommendations had any effect on events, they likely prolonged the disarray.

Since its inception, the FAO has harbored deep institutional suspicions about relying on markets to enhance food security in poor countries. The FAO's clear policy sympathies have lain instead with parastatal and state-owned food boards and with the stockpiling of state grain reserves. Almost everywhere those preferred FAO strategies have been implemented, unfortunately, they have proved to be both inefficient and unnecessarily expensive; in fact, by wasting scarce resources, they may actually have reduced rather than improved nutritional security for the populations subject to them. The FAO has also encouraged low-income countries to pursue "self-reliance" and "trade-oriented self-reliance" in food and agriculture, but in country after country the schemes that the FAO endorsed or assisted have resulted in long-term dependence on food aid from abroad.

The low confidence that the FAO inspires even within the UN system can be inferred from the fact that three additional UN organizations—the World Food Programme, the World Food Council (disbanded in 1991), and the International Fund for Agricultural Development—were subsequently established to deal with international agricultural and nutritional problems.

Then there is the World Health Organization. As one sympathetic critic has noted, "It is virtually impossible to gauge the effectiveness of the WHO because of the vastness of the Organization's mandate."[10] The WHO's reputation today is based to a considerable degree on its earlier initiatives against communicable and tropical diseases—the most famous of which was its role in the successful worldwide campaign to eradicate smallpox. Time, however, seems to have obscured the fact that many of those now-vaunted campaigns were less effective than anticipated, and some—like the Malaria Eradication Programme—were undisguisable failures.

While by no means as hopelessly misguided as the FAO, the WHO today appears to be an agency determined to refight the last war—and it is poorly suited to choose its new battles. Although worldwide improvements in life expectancy and attendant changes in health patterns have shifted the "global burden of disease" from the communicable toward the chronic, and will likely continue to do so, the WHO has largely neglected the critical implications of that transition for low-income countries (not the least of those are issues of health care finance for poor but "greying" populations). Instead, the WHO has opted, somewhat nostalgically, to concentrate on "the re-emergence of traditional diseases." It has also devoted its energy to a drive to codify and enforce an international "Essential Drug List," the inevitable consequences of which have been to restrict the choices and limit the quality of medicines available to patients and to increase the commercial risks of pharmaceutical innovation in the future.

Like the WHO, the United Nations Population Fund (UNFPA), through its financial and administrative support of international family-planning programs, deals with health issues. The UNFPA, however, has stubbornly ignored the medical injunction, "First, do no harm." Fortified by the sectarian conviction that uncontrolled population growth poses a great danger to well-being and development in the world's poorer countries, the UNFPA's leadership has tolerated, indeed financed, "population activities" that expose prospective parents to anti-natal exhortation, pressure, and even coercion. (Emblematically, the UNFPA bestowed its first population award on the minister in charge of China's State Family Planning Commission—at a time when mandatory sterilization, forcible abortions, and infanticide were known to be occurring.)[11] In the real world, involuntarily limiting personal choices about family size automatically reduces the living standards of those concerned; their sacrifice, moreover, offers no sure promise of benefit to others in the future. To the extent that the UNFPA's "overpopulationist" dogma has diverted attention from remediable, but nondemographic, causes of poor economic performance in low-income countries, the UNFPA's international proselytical efforts have also probably served to dissipate the pressure for Third World economic reform.

The United Nation's Children's Fund (UNICEF), for many decades mainly an international clearinghouse that dispensed relief and financed social services for low-income regions, transformed itself in the 1980s into an activist agency focused on advocacy of an international development agenda. UNICEF's new institutional posture was motivated by a shrewd insight into the rhetoric of public policy: namely, that one can champion any given political preference more forcefully by asserting that it is inherently in the interest of children.

According to UNICEF's subsequent explication, market-oriented reforms, privatization of state-owned enterprises, liberalized trade arrangements, and smaller, more limited government were, on the whole, hazardous to children. By contrast, reduced defense spending, augmented social welfare budgets, enhanced state control of local economic activity, greater state-to-state aid flows, and a more overarching restructuring of international trade and finance for low-income areas were generally described as child friendly.

During the Third World "debt crisis," UNICEF devoted much of its energy to arguing that the less developed countries' repayment of debt on the terms originally contracted would be strongly against the interest of children. UNICEF's principal contribution to that debate, *Adjustment with a Human Face*, held up Peru—which had just unilaterally suspended most repayments on its international debt—as a model.[12] (However pleasing Peru's defiant stance may have been to UNICEF's directorate, it proved disastrous for Peruvians; the populist and irresponsible approach to economic affairs pursued by the regime of President Alan Garcia dramatically reduced living standards in the country—including, naturally, the living standards of children.)[13] In the 1990s UNICEF has applied its special perspective on development to the postcommunist region, where it has discovered that an "overly rapid" transition from central planning to market systems is likely to threaten the prospects of children.[14]

Like UNICEF, the United Nations Development Programme (UNDP) is a traditional funding agency (underwriting FAO, WHO, and other parts of the UN system) that has in recent years developed its own high-profile capacity for policy recommendation. The UNDP's development advice is encapsulated in its annual *Human Development Report*, first published in 1990. Although its overall policy perspective overlapped with UNICEF's on most important issues, UNDP's first three reports also discussed the role of political freedom in economic development, finding the relationship to be positive, and proposed developing a political freedom index to supplement the UNDP's new "human development index." That initiative, however, was apparently shelved. The fullest outline of the UNDP's current development agenda appears in its 1994 report. That document states that "it is possible—indeed mandatory—to engineer change" and proposes to do so through "a new design of development cooperation." Features of that design include a North-to-South transfer mechanism for "payment for services rendered and compensation for damages suffered" and "new sources of international [aid] funding that do not rely entirely on the fluctuating political will of the rich nations," which is to say, global taxation to finance development assistance.[15]

Not by coincidence, the UNDP's call for massive, and in large measure unconditional, new resource transfers to Third World governments echoes the themes—and even repeats particular proposals—of the call for a new international economic order (NIEO) of the 1970s. (A number of the principals who drafted the UNDP report were themselves vocal NIEO exponents two decades earlier.) Yet if the originally envisioned NIEO was a fundamentally flawed design for self-sustained development and global economic health (and there is little debate about that today), the updated version of that statist project is if anything even more woefully miscast for its time. Since the 1970s the potential for international development has been substantially recast by the tremendous expansion of world trade, the explosive growth of international private capital markets, and the increasingly important role corporations have come to play in the international transfer of technology.

Although the UN's development agencies have exerted an incalculable but nonetheless real influence on economic and social policies in low-income countries, any discussion of the UN system's overall impact on development policies would be incomplete if it failed to mention the role that smaller specialized UN organizations have played in influencing the Third World's policy climate. Three of those organizations deserve special consideration: the UN Economic Commission on Latin America (ECLA), the UN Conference on Trade and Development (UNCTAD), and the UN Economic Commission on Africa (ECA).

The ECLA's influence on policy circles in Latin America has been profound. Its gifted staff (of whom the late Raúl Prebisch was perhaps the most famous member) offered a diagnosis and prescription for Latin America's economic problems so distinctive as to be called the "ECLA school." The ECLA championed the argument that Latin American economies could not prosper through a trade-led development strategy and advised countries to throw themselves instead into "import substitution" and promotion of "infant industries." More generally, the ECLA's "structuralist" perspective suggested that special peculiarities of the Latin American economies made orthodox macroeconomic policies inappropriate for the region.

To an arresting degree, Latin America has reaped what the ECLA sowed. As economic reformers in the region are now ruefully realizing, the continent today is littered with "infant industries" that have never grown up. While East Asian economies embraced outward-oriented development policies and "orthodox" macroeconomic stabilization policies, Latin America spent the 1960s and the 1970s wandering in a structuralist wilderness. By the 1980s—when the "debt crisis" struck Latin America—no amount of erudite "structuralist" analysis could obscure the fact that borrowed money is more difficult to repay if it has been used for unproductive purposes.

Over the past generation, UNCTAD has been closely involved in shaping the policies of the Group of 77 (an association of "nonaligned," low-income countries in the UN). In the three decades since UNCTAD I convened in Geneva in 1964, this continuing conference has steadfastly lobbied for a relatively fixed set of objectives:

increased unconditional ODA transfers to governments of Third World countries; restrictions on transnational corporate enterprise and direct private foreign investment in Third World countries; international commodity agreements that would raise export prices for, and facilitate formation of cartels by, Third World producers of "primary products"; and nonreciprocity in trade (i.e., preferential access to Western markets while Third World countries maintain their own protectionist tariffs).[16] One critical observer has aptly described that program of action as "predatory poverty on the offensive."[17] To the governments that have taken its advice, UNCTAD has offered a formula for achieving economic slowdown and stagnation for low-income populations.

Pride of place for malign development advice, however, probably goes to the ECA, whose assessments and recommendations are closely followed by the Organization of African Unity. In the face of a prolonged and mounting economic crisis that came to grip virtually the entire continent, the ECA seemed to adopt the official posture that outsiders have no standing to criticize economic performance in Africa. As Adebayo Adedeji, the ECA's director from 1976 to 1991, pointedly put it,

> It is essential that our partners-in-development respect our priorities, perceptions, goals and strategies. That means that the provision of financial and technical assistance from such partners must reflect those African priorities and goals. It is only by so doing that the ghost of suspicion, that the African economy is being manipulated by outside powers with a view to frustrating the achievement of national and economic objectives, can be laid to rest.[18]

At the start of the 1980s, when the dire economic trends in the sub-Saharan region could no longer be denied, the ECA's own proposed remedies for Africa's afflictions included "policy emphases" on "comprehensive planning, large parastatal firm expansion, capital-goods and heavy industry development, increased state intervention in peasant price-setting, and an introverted development strategy."[19] And in the late 1980s, when sheer financial exigence seemed to be creating pressure for far-reaching reform of governmental policies and practices in the sub-Sahara, the ECA went on record as opposing even the relatively buffered "structural adjustments" the World Bank then favored, arguing instead that Africa's fundamental need was for debt relief. Thus the ECA may be said not only to have devised a framework for achieving economic failure in an African context but also to have worked to preserve that framework in the face of forces that might have helped overturn it.

Concluding Observations

Whether Western taxpayer funds have been spent judiciously or appropriately by the UN's development agencies and allied development activities is, of course, an important question, but it is beyond the purview of this chapter. I have considered a more narrow and restricted issue: namely, is there good reason to believe that the tens of billions of dollars—perhaps hundreds of billions of dollars—that the UN system has spent on "development" over the postwar period have on balance made a positive contribution to material advance in the poorer regions of the world?

That would seem to be an exceedingly modest criterion to satisfy. But the argument that UN development activities have in fact met that minimum standard of performance is neither self-evident nor persuasive. Weighing the UN system's overall impact on material advance in less developed regions turns out to be a complex task—and what makes the task complex is the very multiplicity and scope of the factors pressing on the negative side of the scales.

In the final analysis, the most crucial "development resource" that the UN has transmitted to low-income areas may have been, not money, but ideas and advice about policy. It is in that realm that the UN's failures appear most profound. All too often, the development doctrines that have evolved under the aegis of the UN system have played to the worst instincts of ruling circles and opinion shapers in low-income areas, reinforcing the temptations of willful dirigisme while distracting attention from the mundane but necessary tasks of governance and market building. Feckless, irresponsible, or plainly injurious economic policies have been embraced, defended, and subsidized—routinely, and for decades—by the UN's development apparatus. To be sure, there have been notable and honorable exceptions, but they seem to have been just that—exceptions.

With the end of the Cold War, the continuing development of international commercial and financial markets, and growing investor interest in "emerging country" opportunities, conditions today are propitious for material advance in low-income areas—so long as those areas embrace a regimen of enforceable law and relatively liberal economic policies. The UN system's development apparatus promises to be of little help in that undertaking. Although the UN's top development specialists, like all successful survivors within large organizations, seem to be learning the language and the code words of the new era that they face, their acceptance of the new international economic realities typically appears to be grudging and reluctant. Dirigiste dreams die hard, especially in the protected confines of a well-heeled and tenured international civil service. For the foreseeable future, it is more reasonable to expect the UN's development activities to be an anchor tying low-income countries to burdensome policies of the past rather than a pilot boat guiding them toward the currents that could carry them forward.

Notes

1. For these estimates, see Organization for Economic Cooperation and Development, *Development Co-operation: 1995 Report* (Paris: OECD, 1996), statistical annex.

2. A comprehensive assessment would require, at the outset, evaluation of thousands upon thousands of "development" projects, mountains of policy documents, and the by-now nearly countless "action programmes" and agendas that have been spun off from almost half a century of "developmental" summits, conferences, consultative meetings, preparatory committees, and other deliberative gatherings. Here, it must suffice to speak generally about conditions, tendencies, and problems.

3. Angus Maddison, *Monitoring the World Economy 1820–1992* (Paris: OECD, 1995), p. 24; and United Nations, *World Population Prospects: The 1996 Revision* (New York: UN, forthcoming), vol. 1, p. 168.

4. For a fuller treatment of those phenomena, see Nicholas Eberstadt, *The Tyranny of Numbers: Mismeasurement and Misrule* (Washington: AEI Press, 1995), chap. 9.

5. Figures taken from World Bank, *World Development Report 1996* (New York: Oxford University Press, 1996), tables 4, 11, 12, 13.

6. For critical examination of U.S. AID and World Bank/IMF policies, see Nicholas Eberstadt, *Foreign Aid and American Purpose* (Washington: AEI Press, 1988); and Doug Bandow and Ian Vásquez, eds., *Perpetuating Poverty* (Washington: Cato Institute, 1994).

7. For a recap of some of the accountability problems, see Stefan Halper, "A Miasma of Corruption: The United Nations at 50," Cato Institute Policy Analysis no. 253, April 30, 1996.

8. "Asian Rice Shortage," *The Economist*, August 23, 1952, p. 456.

9. For more details, see Eberstadt, *Tyranny of Numbers*, chap. 7.

10. Javed Siddiqi, *World Health and World Politics: The World Health Organization and the UN System* (Columbia: University of South Carolina Press, 1995), p. 199.

11. See John S. Aird, *Slaughter of the Innocents: Coercive Birth Control in China* (Washington: AEI Press, 1990), pp. 3–19.

12. Giovanni Andrea Cornia, Richard Jolly, and Frances Stewart, eds., *Protecting the Vulnerable and Promoting Growth*, vol. 1 of *Adjustment with a Human Face* (Oxford: Clarendon, 1987), pp. 292–93.

13. See, for example, Paul Glewwe and Dennis de Tray, "The Poor in Latin America during Adjustment: A Case Study of Peru," World Bank Living Standards Measurement Study Working Paper no. 56, 1989.

14. The first of such studies was Giovanni Andrea Cornia and Sándor Sipos, *Children and the Transition to the Market Economy* (Bookfield, Vt.: Avebury, 1991).

15. United Nations Development Programme, *Human Development Report 1994* (New York: Oxford University Press, 1994), pp. 2, 4, 5.

16. For one of the earliest (and still the most penetrating) critiques of UNCTAD's economic agenda, see P. T. Bauer, *Dissent on Development* (Cambridge, Mass.: Harvard University Press, 1976), chap. 6.

17. Martin Bronfenbenner, "Predatory Poverty on the Offensive: The UNCTAD Record," *Economic Development and Cultural Change* 24, no. 4 (1976): 825–31.

18. Adebayo Adedeji, *Towards a Dynamic African Economy: Selected Speeches and Lectures, 1975–1986* (London: Frank Cass, 1989), p. 5.

19. E. Wayne Nafziger, *The Debt Crisis in Africa* (Baltimore: Johns Hopkins University Press, 1993), p. 163.

17. Nongovernmental Organizations and International Development Bureaucracies

Michael Maren

Even critical accounts of the United Nations tend to be easier on the UN humanitarian organizations than on the rest of the UN. And the nongovernmental organizations (NGOs) that work closely with the United Nations often get off totally. I hope to rectify that situation, since the NGOs deserve much of the same criticism the UN has received.

International development bureaucracies are distinguished from NGOs by the fact that development bureaucracies don't actually *do* anything. Those bureaucracies include the large UN organizations; the U.S. Agency for International Development (U.S. AID); the British Overseas Development Agency (ODA); and a new and very large player, the European Union, which is now getting very involved in development activities. They fund people, they fund NGOs, they fund studies, they fund academics, and they fund think tanks. With a couple of exceptions, however, they don't do anything on the ground.

The third category of players in the relationship between NGOs and the development bureaucracies is think tanks and academic institutions. Together the three types of players form a sort of closed world that creates the illusion that something good is happening on the aid front. Each of the players has a role. Academic organizations come up with theories. When I first started working in Africa in 1977, all the talk was about meeting basic human needs. So, any time that we had to write a project proposal, the rule of thumb was that the phrase "meeting basic human needs" should appear at least once on every page. After I had been in Africa for a couple of years, I was told, "No, that is now obsolete. Now we're doing women in development, so be sure to include a paragraph in all of your project

227

proposals about how we're going to include women in the project." And then, sure enough, other things came along. The latest catch phrase, which I'm sure you've heard a thousand times, is "sustainable development"—as if that were some sort of light bulb. The fact is, if it's not sustainable, it's not development. Sustainable development is a redundancy.

The triangular relationship among academic institutions, development agencies, and NGOs can be summarized as follows: the academics come up with the theories, the development bureaucracies hold out the money, and the NGOs write the project proposals claiming to pursue whatever the current development theory happens to be.

In addition to working for U.S. AID, I've worked for various NGOs. Their emphasis on the latest development approaches, however, does not change the nature of their projects. A water project is a water project, whether you're carrying it out for sustainable development, women in development, or to meet basic human needs. If you're laying out five kilometers of pipe and bringing water into a village, the nature of the project is unchanged by new rhetoric.

How do development agencies then determine if a project is a success or not? The aid bureaucracies go back to the university and hire the academics (who came up with the development theory to begin with) to evaluate how the NGOs are carrying out the project. Typically, the academics arrive in the capital city, check into the nicest hotel, and hang around the swimming pool until they have to go out to the field. Ultimately, they get into their Land Cruisers or their little airplanes and go out to the field where it's hot and stinky and not very comfortable. They're walking around looking at the project, which was their idea to begin with, and they're thinking about getting back to the hotel as soon as possible. (I can tell you this because I've worked as a consultant on project evaluations for U.S. AID and have observed such conduct firsthand.) At the end of the day, the consultants return to their hotels and write a generally positive evaluation of the project—with a couple of provisions emphasizing the need for more study, thereby increasing the possibilities of future employment at $500 a day.

The result is a closed circle of people and a closed circle of money in which nobody has any vested interest whatsoever in saying that the project stinks, isn't working, and should be shut down. Anybody who has ever gotten a grant knows that the first priority in getting grant money is to spend all the money and account for it. That ensures receipt of a grant the following year.

Although we regard NGOs as private organizations, most of them get the bulk of their money from development bureaucracies. The most prominent NGOs include CARE, Save the Children, World Vision, and other organizations with which you're all familiar. If you go through their annual reports carefully, and go through their books, you'll discover that more than half of the money they spend comes from grants received from UN agencies or national development agencies.[1] The money the public donates to them is generally used for local administration and as "leverage" for obtaining grants. The more money they receive from the public, the more grant money they can get from the bureaucracies. Since NGOs depend so much on doing projects, they generally accept any project that they're asked to do by the aid bureaucracies. The NGOs in general do not show a whole lot of judgment, much less selectivity, about the development projects they undertake.

Somalia: Development without Aid

My observations of the conduct of aid agencies are based on my experience in the past 4 years as a journalist in Somalia, and for 10 years before that as a reporter and aid practitioner in Somalia and most of Africa. I do not consider Somalia an anomaly in any way. Rather, I regard the current state of that country as an extreme but logical extension of what passes for development aid and relief throughout Africa.

I was most recently in Somalia for four weeks in August and September of 1996. I arrived a year and a half after the last UN peacekeeping troops had departed and a year after most UN development agencies and NGOs had left.

Without foreign troops to keep the port and airport of Mogadishu open, both have closed. Two militias are facing off along the airport runway, and both factions are within 100 meters of the port. Each has the power to close those facilities; neither has the power to open them. That creates a serious problem for Somali businessmen and is a huge obstacle to economic development.

Despite the problems associated with lack of any central authority, however, business is booming. The markets are full of goods. A large number of young men (I won't venture an estimate) who once made their living with guns are now in business—especially transporting, importing, and exporting. Though three major political factions control portions of the city of Mogadishu, hundreds of business operators work all sides of the "green" lines, crossing the military and political boundaries as if they didn't exist. Currency markets operate efficiently. Exchange rates between the Somali shilling and a dozen foreign currencies are published daily. Private schools and hospitals are opening up throughout the city. Teachers and medical practitioners are being paid by parents and patients.

There are now two competing telephone systems in Mogadishu. City residents have a choice between AT&T and a Scandinavian carrier for their long-distance calls. In northern Somalia, calls are made via Sprint. From Mogadishu one can call anywhere in the world for $2 a minute, a fraction of the price of a call from most African countries, and in some cases cheaper than a call from New York. It is common to see people standing on bombed-out street corners with cellular phones in their hands.

Improved communication has been a boon to business. Western Union has opened up in Mogadishu, allowing a free flow of funds. By contrast, it is not possible to send a Western Union money order from the United States to a business center such as Nairobi, Kenya. DHL operates in Mogadishu now, and negotiations are under way with FedEx. The owner of one of the Somali phone systems has a plan to bring the Internet to the country within a year.

Moreover, Somalia has just had its best harvest in years. It is definitely the best harvest since the civil war started in 1990, and probably better than those of the final years of the former regime of dictator Mohamed Siad Barre.

Yet Mogadishu remains as dangerous as ever. There are killings, mortar attacks, and robberies. In a sad way, the violence may be the best thing for Somalia. The violence keeps foreigners away, and it keeps foreign aid money out. It stops NGOs from doing what the people are already doing for themselves. The low, but intimidating, level of continuing violence in Mogadishu has been a kind of inoculation against the much more virulent presence of foreign NGOs.

Some people—particularly people who work for NGOs—may be tempted to look at what is happening in Somalia and declare that Somalis have made all of this progress despite the danger and apparent chaos in the city. But it is clear to me that the Somalis have succeeded *because of* the danger in the city. The absence of foreign activists has forced Somalis to use their own resources and set their own priorities. Since they own the infrastructure, they are building only what they can maintain and what they really need when they need it. Having laid waste to their own city, they are now engaged in a process of organic development—that is, development that is rooted in Somali culture and Somali needs—rather than development that is based on the political priorities of international development bureaucracies and the fiscal needs of NGOs. The development that is taking place in Somalia today is what foreign organizations might call "sustainable development." And while sustainable development is often cited as a goal of international organizations and NGOs, it is their very involvement, ironically, that guarantees that the development that takes place under their auspices is not sustainable.

What has happened in Somalia recently reminds me of the children's story, *Stone Soup*. In it some soldiers wander into a town and ask the villagers for food. The villagers lock their cupboards and plead poverty. In turn, the soldiers say that they don't need any food; in fact, they're going to cook a feast for the entire town: stone soup. They light a fire, fill a kettle with water, toss in some stones, and wait. The soup will be delicious, they say, but it would be so much better if they only had a carrot. So someone brings a carrot. And then it would be even better if they had some onions . . . and so forth until the soup is full of vegetables and everyone marvels that soup made of stones can taste so good.

That is what has happened in Hargeisa in northern Somalia (the self-declared republic of Somaliland) and in Mogadishu. The Somalis became so accustomed to foreign aid that they expected it would solve all their problems. But the aid didn't continue to flow. So Somali businessmen gradually began to raise cash and invest. They started with small repairs and eventually began large-scale public works projects. In Hargeisa one businessman constructed a municipal power station, investing more than $1 million in plant and equipment.

That is also what happened with the phone system in Mogadishu. During the civil war the entire phone system in the city was destroyed. The central phone exchange was looted and the wires were torn from the poles. The first postwar system was installed by

David Morris, a multimillionaire New Zealander who was under contract to supply provisions to UN troops. Morris decided that he was the man to put in a phone system, which he did. What he installed might be called "appropriate technology," that is, it was old, cheap technology. It consisted of a central satellite dish linked to microwave handsets. The system worked, though not very well. The connections were horrible and overseas calls were about $4 to $6 a minute.

That system lasted about a year. Morris was murdered in April 1995 and his operation folded. Immediately after that, Somalis moved to install their own systems. Somali investors came up with nearly $4 million in private money, established strategic alliances with foreign companies, and had state-of-the-art cellular systems operating within months. The businessmen didn't ask for help. They hired only the technological assistance they needed from Motorola and other companies, and they used their own resources for the rest. The result is what may be the best phone system in Africa.

Somalia: Development with Aid?

During the UN's heyday in Mogadishu (1993–95), businessmen weren't investing in the city; they were starting NGOs. Nearly 1,000 NGOs had registered with the UN and were seeking funding, and NGO shingles decorated the walls of buildings all over town. They had names like "Feed the Starving Children," "Help the Children," "Somfam" . . . you get the idea. Today all of them are gone.

When the UN was in charge, people made a rational decision about how they were going to invest their time. The amount of money being poured into aid was greater than the amount being directed through commercial channels. NGOs were the biggest businesses in town. Somalis had seen how young foreigners would come in, with hundreds of thousand of dollars in foreign cash. Somalia's NGO economy briefly thrived and then collapsed.

That episode was a far cry from the real progress that has been made in the nearly two years since the UN left Somalia. Today there are certain groups of people eager to get the aid gravy train back on track in Somalia. Some of those people, itching to get their hands on contract money, are waiting in Nairobi at UN offices, at the offices of the European Union (which has an entire Somalia department), and at the headquarters of hundreds of NGOs.

Aid bureaucrats have one purpose in life: spending other people's money. In the absence of a plan that genuinely deals with poverty in the Third World, they spend money. Organizations that claim to be lobbying on behalf of Third World causes have one measurement of their own success—the amount of money they can get governments to spend. They don't pay much attention to how successful or devastating their development projects might be. That's too complex to really measure. Their concern, or lack of concern, for most Third World people is determined solely by the bottom line on the foreign aid budget.

And there is one more group that really wants the aid to resume. That group is already in Somalia; it includes the warlords and their supporters. The spontaneous economic development of Somalia is the greatest threat to the power of the warlords because it is marginalizing their influence. If businesses can supply jobs to young men, those men are likely to put down their guns and work for cash instead of patronage. Political loyalties in Somalia run only as deep as the warlords' pockets. Development aid and relief aid are resources that governments—even those constituted by the warlords—can control. Business is beyond their grasp.

In August 1996 a UN Development Programme delegation paid a visit to "President" Hussein Aidid—who succeeded his late father as leader of one clan—to discuss resuming aid to Somalia. Aidid milked the visit for public relations, proclaiming to his countrymen, most of whom don't regard him as their president, that a United Nations delegation had come to see him. Therefore, he must be the legitimate head of state. The problem is that the UN aid bureaucracy needs a system into which to channel its largesse. It knows only how to deal with governments—with ministers of finance, ministers of planning, and other people with titles. And in the absence of a credible government, as is the case in Somalia, it will try to invent one.

Today the European Union has some $60 million to spend in Somalia.[2] There is an office full of bureaucrats in Nairobi dying to find a way to spend that money. When I returned from my last trip to Mogadishu, a nice young man who was second in command at the EU office called me in and asked me to share my thoughts about what I had seen in Somalia. I told him that any infusion of aid into Mogadishu would make an already volatile situation explode. The warlords would fight over the aid. The aid would inevitably be fed back into the warlords' coffers and be used to buy ammunition, which even now is not in short supply. And it would threaten the progress already made. Aid would give the warlords the prominence that they are fast losing. In short, I told him to stay away and let the political situation sort itself out.

For the next two hours he tried to convince me—and, I suspect, himself—that there was some good that could be done with the EU's $60 million. To admit that I was right would have been to admit that he was doing a pointless job and should probably resign. But here is a young man on the move, a young man with a great job, great benefits, and a bright future. He has no incentive to turn to his bosses and say, "Let's wait a year, two years, before we dump any more money into Somalia." He needs to do something right away. And the EU office in Nairobi needs to spend the money, all the money, if it hopes to get any more next year.

So the EU is doing something. It is carrying out a food monetization program with CARE in an area of Somalia called Gedo,[3] which is peaceful because it is controlled by the Islamic fundamentalist organization Al-Itoihad, a terrorist group that recently set off bombs in Ethiopia and has plans to turn Somalia into an Islamic fundamentalist state. But Al-Itoihad keeps order in Gedo, so NGOs can work there. Money from the EU, via CARE, is now ending up in Al-Itoihad's coffers. Thus, the group can claim to the people that it is bringing peace and aid from abroad, thereby further enhancing its grip on power.

Another area of Somalia in which the EU now proposes to spend its money is the town of Bosasso, a thriving city-state. The port is open, and there is peace and order in the town. That is because the UN has largely stayed away. Although there have been no development projects in Bosasso for the last six years, the economy is booming. Ominously, the EU has decided that Bosasso now needs help.

Not to be left behind, the UN has just produced its plan of action for Somalia, which includes spending $25 million there in 1997. A consultant who helped draw up the plan told me that the UN feels very competitive with the EU and is not willing to abandon Somalia to "those people from Brussels."[4]

The UN's Food and Agriculture Organization is also dying to get back into Somalia, as indicated by the following wire service story:

> FAO Report Warns of Dwindling Food Supplies in Africa
> NAIROBI, Kenya—The United Nations Food and Agricul-
> tural Organization (FAO), has warned that despite an
> improved food supply in sub-Sahara Africa, 13 of these
> nations are suffering from food shortages and emergencies.
> Unless exceptional food assistance is allocated to these coun-
> tries, the agency said in a report, the countries will face
> increased hardships. . . . The hardest hit countries are
> Burundi, Liberia and Somalia.[5]

This UN organization wants nothing more than to bring free food into Somalia, which has just experienced a tremendous one-year jump in food production. Clearly, the only people suffering "increased hardships" are the ones whose jobs are threatened if the aid programs are closed.

And where does the FAO come up with its figures? How do FAO officials know that people are malnourished in Somalia and that UN intervention is needed to stem a famine? Even in the best of times, it was nearly impossible to know what was going on in Somalia. Between 1978 and 1989 the World Bank, U.S. AID, and other donors invested about $600 million in development projects, many of which were intended to generate a knowledge base about how rural Somalis were using natural resources to generate food and cash for survival and socioeconomic advancement.[6] During some periods there were almost 50 expatriate professionals with degrees in statistics, agronomy, sociology, livestock science, ecology, nutrition, public health, demography, fisheries, economics, agriculture, and so forth working in Somalia. Most of those professionals had long experience working in Africa. Many either had been based for long periods in rural areas or had made frequent visits to them. At that time it was possible to drive and spend the night *anywhere* in Somalia. Yet even then, no professionals knew enough to say that *x* percent of the population was malnourished, or that *y* thousand tons of food would be needed to keep those people alive, although droughts and famines did from time to time occur or were claimed to occur.

Ending Incestuous Aid Relationships

The problem is that no one on the supply side of the aid business has a vested interest in saying "I don't know," much less declaring that aid should end. The big aid bureaucracies use aid and relief as a substitute for real policy. And the NGOs depend on money from the bureaucracies for their survival.

Without that government money, the NGOs would actually have to do their work with the money they get from individuals. They would have to cut way back on administrative costs. For that reason, NGOs have rarely seen a development project they didn't like. To complicate matters, aid bureaucracies trust the NGOs as their eyes and ears in the field. NGOs tell the bureaucracies how much aid is needed, and then the bureaucracies get the money for the NGOs.

That also explains why NGOs work in environments where the power structures are often responsible for the problems in the first place. The conflict of interest is obvious. In most of the Third World most economic problems are caused by the very governments through which the NGOs and development organizations must work. No government is going to allow a development organization to undertake projects that aren't in its best interests. In many countries, especially those in Africa, NGOs are in fact supporting the forces of political and economic repression. Their activities ultimately make things worse for the people they claim to be trying to help.

In the end, there is no independent, disinterested analysis of the NGOs or the bottom-line effect of the money that is spent. Everyone just wants the books to look tidy and every penny to be accounted for. That is what I was told by an exceptionally honest officer at U.S. AID in Nairobi a few years ago. CARE had just received an $8 million grant to do development work in Somalia at a time when very little development work was going on. I asked the U.S. AID officer why the money was being spent, and especially why on CARE, which in my opinion had been responsible for hundreds of stillborn or destructive projects in Somalia. "They keep good books," she told me. "With CARE we have no worries when it's time for an audit."[7]

That statement encapsulates the relationship between NGOs and development bureaucracies. It is entirely incestuous. When aid bureaucracies evaluate the work of NGOs, they have no incentive to criticize them. If a U.S. AID officer is responsible for giving CARE a million-dollar grant, he is not going to report back to Washington that CARE completely screwed up the project. It makes him look bad and will result in a drop in funding the next year. In many cases, if you look at project evaluation reports on file, you find that they are self-evaluations. Save the Children, and CARE, and World Vision are allowed to tell the aid bureaucracy what a great job they have done spending the aid bureaucracy's money.

Ultimately, there are no checks or balances in the world of aid. Anyone can practice "development." You need a license to sell hot dogs in New York City, but anyone can be an aid worker. The development business is a cultish, self-serving club of people who strive to make their reports and discussions so boring that no one on the outside will pay attention. And then they go on and on spending money—our money—in ways that help no one but themselves.

Notes

1. See, for example, Save the Children, *Annual Report 1995* (Westport, Conn.: Save the Children, 1995), pp. 3–4; and CARE, *Annual Report 1996* (Atlanta: CARE, 1996), p. 43.

2. Confidential interview with EU official in Nairobi, Kenya, September 1996.

3. Confidential interview with EU official, Nairobi, Kenya, September 1996.

4. Confidential interview with UN consultant, September 1996.

5. Pan African News Agency, "FAO Report Warns of Dwindling Food Supplies in Africa," October 10, 1996. The wire report was based on an FAO press release.

6. Interview with Murry Watson, a consultant to the United Nations High Commissioner for Refugees, September 1996.

7. Confidential interview, June 1994.

18. The Record and Relevance of the World Bank and the IMF

Ian Vásquez

The World Bank and the International Monetary Fund (IMF) were created in Bretton Woods, New Hampshire, in 1944 at a conference of what would soon become the United Nations. The broad goals of the institutions were to promote global trade and, initially, the reconstruction of postwar Europe through stimulation of the international flow of capital.[1] In the aftermath of the Great Depression and as the end of World War II approached, the main architects of the Bretton Woods agencies, John Maynard Keynes and Harry Dexter White, argued that international commerce and development could not flourish without the mediation of multilateral public institutions.

Since their founding, the lending agencies have grown in size and influence as independent members of the UN system. Although the World Bank played a marginal role in the rebuilding of Europe, it soon began providing credit to poor countries and has made more than $370 billion in loans to nations around the globe.[2] The IMF, for its part, has given billions of dollars of aid and advice to most of the same countries.

Five decades of transferring massive amounts of wealth from rich countries' governments to those of poor countries have not, however, led to a corresponding transfer of prosperity.[3] As the United Nations reported in 1996, "Growth has been failing over much of the past 15 years in about 100 countries," with 70 of those countries experiencing lower average incomes than in 1980 and 43 countries seeing income fall below 1970 levels.[4] During the post–World War II period, economic stagnation, debt accumulation, and declines in productivity have afflicted much of the Third World. Judged by those measures, the multilateral lending institutions do not appear to have achieved great success, much less lived up to their "single ideal—that happiness be distributed throughout the face of the earth," as one overly enthusiastic founder put it in 1944.[5]

At the same time, a small group of developing nations, some of which received multilateral aid, did manage to avoid or overcome severe economic maladies. Naturally, the bank and the fund like to draw attention to a handful of such high-growth countries as South Korea and Chile as evidence of their success. But a country's progress depends on an array of factors, not on any single determinant, including foreign aid. A fair evaluation of the record of multilateral aid must, therefore, not confuse correlation with causation. It must take into account the real causes of nations' growth and the ways in which bank and fund aid has been used.

A Chronicle of Multilateral Lending

The World Bank began as a relatively conservative institution, lending only under a strict set of criteria intended to support viable investment projects in a world where international capital markets were undeveloped. One stipulation for access to credit, for example, was that bank-backed industrial projects be transferred to the private sector.[6] Unlike the IMF, the bank would lend money specifically to support development projects, particularly infrastructure.

The IMF, on the other hand, was created to ensure exchange-rate stability in a world of fixed exchange rates. Thus, its main function was to provide short-term loans to countries experiencing balance-of-payments difficulties. Unlike the World Bank's, the IMF's aid was aimed at correcting a country's macroeconomic policies. Since their inception, both agencies have been financed by governments and have lent only to governments, primarily in the developing world.[7]

Government-to-government transfers of wealth were inspired by the belief that the private sector could not bring economic progress to developing countries and that poor countries were poor because they lacked capital. Development planning, often modeled after Soviet-style five-year plans, was actively encouraged by Western advocates of aid. In 1950 the World Bank itself stated, "The Bank would prefer to ... base its financing on a national development program, provided that it is properly worked out in terms of projects by which the objectives of the program are to be attained."[8]

It was not until the 1960s, however, that the bank began significantly expanding its activities. In 1960, for example, the bank created the International Development Association, a branch that provides highly concessional credits to the world's poorest countries. In 1968

Robert McNamara became president of the World Bank, and his zeal to increase aid flows led to a 13-fold rise in bank lending by the time he left office in 1981.

The IMF began transforming itself during the 1970s. The collapse of the international system of fixed exchange rates eliminated the agency's official mission. Instead of closing down, however, the IMF doubled its lending from 1970 to 1975 and has been finding new missions for itself ever since. It reasoned, for instance, that it must lend to poor countries affected by high oil prices in the 1970s. In the 1980s the IMF became deeply involved in addressing the Third World debt problem and received increased funding as a result. Since the 1970s the fund has created a series of lending facilities designed to provide credit on terms even more lenient than those of previous programs.

World Bank and IMF lending has fueled the expansion of state control over Third World economies. Throughout the developing world, for example, the bank established and financed state-owned enterprises, many of which became a drain on poor nations' wealth and undermined private-sector development.

Indian economist Shyam Kamath notes that between 1951 and 1989 the bank poured more than $20 billion into his country's economy, most of it going to support public-sector projects.[9] Mexico, one of the bank's favorite clients, increased the number of its state-owned enterprises from 391 in 1970 to more than 1,100 by 1982. In areas as diverse as agriculture, the provision of credit, industry, transportation, and energy the state became the dominant, if not the sole, economic actor.

As a result, the World Bank and the IMF have helped Third World governments politicize their countries' economies. The inevitable effect of such largesse has been to turn people's energies toward rent-seeking behavior and political patronage and away from productive activities, thereby allowing ruling elites throughout the Third World to squander their countries' resources on a massive scale. That outcome cannot be explained solely or even mainly by the presence of corruption in the aid process (a phenomenon well documented by numerous authors including Graham Hancock in his devastating book, *Lords of Poverty*).[10]

A more serious problem plagues the World Bank and the IMF. They provide financing to countries whose economic policies are inimical to growth. Regimes that impose an extensive range of harmful measures—price controls, capital controls, trade protectionism, state-run agricultural marketing boards, byzantine licensing schemes, and nationalization of industries—receive generous subsidies from the multilaterals. Under such conditions, no amount of aid can lead to self-sustaining economic growth. Sadly for people in the developing world, the result of such lending is debt, not development.

Even the World Bank self-evaluations repeatedly offer discouraging evidence of the quality of bank projects. A 1987 bank review of annual project performance found that 75 percent of its agricultural projects in Africa were failures. That review echoed a 1981 bank evaluation of Africa that found that "much of the investment in agriculture, especially the domestic component, has gone into state farms, big irrigation schemes and similar capital intensive activities. These have turned out to be largely a waste of money: their impact on output has been negligible in most cases."[11]

Similarly, the bank's latest annual evaluation of its operations (for 1994) judged "one in three [bank operations] . . . not to have met its major relevant goals and/or not to have made an acceptable contribution to development . . . [a success rate] still far too low to be acceptable."[12] That review followed a 1992 internal report that found a "gradual but steady deterioration in portfolio performance"; 37.5 percent of bank projects completed in 1991 were deemed "unsatisfactory."[13]

It is also difficult to find evidence of successful IMF performance. After all, most of the same failed economies that the bank has financed have also received credit from the IMF. Yet despite making loans available on the condition that recipient governments undertake certain policy changes, the IMF has had little incentive or ability to enforce its conditions in practice. Rather, it appears that the IMF has helped turn poor nations into loan addicts. A review of its "short-term" loans is revealing. Through 1993, for example, 11 nations had been relying on IMF aid for at least 30 years; 32 countries had been borrowers for between 20 and 29 years; and 41 countries had been using IMF credit for between 10 and 19 years.[14]

In effect, governments that have been uninterested in reform have received IMF subsidies for years. The fund sometimes does, of course, discontinue credit to countries that blatantly disregard their agreements, and recipient governments sometimes do introduce policy changes consistent with IMF recommendations. In either case, both sides create the appearance rather than the reality of living up to their responsibilities. In cases in which the fund cuts recipients off, it usually resumes lending after receiving further promises that more credit will produce real reforms. In cases in which poor nations undertake measures urged by the IMF, policy changes are often cosmetic or half-hearted, thus precluding the possibility that fund credit will lead to sustained economic growth.

By the 1980s, during the height of the Third World debt crisis, it became clear that developing countries needed to reform their economies. The 33 most indebted countries had accumulated a debt of more than a half trillion dollars.[15] Obviously, lack of capital was not a problem for poor countries.

The bank and the IMF moved to "help" countries resolve their crises by providing more credit based on more conditionality. The bank thus stepped up its structural adjustment lending programs, initiated in 1980, that were intended to induce macroeconomic policy changes in highly indebted recipient nations. Many observers noticed that the bank's functions now overlapped those of the IMF. That caused some people to question the need for two multilateral institutions.[16]

Nevertheless, the IMF responded to the debt crisis by increasing its exposure in the highly indebted countries, thus allowing commercial banks to reduce theirs. Although most highly indebted countries responded to their economic crises by reducing expenditures, little in the way of structural reform occurred. With fresh IMF monies, the major Latin American debtors, for example, addressed the crisis by raising tariffs and increasing taxes. Once again, instead of promoting economic reforms in the developing world, IMF loans allowed politicians in those countries to postpone the introduction of necessary policy changes. As Sebastian Edwards, until recently the World Bank's chief economist for Latin America, explained when reviewing the IMF's role in the 1980s, "In many cases, by approving stand-by programs whose targets everyone knows will not be met, the IMF is participating in a big charade."[17]

For many of the same reasons, the bank's policy-based lending has been ineffective. Because of its own institutional incentives, the bank, like the IMF, cannot afford to allow countries to reform without its intervention. Yale University development economist Gustav Ranis emphasized the impact of institutional incentives in his review of the bank's structural adjustment lending:

> While the program loan instrument may be loaded with conditionality, ultimately the need to lend will overcome the need to ensure that those conditions are indeed met.
>
> At the same time, while the additional resources are supposed to ease the pain of adjustment, they serve to take the pressure off and permit the recipient to avoid adjustment. What usually occurs, at the risk of some exaggeration, therefore, is a rather time-consuming and expensive ritual dance. Few [structural adjustment loan] tranche releases have ever been canceled—at most they are delayed. Few countries, certainly not large ones, have ever had prolonged breakdowns in their relations with the World Bank.[18]

A widespread collapse of development planning finally took place in the late 1980s and early 1990s as numerous developing countries initiated serious market-oriented reforms. Countries such as Mexico, Peru, and Argentina undertook radical programs of deregulation, privatization, and trade liberalization. But they did so out of economic necessity. In the end, the market-liberal revolution that has swept much of the developing world has occurred despite, not because of, multilateral aid. It is simply not credible, economist Deepak Lal explains, "that it was the 'conditionality' of the structural adjustment and stabilization programmes and the money which accompanied them which turned the debt crisis countries (and others), however haltingly, from the plan to the market. . . . The economic liberalisation that has occurred was due to the 'crisis' in governability which past dirigisme had engendered."[19]

And it cannot be said that the multilaterals have helped the transition of postsocialist countries to the market. The dynamics of IMF lending in Eastern Europe and the countries of the former Soviet Union have been the same as elsewhere. Warning against further IMF aid to Russia, Boris Fyodorov, President Boris Yeltsin's former deputy prime minister for finance, stated, "The sooner this money is handed over, the sooner we shall see a change in policy—in the wrong direction. I recall how Mikhail Gorbachev, after each new loan, would lose interest in any kind of economic reform."[20] Since approving a $10 billion loan to Russia in early 1996 (just before national elections), the IMF has twice been forced to suspend the aid because of Russia's noncompliance with the terms of the loan. The IMF has also sought to encourage reform in Ukraine by *cutting off* aid after learning that that country had failed to meet its conditions. Those experiences suggest that a suspension or cutoff of aid is far more likely to promote market-oriented reform than are ongoing infusions of credit based on conditionality.

Aid and Growth

While not all multilateral aid has been wasted, the overall record is clear: the IMF and the World Bank have done far more harm than good. Moreover, numerous studies have shown that the relationship of foreign aid and economic growth is not positive. Peter Boone of the London School of Economics, for example, reviewed aid flows to 96 countries and concluded that "aid does not increase investment and growth, nor benefit the poor as measured by improvements in human development indicators, but it does increase the size of government." "Virtually all aid," Boone found, "goes to consumption."[21]

Another review of aid flows from major sources to 73 countries from 1971 to 1994 found no significant correlation between foreign aid and economic growth. Neither World Bank aid nor IMF aid was found to correlate with economic growth. Nor, contrary to the claims of many aid officials, is there any correlation between World Bank or IMF aid and market-oriented reforms.[22]

On the other hand, numerous studies have found that economic growth is strongly related to other factors. Economists James Gwartney, Robert Lawson, and Walter Block tracked the level of economic freedom in 102 countries from 1975 to 1995. The authors examined 17 variables ranging from inflation variability to openness of the economy in each country as an empirical measure of economic freedom. They found that "increases in economic freedom and maintenance of a high level of freedom will positively influence growth," and that "countries that achieve and sustain high levels of economic freedom over a lengthy time period will tend to be high income countries."[23]

Historical and empirical evidence—dating from long before the creation of the multilaterals—suggests that economic development does not depend on outside factors such as foreign aid or the economic policies of foreign countries or even a nation's natural resources or geographical location. Instead, as economist Mancur Olson has found, the evidence implies that "a country's institutions and economic policies are decisive for its economic performance."[24] To the extent that those domestic factors tend to be market oriented, they will foster economic development.

Multilateral agencies have not been a cause of self-sustaining growth. They have instead slowed nations' transitions to the market and contributed to the conditions afflicting the world's poor. Indeed, especially in the world's poorest countries, the World Bank and the IMF continue to support regimes whose policies are the principal cause of poverty and misery in the first place.

Viewed in that context, the comments of World Bank president James Wolfensohn that the bank "is the lifeline for three billion people living in the world's poorest countries" or of Vice-President Al Gore that "sustainable economic development and growth" in poor countries cannot occur "without the continued strong support and encouragement of the developed countries" appear ludicrous and patronizing.[25]

Hazardous Proposals

The World Bank and the IMF nevertheless continue to view themselves as essential to international development. From a bureaucratic perspective, such an attitude of self-importance is to be expected.[26] Both institutions, moreover, have been successful at greeting changes in international conditions as opportunities to expand their roles in the world economy. The collapse of the Soviet empire, for example, provided the agencies with a number of new clients and was used to justify increasing the IMF's resources by 50 percent in 1992. In recent years the fund and the bank have achieved record lending rates.

That pattern has occurred despite the fact that official aid flows to the developing world are now dwarfed by private capital flows. About $240 billion of private capital went to poor countries in 1996— more than four times the amount disbursed by all official aid agencies. Most of that private money, moreover, is going to approximately a dozen countries that have done the most to reform their economies—countries mainly in East Asia and Latin America. Nations that have been unwilling to reform—such as most sub-Saharan states—have not succeeded in attracting private money. It seems clear that the ability to attract capital is determined, not by any flaw or virtue inherent to a country, but rather by the types of policies a country embraces.

Given the more liberal international environment and the multilaterals' poor record at promoting it, it is important to briefly evaluate new proposals that would expand yet again the agencies' functions. Those proposals include a debt-relief initiative for highly indebted countries, the creation of an emergency fund to prevent Mexico-style crises, a general increase in the IMF's resources, and the distribution of additional IMF credit without a corresponding increase of resources to back that credit.

The first proposal seeks to reduce the debts of some 20 highly indebted countries.[27] The World Bank, the IMF, and national donors would contribute funds to the $7.7 billion initiative that would be used to pay off part of those countries' debts. (Not coincidentally, at least one-fifth of those debts, which total more than $100 billion, is owed to the multilaterals.) The debt-reduction initiative is, of course, an implicit recognition of the failure of past lending to produce sustainable economic growth. Indeed, most of the countries on the list have been financed primarily by official aid agencies. Sixteen of the 20, for example, are countries in sub-Saharan Africa, a region where 75 percent of long-term debt is public or publicly guaranteed.[28]

The problem with the proposed initiative is not that it reduces poor countries' public debt. It is indeed difficult to justify forcing citizens of the poorest countries to pay for the mistakes of their rulers and the government aid agencies that financed them. Rather, the debt initiative promises no end to the borrowing treadmill that caused the problem to begin with. Countries that receive debt relief will be eligible for further multilateral loans on the condition that the recipient governments undertake certain reforms. Proponents of the debt-relief initiative have failed to explain how that new conditionality will be more effective than previous conditionality. The governments of Sudan, Niger, Zaire, and others on the list show little interest in undertaking serious reform in any case. It is doubtful that yet another round of new funds to those regimes will encourage responsibility.

The best solution would be to forgive poor countries' debts and terminate lending. However, the World Bank and the IMF have ruled out either possibility. It appears that their "debt reduction" scheme is as much, if not more, of a help to the multilaterals as it is to poor countries. Because of their AAA credit rating, the bank and the fund cannot afford to recognize their poor lending record and write off debts. Thus, the multilaterals have sought to use the debt initiative as a way of avoiding jeopardizing their financial standing by funneling new money to themselves through the debtor countries. In the end, the proposed debt initiative is a financial shell game that promises little in the way of real reform or sustainable growth.

The next two proposals would expand the size and functions of the IMF. Michel Camdessus, managing director of the IMF, has campaigned for a doubling of his agency's resources from the current capital base of about $200 billion.[29] Given the fund's record in the Third World and postsocialist countries, and given the dramatic change in world conditions since the IMF's founding, such a request seems especially out of place.

IMF enthusiasts have also called for the establishment of a special $50 billion fund (known as the New Arrangements to Borrow), about half of which would come from already available resources, to address future Mexico-style financial crises. Yet the very creation of such a fund would set up a moral hazard; countries that behaved irresponsibly could count on IMF bailouts if they precipitated a crisis. An emergency bailout fund would likely promote, rather than prevent, financial meltdowns. Moreover, as many economists have pointed out, IMF intervention to address Mexico's latest currency crisis was unnecessary and circumvented superior, less expensive, market solutions.[30]

Finally, the Clinton administration and most IMF member countries have advocated increasing the issuance of Special Drawing Rights (SDRs), the IMF's paper money, or unit of account. In effect, developing countries would be given new IMF credit not based on a corresponding increase in new commitments to the IMF from its donor nations.

Economist Allan Meltzer notes that with the administration's support, the IMF can in this way bypass Congress in distributing additional resources from the United States (and other developed countries) to developing countries. Allowing the IMF to print SDRs would cost rich nations "the value of the goods, services, or existing assets that [developing countries] buy [from developed countries] with the new SDRs. No wealth is created. Wealth is transferred and redistributed."[31] Economist Raymond Mikesell, a participant in the 1944 Bretton Woods conference, also warns that "a general expansion of SDRs is a poor form of foreign aid. It is neither targeted to specific purposes nor countries in need. Expanding the total volume of international liquidity serves no global function and might contribute to world inflation."[32] In short, the major proposals to expand the functions of the multilaterals are potentially reckless and certainly unnecessary.

The world has changed dramatically since 1944. The conditions in which the bank and the fund were established changed long ago, along with many of the institutions' original functions. The dismal record of multilateral lending agencies and their relevance to sustainable economic growth suggest that the world would be better off without the IMF or the World Bank.

Notes

1. The official name of the World Bank, the International Bank for Reconstruction and Development, reflected the bank's immediate priorities.

2. World Bank, *World Bank Annual Report 1996* (Washington: World Bank, 1996), p. 243.

3. For a discussion that distinguishes the transfer of wealth from the transfer of prosperity, see Melvyn B. Krauss, *Development without Aid: Growth, Poverty and Government* (New York: New Press, McGraw-Hill, 1983), pp. 109–25.

4. United Nations Development Programme, *Human Development Report 1996* (New York: Oxford University Press, 1996), p. 1.

5. Souza Costa, quoted in Bruce Rich, *Mortgaging the Earth: The World Bank, Environmental Impoverishment and the Crisis of Development* (Boston: Beacon, 1994), p. 56.

6. Doug Bandow, *The Politics of Envy: Statism as Theology* (New Brunswick, N.J.: Transaction, 1994), p. 151.

7. The World Bank can also make loans to government-guaranteed projects.

8. World Bank, *Fifth Annual Report (1949–50)* (Washington: World Bank, 1950), p. 8, cited in Shyam J. Kamath, "Foreign Aid and India's Leviathan State," in *Perpetuating Poverty: The World Bank, the IMF, and the Developing World*, ed. Doug Bandow and Ian Vásquez (Washington: Cato Institute, 1994), p. 215.

9. Ibid.

10. Graham Hancock, *Lords of Poverty: The Power, Prestige, and Corruption of the International Aid Business* (New York: Atlantic Monthly Press, 1989).

11. Quoted in James Bovard, "The World Bank and the Impoverishment of Nations," in *Perpetuating Poverty*, pp. 64, 65.

12. World Bank Operations Evaluation Department, *1994 Evaluation Results* (Washington: World Bank, 1996), p. 25.

13. World Bank Portfolio Management Task Force, "Effective Implementation: Key to Development Impact," Washington, World Bank, 1992, p. ii.

14. International Monetary Fund, *Annual Report* (Washington: International Monetary Fund, various years).

15. William R. Cline, *International Debt Reexamined* (Washington: Institute for International Economics, 1995), p. 41.

16. See, for example, Peter Korner et al., *The IMF and the Debt Crisis* (Atlantic Highlands, N.J.: Zed Books, 1986), p. 146; James B. Burnham, "Understanding the World Bank: A Dispassionate Analysis," in *Perpetuating Poverty*, p. 84; and Raymond F. Mikesell, "Proposals for Changing the Functions of the International Monetary Fund (IMF)," Jerome Levy Economics Institute Working Paper no. 150, December 1995, p. 43.

17. Sebastian Edwards, "The International Monetary Fund and the Developing Countries: A Critical Evaluation," in *IMF Policy Advice, Market Volatility, Commodity Price Rules and Other Essays*, ed. Karl Brunner and Allan H. Meltzer, Carnegie-Rochester Conference Series on Public Policy, vol. 31, Autumn 1989, p. 39.

18. Gustav Ranis, "On Fast-Disbursing Policy-Based Loans," Paper prepared for the Center for Strategic and International Studies Task Force on Multilateral Development Banks, July 1996, p. 6.

19. Deepak Lal, "Foreign Aid: An Idea Whose Time Has Gone," *Economic Affairs* 16, no. 4 (Autumn 1996): 12.

20. Quoted in Doug Bandow and Ian Vásquez, "Time for Reform: Misguided Hopes in Russia and Elsewhere," *San Diego Union Tribune*, July 31, 1994.

21. Peter Boone, "Politics and the Effectiveness of Foreign Aid," London School of Economics and Center for Economic Performance, November 1994; and Peter Boone, "The Impacts of Foreign Aid on Savings and Growth," London School of Economics and Center for Economic Performance, October 1994.

22. For example, Lawrence Summers, formerly chief economist at the World Bank and now deputy secretary of the U.S. Treasury, has claimed that the mission of the multilaterals "over the past half-century has been to support the developing world's evolution to a market economy." See Lawrence H. Summers, "An IFI Question: Are Multilaterals the Solution?" *Wall Street Journal*, October 12, 1995, p. A22. Details on the aid correlation review can be provided upon request.

23. James Gwartney, Robert Lawson, and Walter Block, *Economic Freedom of the World: 1975–1995* (Vancouver: Fraser Institute: 1996), p. xvii. For similar findings, see also Richard E. Messick, ed., *World Survey of Economic Freedom: 1995–1996* (New Brunswick, N.J.: Transaction Publishers, 1996); and Kim R. Holmes, Bryan T. Johnson, and Melanie Kirkpatrick, *1997 Index of Economic Freedom* (Washington: Heritage Foundation and Wall Street Journal, 1997).

24. Mancur Olson Jr., "Big Bills Left on the Sidewalk: Why Some Nations Are Rich, and Others Poor," *Journal of Economic Perspectives* 10, no. 2 (Spring 1996): 19. See also Ralph Raico, "The Theory of Economic Development and the 'European Miracle,'" in *The Collapse of Development Planning*, ed. Peter J. Boettke (New York: New York University Press, 1994), pp. 37–58; Nathan Rosenberg and L. E. Birdzell Jr., *How the West Grew Rich: The Economic Transformation of the Industrial World* (New York: Basic Books, 1986); Gerald W. Scully, "The Institutional Framework and Economic Development," *Journal of Political Economy* 96, no. 3 (June 1988): 652–62; and Stephen Knack and Philip Keefer, "Institutions and Economic Performance: Cross-Country Tests Using Alternative Institutional Measures," *Economics and Politics* 7, no. 3 (November 1995): 207–27.

25. See James D. Wolfensohn, "1996 Annual Meeting Speech," World Bank, Washington, October 1, 1996, p. 2; and Al Gore, "Remarks by the Hon. Al Gore, Vice President of the United States, at the Joint Plenary Session of the Annual Meetings of the International Monetary Fund and the World Bank Group," Washington, October 1–4, 1996, p. 4. Transcript in author's possession.

26. For analyses of multilaterals as government bureaucracies, see Burnham, pp. 75–85; and Roland Vaubel, "Bureaucracy at the IMF and the World Bank," *The World Economy* 19, no. 2 (March 1996): 195–210.

27. The final list of countries eligible for debt-reduction facility benefits has not yet been established, but a list of potential beneficiaries includes Bolivia, Cameroon, Congo, Côte d'Ivoire, Ethiopia, Guyana, Madagascar, Myanmar, Niger, Rwanda, Tanzania, Uganda, Burundi, Guinea-Bissau, Mozambique, Nicaragua, São Tomé and Principe, Sudan, Zaire, and Zambia. *IMF Survey*, July 15, 1996, p. 230.

28. See World Bank, *World Debt Tables, 1996* (Washington: World Bank, 1996), pp. 38, 216.

29. See Michel Camdessus, "Address to the Board of Governors of the Fund," October 10, 1995, p. 6. Transcript in author's possession.

30. See, for example, W. Lee Hoskins and James W. Coons, "Mexico: Policy Failure, Moral Hazard, and Market Solutions," Cato Institute Policy Analysis no. 243, October 10, 1995; Anna Schwartz, "Trial and Error in Devising the Mexican Rescue Plan," Paper presented at the semiannual meeting of the Shadow Open Market Committee, Washington, March 5, 1995; and Peter Ackerman and James A. Dorn, "Dose of Financial Morphine for Mexico," *Financial Times*, February 15, 1995.

31. Allan H. Meltzer, "End the IMF," Paper presented at the Cato Institute's 13th Annual Monetary Conference, Washington, May 25, 1995, p. 3.

32. Mikesell, p. 40.

Contributors

Ronald Bailey is a senior producer at New River Media, an independent television company based in Washington, D.C., where he produced the national weekly public television series *Think Tank with Ben Wattenberg*. An expert on environmental issues, he is the author of *Eco-Scam: The False Prophets of the Ecological Apocalypse* (1993) and the editor of *The True State of the Planet* (1995).

Bailey has an extensive background in television and print journalism, including producing PBS's *Technopolitics* in 1992 and 1993 and editing the award-winning *TechnoPolitics Report* newsletter. His articles and reviews have appeared in the *Wall Street Journal*, the *Washington Post*, the *New York Times Book Review*, *Smithsonian*, and many other prominent publications.

Doug Bandow is a senior fellow at the Cato Institute and a nationally syndicated columnist. He is a frequent contributor to a number of publications, including the *New York Times*, the *Wall Street Journal*, the *Washington Post*, *USA Today*, *National Review*, *The New Republic*, and *Foreign Policy*. He has written or edited numerous books, including *Tripwire: Korea and U.S. Foreign Policy in a Changed World* and *Perpetuating Poverty: The World Bank, the IMF, and the Developing World* (coedited with Ian Vásquez). He also appears regularly on radio and television programs, including *Nightline, ABC Nightly News, Good Morning America,* and *Crossfire*. Before joining the Cato Institute in 1984, Bandow worked at the White House as a special assistant to President Reagan.

John R. Bolton is senior vice president at the American Enterprise Institute. From 1995 to 1997 he was president of the National Policy Forum. He served as assistant secretary of state for international organization affairs in the Bush administration from 1989 to 1993. In that capacity, he managed the formulation, articulation, and implementation of U.S. policy and diplomacy within the UN system.

Bolton also served in the Reagan administration as assistant attorney general of the Civil Division and as assistant attorney general, Office of Legislative Affairs (1985–88).

Ted Galen Carpenter is vice president for defense and foreign policy studies at the Cato Institute. He is the author of *The Captive Press: Foreign Policy Crises and the First Amendment* (1995), *Beyond NATO: Staying Out of Europe's Wars* (1994), and *A Search for Enemies: America's Alliances after the Cold War* (1992) and has edited numerous other books.

Carpenter's work has appeared in various policy journals, including *Foreign Affairs, International History Review, Foreign Policy, The Journal of Strategic Studies,* and *The National Interest.* His articles have also been published in the *New York Times,* the *Washington Post,* the *Wall Street Journal,* the *Los Angeles Times,* and many other newspapers and magazines. He is a frequent guest on radio and television programs and networks including *CBS Evening News, NBC Nightly News, Crossfire, Larry King Live,* Voice of America, and BBC television and radio.

Nicholas Eberstadt is a researcher with the American Enterprise Institute in Washington, D.C., and the Harvard Center for Population and Development Studies in Cambridge, Massachusetts. He has served as a consultant to the World Bank, the U.S. Agency for International Development, the Department of State, the Bureau of the Census, and the Congressional Budget Office and has testified before Congress on aid and development questions for more than a decade. He has published more than 200 scholarly and popular articles and is the author or editor of eight books and monographs, including *Foreign Aid and American Purpose* (1988), *U.S. Foreign Aid Policy—A Critique* (1990), and *The Tyranny of Numbers: Mismeasurement and Misrule* (1995).

Daniel Gouré is deputy director of political-military studies at the Center for Strategic and International Studies in Washington, D.C. From 1991 to 1993 he served as director of the Office of Strategic Competitiveness in the Office of the Secretary of Defense. He has also held a number of other positions with members of the defense community, including the U.S. Arms Control and Disarmament Agency and private-sector consulting firms.

Gouré has published widely in such journals as *Orbis, Competitive Strategy, Signal, Military Technology,* and *NATO's 16 Nations.*

Stefan Halper is executive editor and host of *This Week from Washington* and *Reflections,* which are syndicated each week on 170 stations across the United States by Radio America. He is also executive editor and host of NET television's *WorldWise,* a weekly prime-time program on international security affairs. Halper is a syndicated columnist who has been widely published across the United States, Europe, and Japan in a variety of newspapers and journals. He has appeared regularly on CBS, NBC, ABC, CNN, C-SPAN, the BBC, Romanian television, Russian television, the Canadian Broadcasting Corporation, South African Television Network, and on Japanese, Korean, Chinese, and Taiwanese television programs.

Halper served in the Nixon White House, the Office of Management and Budget, and the White House Office of the Chief of Staff under President Gerald Ford. He was policy director for the 1980 Bush presidential campaign and director of policy coordination for the Reagan-Bush ticket in 1980. He served as deputy assistant secretary of state in the Reagan administration and was a senior foreign policy adviser to the Republican National Committee in 1996.

John Hillen is a defense policy analyst at the Heritage Foundation. He is a former regular U.S. Army officer and is still active in the U.S. Army Reserve. Before joining Heritage, Hillen was an overseas research scholar at the University of Oxford in England.

Hillen has published extensively on UN peacekeeping and peace-enforcement issues. His articles and op-ed pieces have appeared in the *International Herald Tribune,* the *Los Angeles Times,* the *Christian Science Monitor, Foreign Affairs,* and many other publications. Hillen is the author of *Blue Helmets in War & Peace: The Strategy of UN Military Operations,* which will be published by Brassey's in September 1997.

Edward C. Luck is an independent consultant with several affiliations. He is president emeritus and senior policy adviser of the United Nations Association of the United States and senior consultant to the Open-Ended, High-Level Working Group on Strengthening of the United Nations System of the UN General Assembly. A frequent media commentator, he has published and testified widely on arms control, defense, and foreign policy.

Luck is currently writing a book on the sources of American ambivalence toward international institutions for the Twentieth Century Fund.

Michael Maren is a journalist and former aid official who has worked in Africa for 20 years. He has written for the *New York Times, Harper's, The New Republic, Forbes Media Critic, New York Times Magazine*, and many other publications. He is the author of *The Road to Hell* (1997), which exposes the role of foreign aid in Somalia and other African countries.

Roy D. Morey is director of the United Nations Development Programme office in Washington, D.C. Previously, he served as UN resident coordinator for overall development management of the UN system and as UN Development Programme resident representative for Vietnam. He has held numerous other posts within the UN system since joining the organization in 1978. Before that, he served as deputy assistant secretary of state for international organization affairs and in various other U.S. government positions.

Morey is the author of a number of books, including *An Act of Congress: The Legislative Process and the Making of Education Policy* (with Eugene Eidenberg), and his articles have appeared in numerous policy journals.

Robert B. Oakley served as the U.S. special envoy to Somalia for Presidents Bush and Clinton. He is a veteran of the U.S. Foreign Service, where his overseas postings included serving as ambassador to Zaire from 1979 to 1982, ambassador to Somalia from 1982 to 1984, and ambassador to Pakistan from 1988 until his retirement in 1991. He has also held senior positions in the State Department and on the National Security Council.

Oakley is currently affiliated with the Institute for National Strategic Studies at the National Defense University and is the coauthor of *Somalia and Operation Restore Hope: Reflections on Peacekeeping and Peacemaking* (1996).

Gareth Porter is a consultant to the World Wildlife Fund, the World Conservation Union, the United Nations Environmental Programme, and the Center for International Environmental Law. He served as the director of the Environmental and Energy Study Institute's International Program from 1990 until early 1996. Before that, he taught in the School of International Service, The American University, and the City College of New York.

Porter is the author of several books and monographs on the environment, including *Global Environmental Politics* (second edition, 1996). His articles on environmental issues have appeared in numerous publications, including *Current History, EPA Journal,* and *Environmental Change and Security Report.*

Sheldon Richman is vice president of policy affairs at the Future of Freedom Foundation. Previously, he was a senior editor at the Cato Institute.

Author of *Separating School and State: How to Liberate America's Families* (1994), Richman has written widely on a variety of topics, including population and the environment, federal disaster policy, and international trade. His articles have appeared in the *Washington Post,* the *Wall Street Journal,* the *Christian Science Monitor,* the *Chicago Tribune,* and many other prominent publications. A frequent media commentator, Richman has appeared on numerous radio and television programs, including *Crossfire, This Week with David Brinkley,* and *Montel Williams.*

Michael Stopford is the chief of media relations at the International Finance Corporation. After five years with the British Diplomatic Service, from 1979 until May 1996 he held a variety of positions within the United Nations system, including those of chief of staff of the UN Office in Geneva and director of the United Nations Information Center in Washington, D.C.

Stopford speaks frequently on the United Nations. His articles on UN-related topics have appeared in such journals as *The Virginia Journal of International Law* and *The Detroit Mercy Journal of International Law.*

Alan Tonelson is a research fellow at the U.S. Business & Industrial Council Educational Foundation. He has also served as a fellow at the Economic Strategy Institute and as associate editor of *Foreign Policy.*

Tonelson's articles on American politics and foreign policy have appeared in numerous publications, including *The Atlantic Monthly*, the *New York Times*, the *Washington Post*, the *Wall Street Journal*, *Foreign Policy*, and *National Interest*. He is the coeditor of *Powernomics: Economics and Strategy after the Cold War* (1995). He is also a frequent commentator on radio and television.

Ian Vásquez is director of the Cato Institute's Project on Global Economic Liberty. He is the author of several Cato policy studies. His articles have appeared in newspapers throughout the United States and Latin America.

Vásquez has appeared on CNBC, NBC (in Latin America), C-SPAN, Telemundo, Univisión, and Canadian Television discussing foreign policy and development issues. He has also appeared on the Voice of America radio network and other radio programs. In addition, he coedited (with Doug Bandow) *Perpetuating Poverty: The World Bank, the IMF, and the Developing World* (1994).

Richard Wagner is the Holbert L. Harris Professor of Economics at George Mason University, a position he has held since 1988. He has published widely on a variety of economic and public policy issues. His books and monographs include *The Fiscal Organization of American Federalism* (1971), *Inheritance and the State*, *Democracy in Deficit*, written with James M. Buchanan (1977), and *To Promote the General Welfare* (1989).

Wagner's articles have appeared in *American Economic Review*, *Journal of Law and Economics*, *Public Choice*, *National Tax Journal*, and numerous other journals.

Index

Cato Institute

Founded in 1977, the Cato Institute is a public policy research foundation dedicated to broadening the parameters of policy debate to allow consideration of more options that are consistent with the traditional American principles of limited government, individual liberty, and peace. To that end, the Institute strives to achieve greater involvement of the intelligent, concerned lay public in questions of policy and the proper role of government.

The Institute is named for *Cato's Letters*, libertarian pamphlets that were widely read in the American Colonies in the early 18th century and played a major role in laying the philosophical foundation for the American Revolution.

Despite the achievement of the nation's Founders, today virtually no aspect of life is free from government encroachment. A pervasive intolerance for individual rights is shown by government's arbitrary intrusions into private economic transactions and its disregard for civil liberties.

To counter that trend, the Cato Institute undertakes an extensive publications program that addresses the complete spectrum of policy issues. Books, monographs, and shorter studies are commissioned to examine the federal budget, Social Security, regulation, military spending, international trade, and myriad other issues. Major policy conferences are held throughout the year, from which papers are published thrice yearly in the *Cato Journal*. The Institute also publishes the quarterly magazine *Regulation*.

In order to maintain its independence, the Cato Institute accepts no government funding. Contributions are received from foundations, corporations, and individuals, and other revenue is generated from the sale of publications. The Institute is a nonprofit, tax-exempt, educational foundation under Section 501(c)3 of the Internal Revenue Code.

CATO INSTITUTE
1000 Massachusetts Ave., N.W.
Washington, D.C. 20001